W9-DCE-614

It's Not Rocket Science
Using Marketing to Build a Sustainable Business

Mitchell Goozé
with Jane Broida Drake

THE INSTITUTE FOR MARKETING AND INNOVATION   SANTA CLARA, CA

ISBN 1-889772-04-6
Library of Congress Catalog Number 96-78204

Designed by London Road Design
Printed in the United States of America

First printing 1997
Second printing 1998
First paperback printing 2001
Revised paperback printing 2002

To Carol
From Scott
Love Daniel

Acknowledgments

It's tough to acknowledge everybody who's been a part of this book, but some of the ones who stand out for me are: Marty Ehrlich, who, as Vice President of Engineering at Lloyd's Electronics, allowed me my first look at marketing . . . even though I was "only" an engineer; Francis Christian, who, as a Product Marketing Engineer at Motorola, convinced me to make the "career shift" to marketing; Bill Toon, who, as Marketing Manager for the Microprocessor Group at Motorola, offered me that first, full-time marketing job; George Nelson, who, as Applications Engineering Manager, traveled with me on the technical seminar circuit and showed me how much fun speaking and training could be; Don Bell, who, as Vice President of American Microsystems (AMI), offered me my first Marketing Manager position and convinced me to come to AMI rather than to Advanced Micro Devices (AMD), which, for better or worse, was, no doubt, a major fork in the road; Carm Santoro and Glenn Penisten, who, as Vice President and President, respectively, of AMI, gave me my first P&L position as Director of the Microprocessor Product Line; Henry Davis, who created another major fork in the road with the opportunity to try a high technology start-up, which among other things, allowed me to join The Executive Committee (TEC); Ron Jackson, who encouraged me to start speaking on marketing, and who, after reading the first draft of this book, helped dramatically shape its tone and direction; the members of TEC 27 who allowed me to give my first marketing presentation to favorable review; the two thousand TEC members in North America whose positive feedback kept me going; Ted Steinberg, who, for the last twelve years, has challenged me to "think right;" David Palmer who's been after me to "write a book already;" my other partners and co-workers, Bayard Bookman, Jeff Krawitz, Liz Miller, Ralph Mroz, Neil Reckon and James Schaeffer who help make working fun; and, of course, my Mom and Dad, without whom I wouldn't be possible.

This book is dedicated to all the CEOs, presidents, general managers, business owners and marketing executives who have taught me enough over the last 10 years to make me believe I had the right to write this book.

Preface

This book is an attempt to capture, in writing, ideas on marketing I've been presenting around the world. It was created using the taped versions of many of my speeches as a foundation.

Over the years, some members of my audiences have concluded that this is Marketing 101. In truth, they're right. As a business person, all you really need to win is Marketing 101. Vince Lombardi won championships with Football 101. You can succeed in business if you will just master Marketing 101. You see . . . it's not rocket science.

Mitchell Goozé
August, 1996

The publisher asked me to update this book as it went into paperback release. Rereading the entire book for the first time in a few years, I am please to see that, as many readers have said to me, the ideas are still solid. I have updated some of the stories but have chosen to not add many newer ones, as the examples included have proven to be useful to readers and are still valuable today. I should also tell you that my father, who was a rocket scientist, has read the book and assured me that this is *not* rocket science!

Mitchell Goozé
March, 2002

Contents

Introduction

The book's title, *It's Not Rocket Science: Using Marketing to Build a Sustainable Business,* means what it says. In most cases, marketing is not extraordinarily difficult, but it seems to be a forgotten or neglected part of too many businesses. Perhaps because we confuse it with sales or advertising. Building a long term business is a goal some people achieve . . . but more fail to make happen. While it may not be rocket science, it does take understanding and attention to succeed.

The Small Business Administration estimates that over one million companies start up every year. The majority quickly fail. Of those that survive past their first anniversary, most will close their doors before the employees, including the owner, can afford to retire.

In 1837, there were eighteen soap and candle manufacturers in Cincinnati. None was appreciably larger than the others, and each served a roughly equal share of the city's market. It would take research to discover the names of seventeen of them. The eighteenth was Procter and Gamble, the company that eventually developed and sold Ivory soap to the nation.

Why did that firm survive over a hundred years to invent Tide, another winning cleanser? They survived for many of the same reasons any business outlasts its contemporaries. This book makes clear the basis for a firm's potential success in the market regardless of its size.

Most entrepreneurs don't want to build a firm as large as Procter and Gamble. However, many would love to have a firm that survives through their own life and can be passed on to the next generation, or sold for a profit that allows a more than comfortable retirement. Of course, what we want to do in life doesn't always resemble what we actually do. For most of us, that idea relates to disappointment, but it can also have a pleasant connotation. First, a business has to grow strong. Only then does anyone get to decide if he or she wants to stay with the company, and help it grow larger.

The question remains, what did Procter and Gamble do that seventeen others did not, so it survived to keep growing? That's what we must understand. Not just in academic theory or "mom and pop" company tactics. But in sustainable business practice that gives you the options to control your future. It is said that there are three kinds of people: (1) Those who make things happen, (2) Those who watch things happen, and (3) Those who wonder want happened. If you'd like to be a part of the first group, this book can help. It may also answer the third question for some of you.

People who go into business usually know how to *sell* their product or service. They also know they can hire salespeople, when the need arises. The majority give no thought to *marketing* their goods. Some think a company markets its wares through advertising—and the more, the better. Others believe only large businesses can afford marketing . . . whatever it is. Excellent marketers guided Procter and Gamble from its inception. Their insight enabled the firm to succeed.

The surest and quickest way to recognize what a business needs, to help it grow, is to examine it through the eyes of marketing. That is the vision this book imparts.

There are numerous books on marketing that discuss the all-important Marketing Plan. Their suggestions on goals and strategies can be remarkably helpful in getting you to consider how to translate your thoughts to paper, and they don't need repeating here. In *It's Not Rocket Science: Using Marketing to Build a Sustainable Business,* the Marketing Plan is only discussed briefly near the end of the book. My intention here is to acquaint readers with the nuts and bolts of the *real* job of marketing.

Marketing concerns itself with everything a business needs to do to accumulate and keep customers. But it does not include selling. Despite academic theory to the contrary, selling is not a subset of marketing. Marketing and selling are two different disciplines. However selling overlaps with, and is most effective when it is supported by marketing, as manufacturing overlaps engineering, while each remains distinct from the other.

Somebody must do the *real* marketing in a company. If there are no marketing professionals on staff, then either the president does it or the individual sales people do it as best they can, because it must be done. Just as a lack of proper design engineering must be made up for in the manufacturing department—assuming they can—lack of proper marketing will be made up for in the sales department . . . assuming they can. Perhaps the real reason so few salespeople seem to do really well, despite massive amounts of training, is a lack of marketing skills within the company, not a lack of sales skills.

In 1984 Scott McNealy, then Vice President of Manufacturing for Sun Microsystems, told me that Sun wasn't going to ". . . waste their money on marketing flakes." Fortunately for the other employees and investors in Sun, Scott, Vinod Kohsla and other Sun people were great at marketing even though they weren't professional marketing "flakes." Without great marketing Sun would not have been the success they've become. In the early 1980s there were at least three other companies who had licensed the exact same hardware that Sun was making.

This book has something to give anyone who wants to or does own, work for, invest in, or trade with, a firm that can be a long lasting success. In essence, it contains food for all those who like to ponder what business might do for them . . . and to them!

A marketer does not always work in a marketing department. She may be in advertising, public relations, merchandising, or management. (My use of the word, *he or she* throughout the text, is a literary device. If you choose to, you can substitute either for the other in all generic instances.) A potentially fine marketer does not need a particular college degree. He could begin in shipping and receiving or as a receptionist.

Charles Luckman served as the President of Lever Brothers for a number of years. He is one of those rare individuals who has innumerable talents, while most of us hope we have one that can adequately support us. Luckman was a natural born marketer, salesman, and leader, among other distinctions. Two of his exploits are described later in the book. But a story of his boyhood neatly illustrates my point.

When he was nine years old, Charlie acquired a newsstand position in a busy location in Kansas City. He had one corner, and three older boys sold the same paper on each of the other corners of the intersection. After a few weeks, Luckman realized that some people were deliberately crossing the street to buy a paper from him. He finally worked up the courage to ask one woman why she did it. She replied, "Because you always say, 'thank you.'"

The salesmanship, innate in the boy made him appreciative of his customers, and cognizant of their behavior. The inherent marketer persuaded him to ask his customer for the reason behind her actions.

Everybody goes to the market as a consumer. Manufacturers, wholesalers, and retailers fill the shops with every kind of product or service they believe we'll buy. The diversity of the modern marketplace . . . and the multiple versions of the same goods . . . approaches the unbelievable. Innumerable competing companies are trying to sell their wares to us. As customers, we know the free enterprise system does much *for us*. Sometimes, we have to seriously question what it is doing *to us*.

Regardless of our love/hate relationship with business, most of us appreciate a competitive marketplace. In 1990, the headline of a featured article in a Copley newspaper conveyed a surprising and welcome message. It proclaimed, "Capitalism, not defense secrets, interests Soviets." The report described how visiting foreign students, enrolled at Loyola-Marymount University, were taking a crash course in business.

Though adults in the United States basically understand capitalism, some are more aware of the system's faults than its virtues. They know how difficult it can be to find a decent paying job . . . and to hold on to it. Others know how hard it is to raise the capital to start a business, and how merciless a marketplace can be.

To survive, a company must continually sell its goods, while fending off competitors. In 1990, Mort Segal, a publicist for the film industry, gave a seminar on marketing to the Soviets. During his talk, he used the word, *competition*. His audience actually asked him, "What's competition?" While this may seem unbelievable to most of you, even in 1995 as the electric utility industry was preparing to be deregulated in the United States, many high-level marketers in those companies were just coming to grips with the reality of competition . . . not just the theory.

Because the word is so familiar to Americans, many people believe they understand its connotations. After all, they shop and work in a competitive marketplace every day. When a promising opportunity appears, they mortgage their future and invest in a business, never doubting they know how to compete.

Their company grows, but their competitors grow, too. They begin to wonder if their firm can keep up . . . or stay ahead. Or, their business begins well, but later slows down. They realize they're unsure of the cause, and understand even less how to reverse the trend. At those times, marketing . . . whether identified as such or not . . . will separate the winners from the losers.

There is an enormous amount of information in the pages that follow. Moreover, I strongly believe that if one story does not impress you, another will. Therefore, I often use several adventures—or misadventures—to illustrate the same idea.

Occasionally, the tales concern multibillion dollar corporations. This could cause you to think you can't relate to them. You may want to tell me, "The company I'm with doesn't have anything like the giants' money. Reading about what they do can't help me with my problems."

A corporation's vast wealth does not negate the knowledge you can gain from their experience. In actual practice, knowing what the giants did can help you avoid their mistakes. They do stumble, badly, and in the same areas that you must tread. The price they pay for their errors simply includes more zeros to the left of the decimal point.

The more of those zeros in a company's financial statement, the better chance it has to survive mistakes. Hence, the less zeros your firm can draw upon, the more you need to tread carefully.

When you're through reading this book, you may rightly decide your business employs excellent marketing techniques. Or, you could realize you're too lazy to market your goods. There is one statement, however, that you can't *accurately* make. If you say your firm can't afford a marketing program, you cannot be right. It doesn't take a large bankroll to plan for tomorrow. It does require a measureless investment of thought. Much of what you read in these pages may seem elementary on the surface. I encourage you to look and *think* below the surface.

Without marketing, a company will be just one of the many. With marketing, done well, a company will be one of the few. Only a few succeed in the long term. The rest just survive for awhile.

Almost everything said in this book applies equally to product and service businesses, but I seldom use both words because it would be cumbersome. At times, I describe obstacles a particular industry is subject to encounter. To some degree, everyone has to jump the same hurdles.

By now, those readers who perceive their product as a commodity, may be thinking, "Concrete is concrete is concrete. Nothing I read in a book is going to make mine different from anybody else's." That's true, but you can create a difference between your company and its competitors in a way that's valuable to *your* customers. That takes marketing. Your business sells concrete; many of the people who buy concrete also buy something more.

A nursery rhyme that sounded especially silly to me in my childhood was:

> To market, to market, to buy a fat pig,
> Home again, home again, dancing a jig.

I now recognize a truth about human nature: Whether we live in a primitive village or a cosmopolitan city, we all like to come home from a marketplace "dancing a jig." Male or female, young or old, sophisticated or unspoiled in our tastes, everybody enjoys buying something new.

Why do so many people trade with certain companies and reject others? Why can one business swiftly initiate profitable ideas, while its competitors hesitate and debate? Within these pages, you can learn the answers to those questions, and understand how to use your knowledge. Then you, along with your customers, can go home from *your* market "dancing a jig."

PART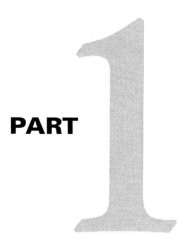

A Marketing View of Business

A Definition of Marketing

O wad some Pow'r the giftie gie us
To see oursels as others see us!

Robert Burns,
To A Louse

Marketing vs. Selling

Have you noticed many people use the words *selling* and *marketing* interchangeably? It's commonplace. Businesspeople substitute one word for the other in conversation . . . and no one notices.

A CEO announces, "We have to improve our marketing," and then calls the sales force together to devise new strategies. Or, key employees spend days putting a marketing program together, but actually create a sales approach. Even for that purpose, it's inadequate, because it does not contain the vital additional information a real *marketing* plan provides.

The words *selling* and *marketing* denote different responsibilities. When companies confuse them, they commit a costly error. Eventually, the error reveals itself in the financial statements. By that time, profits have decreased and economy measures must take precedence over all other concerns. Long time employees find themselves going to interviews and learning the latest procedures at the unemployment office.

The owners blame the company's problems on slow sales and employee indifference. The employees complain about corporate greed and misspent money. Rarely does anyone question whether the business had a proficient marketing program.

Marketing Defined

Peter Drucker, the father of modern business management, described marketing as much broader than selling. He tells us that marketing encompasses the *entire business* . . . as seen from the customer's point of view.

His definition does not imply that marketing is more important than selling. It does not suggest that one is harder to do than the other. Nor does he infer that marketers are smarter than salespeople. Drucker was simply defining one of two different but crucial aspects of business practice.

Marketing Eyes

To see your business from a marketing viewpoint, you have to step outside of it and stand in your customers' shoes. It's not easy to perceive your company through the fickle eyes of consumers. Not only are their tastes forever changing, but your own view is difficult to disregard. Therefore, seeing your business as others see it, through marketing eyes, is a skill most of us have to work to acquire.

Your Challenge

An incredible number of ardent vendors court retail and industrial consumers. Your challenge, as a marketer, is to keep the customers your company has acquired and to create new customers. To do so, you must convince people to trade with your firm instead of others. To be successful you may have to alter what your company offers, or the way you market it, or both.

Your goods, and the people who use them, will be discussed in Part Two. For the moment, we'll presume your product or service is all that it needs to be. Consequently, you'll need to practice better marketing to prompt more people to trade with you.

All businesses reflect an effort to provide something people want. When customers buy something from your firm, you know their motive is not to help your company succeed! They're expecting to gain a product or service that is more valuable to them than their money. Hence, marketing has to recognize the *value* of the firm's offer . . . as customers perceive it.

I once heard a concise definition particularly relevant to service businesses: marketing is the process of helping others *value* your service. Though it is easy for you to see its worth, the challenge is to convince others of it.

Advertising vs. Marketing

Many people believe the value attributed to most products is merely the result of clever advertising. With some offers, this is undeniably true. Advertising, however, is only a subset of a marketing program. It primarily serves as a sales tool.

In 1905, Albert Lasker, one of the pioneers of advertising who built Lord & Thomas, found the precise definition of advertising he had been seeking for years. In his book, *The Lasker Story*, he told how John E. Kennedy coined the phrase that remains superbly applicable a century later. Advertising is simply "salesmanship in print."

When your company is ready to implement your marketing program, your first act may be to advertise. The content of the advertisements must grow out of your marketing plan. Consequently, think about advertising at the end of your planning. For this reason, we'll examine advertising near the end of the book in Chapter 20. Advertisements convey messages. *Marketing enables a firm to have messages worth conveying.*

Marketing at the Ground Level

The following tale is probably fictional. However, it illustrates part of the difference between marketing and selling in actual practice.

A fourteen year old boy in a suburban community went into a neighborhood shop one afternoon. He asked if he could use the telephone for a brief call. The proprietor gave him permission and he dialed a number. The owner was stocking shelves nearby, so he could not help overhearing the boy's end of the conversation. It began promisingly.

"Hello, Mrs. Smith. I go to school near your house and I'm a gardener. I was wondering if you'd like me to take care of your yard?

"You already have somebody. Well, I'm a good worker, Mrs. Smith. I know the right time to plant certain flowers, and I'm very reliable.

"I understand, ma'am, but I don't charge a lot. If you'll give me a chance, I'm sure I could save you some money.

"You wouldn't want to change gardeners. Okay, then. Thanks anyway."

The boy sighed and hung up the phone. He thanked the proprietor, placed some coins on the counter, and started to walk out.

The man felt sorry for the youngster so he said, "Wait a minute, son. You don't have to pay me. I couldn't help hearing you didn't make the sale. The call didn't cost me anything, so keep your money."

"No, sir," the boy replied. "I'm glad to pay for it. The call was great."

The businessman became annoyed because the boy was obviously lying. "Young man, you don't have to pretend the call was successful. No one makes every sale they go after, but you can't let that discourage you. Just do good work and keep calling people. You'll sell your service."

"You don't understand, sir," the youngster answered. "That wasn't a sales call. Mrs. Smith is my customer. I just needed to make sure I'm doing everything she wants."

That's marketing on the ground level.

Marketing View

Marketers take the long view: they want to think about the future. They like to envision products or services that could better satisfy customers' needs in the months and years to come. They seek ways to serve more people, and to reach a wider area. They try to identify problems in the marketplace their company could help resolve. Ideally, they conceive of something their firm can provide that will be useful, before an industry that needs it has thought of it.

Sales View

Salespeople, on the other hand, concern themselves with the here and now. Salespeople want the order yesterday; they'll settle for today; it taxes their patience to wait until tomorrow. Thank goodness for people who love to sell. Companies could not meet payrolls without them.

The need for short-term results is an intrinsic quality of a good salesperson's nature. Her compelling interest in *today's events* enables her to present a product, day in and day out, in a marketplace rife with competitors.

Ironically, salespeople's indispensable concern with current demand can be a trap for marketers. You need to be cautious when you ask your sales force for suggestions about new lines to carry, or another service to offer. They'll usually tell you what people are asking for *today*. If you can quickly respond to the need, then the sales force can help you. Beware, however, if it is going to take six months or longer to get the disk drive they assured you they could sell. They may not want it by then. Their customers will probably be buying something else.

Firsthand Information

In reality, your firm's future rests in your customers' hands. Close attention to them and their comments will help you tailor your product or service to their real needs. This means they have to talk to the person in charge of, or directly involved with, the company's marketing on an on-going basis.

If you act on information about customers gleaned solely from a sales force, you are relying on secondhand material. This reliance has several drawbacks. First, you are only hearing an *interpretation* of ideas someone else *thinks* he heard. Interpretations do not always accurately convey what the original speaker said. Second, your salesperson may only mention the matters he wants to discuss, or the facts he thinks you want to hear. Third, you won't learn anything he doesn't want you to know.

Your own frequent conversations with the persons your company serves, or hopes to serve, are your most dependable protection against misguided moves. False assumptions lead to ruinous actions. These conversations also yield a valuable side benefit. Firsthand knowledge of your customers enables you to evaluate the accuracy of your other sources of information about them.

These warnings do not imply that you should avoid talking to your sales force. On the contrary, regular communication between management, marketing, and sales allows everyone to become familiar with and involved in the marketing program. Salespeople make unique contributions to the plan which will be explored more fully in Chapter 18. The point to appreciate at this moment is less complicated. A marketing person thinks about the future; a salesperson focuses on the present. Hence, your sales force will usually talk about what their customers want today.

A Basic Marketing Tenet

Anyone who decides to start or enlarge a business studies the goods people are buying in the current marketplace. On this basis, she then decides what she should offer her target clientele. She prepares the company to deliver, readies her sales staff for action, and anticipates a deluge of orders. This is the most common procedure in a start-up or turnaround operation, and it sometimes does the job.

When marketers approach a business, to improve or rescue it, they try to identify what customers *are actually buying*. Customers take delivery of a particular product or service, but *this is not all they bought*. Customers buy the value they want to receive (holes) not just the product or service that delivers that value (drills). In that statement rests the basic tenet of marketing.

Marketing by Familiar American Companies

John Gilpin was a citizen
Of credit and renown, . . .

William Cowper,
The Diverting History of John Gilpin

In the weeks before Christmas, customers are often waiting outside when the Manhattan branch of Tiffany & Company opens each morning. Once inside, some purchase uniquely Tiffany merchandise. Many buy items they know they could find at other fine shops, sometimes at a lower price.

What Are They Buying?

Why do people stand outside, on a winter day, waiting to pay top dollar for something they could easily buy elsewhere? They wait because they want something more than the article they select. They want the store's blue box. What's so important about a blue box? Even unopened, it delivers a message: "To show you how much you mean to me, I'm giving you something from Tiffany's." The box may contain the same crystal vase other stores sell, but this gift comes in *the blue box*.

Tiffany & Company has spent over one hundred and fifty years associating its name with exquisite merchandise and an aura of exclusivity. Now, anything that comes in its box has a greater value than its counterpart from other shops. A Tiffany sales clerk may think a customer is merely selecting a beautiful Christmas gift, management understands that many once-a-year shoppers are there mainly to get the blue box.

The company advertises a "Tiffany diamond." Other than the one famous gem bearing that name, what is such a diamond? Does the firm own a mine? Not really, but they do have a blue box. Into it, they'll place a patron's diamond. By that simple act, they create, forevermore, a "Tiffany diamond."

Diamonds vs. Rubies

Rubies are at least forty times rarer than diamonds. Knowing that indisputable fact could persuade you to give the important person in your life a ruby ring. You may want to say, "I chose this gem for you, especially, because rubies are so much rarer than diamonds." When you present it, you should prepare yourself. Your gift . . . and the recipient's response . . . may prove disappointing!

In 1889, De Beers Consolidated Mines, Ltd. set up an effective monopoly over the diamond industry. In time, most major producers joined in a marketing cartel. Their intention was to maintain the price of diamonds at a high level. They also launched an aggressive marketing campaign, and we cannot doubt their program's success. Almost a half a century later, Leo Robin and Jule Styne wrote a delightful song explaining how ". . . diamonds are a girl's best friend."

There's no tangible reason for the high price of diamonds. Rubies, by virtue of real supply, are inherently more precious.

Diamonds, by virtue of demand, have usurped the ruby's place. The diamond cartel created the demand.

They imprinted an exclusive value on their product before the ruby industry realized what was happening. Now, a young engaged couple will joyfully select a tiny diamond ring. The way they see it, the gem's size does not reflect the worth of their purchase. They know they actually bought a symbol that their love . . . like the diamond, "is forever."

This slogan, which carries the force and conviction of an ancient adage, is in fact the brainchild of an inspired group of marketers. You could say the brilliance is less in the diamond than in the marketing plan.

Snow Throwers—Machine or Concept

A retail merchant of snow throwers locates the business in an area where people expect their driveways to be buried regularly beneath a foot of snow. As the merchant sees it, the choice is between the old fashioned and laborious shovel, or a power driven snow thrower. But customers only want to get the snow out of their way with as little aggravation and delay as possible and in fact, snow throwers provide plenty of both.

If anyone invents a contraption that is easier to use, or faster, snow throwers will become more obsolete than the ancient shovel. People only buy them now because someone has convinced them snow throwers are more efficient. But the shape of the hardware is virtually irrelevant. It's the concept of easy snow removal that customers are actually buying.

A Chicken Is a Chicken Is a Chicken, or Is It?

Most of us don't buy a chicken because we collect chickens. We need something for dinner; we want chicken; so we buy one. People pay for an item, and take possession of it, but invariably they also bought something else. When buying chicken for eating, the question is how does the consumer determine which chicken to select? Even a collector buys an article to improve his collection in some way. Marketing needs to identify, precisely, the "something else" certain people want to buy, in chickens or diamonds. The additional attributes come in a myriad of forms, and serve as basic tools. After the overview, we'll return to the subject, and examine how you can discover and use such tools, to differentiate your product or service.

Have a Plan

You *sell* products and services; you *market* what the customer is actually buying. When you market, you may be enlarging upon a well known need certain people share. Or, you could be building on your own perception of what people would want if it were available. Before your company invests money to implement your idea, you need to prove the validity of your proposal. You do this by developing a carefully constructed plan.

Without a well formulated plan, anyone, no matter how credible or renowned, can send his company in the wrong direction. Bad moves can be helpful . . . provided someone else makes them. When your competition becomes misdirected, you have an opportunity to gain market share. Sooner or later, everybody makes mistakes. This truism guarantees room in the marketplace for all who want to take on its challenge.

Avon

In 1979, Avon Products, Inc. bought Tiffany & Company. Avon's door-to-door cosmetic business had started to decline. Too many women were no longer home in the daytime, fulfilling the role of budget-minded housewives. The firm decided their wisest move was to add another dimension to their holdings. By choosing Tiffany's, they proved they had lost sight of their real expertise. Remember, the successful marketing of any goods requires an ability to see your business through your customers' eyes. Avon was unfamiliar with the clientele of elite establishments. Their style of merchandising, promotion, and other business practices, did not suit Tiffany's aura. And that may be an understatement!

Today, Avon admits their employees were not sufficiently malleable. They could not relate to their new clients' needs. The company cites their later acquisition of Giorgio's as proof they can successfully manage an up-scale venture. Perfume, however, is more in keeping with their basic cosmetic business than the selling of $50,000 diamond bracelets.

Avon's present position proves something more important than their ability to succeed with higher priced merchandise. They were smart enough to learn from their mistakes. Financially they were in a position to survive their serious blunder. A comparable error, committed by a less prosperous business, could have been fatal.

In 1984, Tiffany's original management repurchased the business while the firm's credibility was still intact. If they hadn't, a piece of Baccarat crystal in a Saks Fifth Avenue box could now have the same, or more, value than one in a Tiffany blue box.

There are three significant points to this story. First, as a marketer, you need to recognize the skills your company possesses, and the customers such skills enable your firm to serve. Second, you need to respect the real dangers inherent in an incompletely thought-out plan. The third is a reminder of an old truth that is so well known it is easily forgotten. Any name, no matter how old and prestigious, can lose its value if its image becomes blurred in the public mind.

What's in a Name?

The importance of a company's name is an accepted axiom. Two more time-proven rules have grown out of it. Consumers associate only one product with one name, so a name carries an implication that may be vital to a company's financial well-being.

It is common for us to hear "Heinz" and think "ketchup." Or, if we are old enough, we think "pickles," because that used to be the firm's most popular product. No matter which item comes to mind, we think of one . . . not both.

Of course, there are times when we select something new simply because the brand is familiar. Still, the public's association of one brand name with one product has a proven impact on sales. For this reason, smart manufacturers give their various products different brand names.

Similarly, the name of a business, or a product, suggests merchandise of a certain monetary value. A company ordinarily abides within the price range the public associates with their goods. If, however, management decides to upgrade their firm's image, they'll need enormous resources, and unlimited patience, to market their new concept.

Gallo

For instance, Gallo wine has always occupied a low-end position in the marketplace. How much advertising do you think it would take to convince consumers that Gallo produces premium wines? How long would it take to persuade you to serve their brand as a reflection of your good taste?

In the 1980s, the Gallo brothers set out to make their name synonymous with superior. They told us they were going to produce high-line wines, and they refused to give them a new brand name. I don't doubt the Gallo winery can yield prime beverages . . . possibly as good as any in the world. Nevertheless, that's not how the American public has ever perceived the brand.

Time, and an immense financial investment, may eventually create an association of excellence with the Gallo family name. In the meantime, many people use the cheap products solely for cooking. Moreover, some liquor stores continue to speak of parts of the line as a "wino's wine." To rid themselves of this image, the company would have to eliminate some of their products. They'd be forfeiting a large portion of their sales, without assurance of the outcome.

In the late 1990s, the Gallo children took over day-to-day management of the firm. They brought a different perspective on how to capitalize on their company's ability to produce a "better" product without sacrificing its substantial "low-end" market share. A new brand, Turning Leaf, was created to focus on this mid-priced market.

Beefeater Gin

Once in a while, if everything falls into place, it can be possible to increase a product's value. Beefeater is a low-end brand in England. When it first came to the United States, nations knew less about each other's products than they do now. The American public was unaware of the lowly position Beefeater had always held in English pubs . . . and most people cannot distinguish one gin from another by taste anyway.

The importers introduced it in the U.S. as a high-line, imported gin. They advertised it as the brand to select when a person wanted a superior liquor. Naturally, its shelf price was in keeping with this image. And in this case . . . perception was reality.

A carefully thought-out marketing plan gave Beefeater a new value in the "new world." But the distillers did not attempt to reprise their success in England. English consumers had decided, long ago, how much the brand was worth. The company took the sensible path. It is usually far more profitable to capitalize on an existing concept than to try and change it.

Corona Beer

The tale of Corona beer offers a unique variation on this theme. The producers priced it to attract the low-wage earners in Mexico. In the United States, although it began as a low-end product, the Yuppies upgraded it. "Everybody" drinks beer. So if you wanted to order something that would distinguish you from the crowd, you chose the brand that has the label painted instead of pasted on the bottle. In this case, the company was not the instigator of the change, which may only prove that it is sometimes better to be lucky than smart.

A business acquaintance of mine committed a potentially serious error because he was unaware of the beer's market position in Mexico. He had invited a visiting executive, from a large firm in Mexico, to lunch. My friend, to be considerate, asked his guest if he wanted a Corona. The expression on the man's face instantly bespoke the real offense he took at the suggestion. The embarrassed host quickly explained that the beer was very popular in the States. Finally, his guest shrugged his shoulders, and said, "Maybe so, but give me a Bud." Ironically, he was unaware of Bud's "working man" image in the USA.

Kellogg's Frosted Flakes

Sometimes you have to adapt a concept to move with the customer base. Kellogg's Frosted Flakes satisfied a generation of children. Suddenly the company's advertising spoke of it as an adult cereal, but they hadn't changed its contents. What had happened? The children had grown up. Kellogg's simply chose to persuade their original customers to keep eating Frosted Flakes. Their offspring would possibly join them.

It was a prudent decision. If the company had aimed a whole campaign at a new generation, the youngsters may have rejected the conventional taste of Frosted Flakes. The cereal market is overflowing with exotic flavors. In this case, the adults had pleasant memories of the product from their childhood. They simply needed to think of it as still tasty and sufficiently nutritious, no matter their age.

Remember, marketing has to look for a product's value from the customer's side of the counter. From this vantage point, value has a subtle appearance.

Quality Inns

The selling of franchises offers spacious terrain for the marketing of concepts. In the 1980s, Quality Inns International (the firm became Choice Hotels International in 1990) decided to develop a chain of economy hotels with standardized rooms and amenities. They wanted to call them "McSleep."

In the moment you read that name, did you immediately think of a frugal Scottish person? If, instead, you thought of the McDonald's hamburger chain, so did a court of law when Quality Inns posed the frugal Scotsman argument.

Most people know how Ray Kroc bought a hamburger stand in Riverside, California, and transformed it into a world-wide franchise. He marketed the idea of a uniform fast food menu, with consistent quality in every location. McDonald's international reputation allows them to protect their name from variations . . . even against such an unrelated business as hotels. Quality's new chain eventually became Sleep Inns.

There is a less well known side of the lawsuit. Few people appreciate how thoroughly Quality's marketing people planned the whole program. Quality Inns International sold franchises. They did business with people who wanted to own hotels. McDonald's had begun to send letters, and in other ways express their dissatisfaction with what they considered a trademark infringement. Quality decided to sue for the right to use the name.

Actually, they believed they couldn't lose, no matter what the court decided. If they won, they'd get to use "McSleep," which was a dynamite name. If they lost, they'd be the company that had tried to be "McSleep." The publicity created by the court case helped sell franchises. A franchiser who had the creativity to think of the name, and the nerve to try to use it, made a deservedly strong impression on potential franchisees.

Robert Hazard, Jr., Choice Hotels' CEO, was the man behind the concept. He often joked while he waited for the outcome of the case. "If we lose McSleep," he'd say, "we can use 'Jack-In-The-Sack.' " Obviously, the Jack-In-The-Box hamburger chain did not enjoy McDonald's widespread renown, but the pun again displays Hazard's inclination to play skillfully with words.

Quality Inns International wanted to make their new franchises memorable and therefore more valuable, by associating their name with a trademark known around the world. Remember, your marketing should give more worth to your product than the money your customers trade for it. This remains true whether you are offering an easy to remember franchise, or a device that easily removes snow.

Franchisees actually have little influence on the concepts attached to a franchise they buy. A franchiser sells locations, along with products and other needed items. He usually retains the right to initiate or discontinue all marketing programs. The buyer takes possession of a location, which bears a crucial role in the success of the business. The main value of the purchase, however, rests in the "wit and wisdom" of the franchiser. A franchisee's responsibility is to create a sales plan that takes full advantage of the franchiser's marketing skills. Nevertheless, if you own or work for a franchised business, the better you understand marketing, the more you can use it . . . or play a part in improving it.

The Service Sector Dilemma

Before we complete the overview, we need to look at a problem that service businesses commonly face.

A customer can see a diamond ring or a designer pen, and determine its worth before she pays for it. Even then, it may fall short of what she thought she was buying. A client can never see an audit before he orders it. He only has the accountant's promise that the finished report will live up to expectations. A firm can provide references, but the list will not include dissatisfied persons . . . and everyone knows it. Thus, the client is initially buying a promise: "a pig in a poke." On top of that, no matter how much someone needs an audit, most people find it hard to want one!

Service businesses offer promises, before anything else. They may promise to design someone's dream house, or find her expert personnel, or fix his car by late afternoon. Somehow the firm has to convince customers that its promise will become *tangible*. You'll find out more about this in later chapters.

The Importance of the Promise

The critical point for now is the importance of a promise, regardless of what industry you work in. If your firm is going to succeed over the long term, you have to make all stated or implied promises tangible. Donald Trump, in his book, *Trump: The Art Of The Deal,* phrased the idea colorfully. No matter what befell him later, his plight cannot diminish the truth of his words.

"You can't con people, at least not for long. You can create excitement, you can do wonderful promotion and get all kinds of press, and you can throw in a little hyperbole. But if you don't deliver the goods, people will eventually catch on."

Japan's
Marketing Style

. . . But you'll look sweet upon the seat,
Of a bicycle made for two.

Harry Darcy,
Daisy Bell

A 1989 article in *The Wall Street Journal* included this statement: ". . . new cars are fundamentally becoming more alike. Differences in quality are narrowing, and most companies now can offer a quick, smooth ride with reasonable fuel economy."

In the same year, a J. D. Power & Associates' report revealed that new car owners saw little difference between brands. They based their satisfaction primarily on dealer service. The better rated vehicles received high marks because the dealer networks were more supportive of their customers.

The next logical question is, if differences in quality are becoming insignificant, why do people still buy expensive automobiles? The answer is obvious. A car's value largely rests in the image a manufacturer imprints on it. The difference between buying a vehicle for transportation, and a concept to ride around in, begins with $40,000 and can exceed $200,000.

The high price of owning a concept does not imply you overpaid if you own a Mercedes, Jaguar, or BMW. Those brands are unquestionably worth the money they command. Presumably, you found something you wanted. If the dealer delivered everything you expected, you made an excellent trade of your money for a product.

Many women admit they'd become uncomfortable if they found themselves standing next to a woman wearing the same dress. It would be disconcerting, to say the least, to have their lack of originality made so obvious. The same principle applies to drivers who don't want to see the car they selected everywhere they look.

Keep in mind that concepts can become tangible or intangible benefits. Often, they are both. For years, people bought a Porsche because it could go 160+ miles an hour. It was worth its price to those who wanted the feeling they could command such power. Buyers knew they'd have to watch for an opportunity to let the energy loose, but the restriction didn't deter them. They were buying the *idea* of extraordinary speed. Occasionally, they'd even get to use it.

People who want and can afford to buy a vehicle that's not commonplace, can now choose from a variety of notable cars. Marketing, far more than technology, is responsible for the abundance. If, however, someone's primary reason for selecting a particular brand is to impress others, his success will depend upon where he drives it. In areas of Los Angeles, parking valets delivered so many BMWs to waiting patrons, the car stopped attracting attention.

Any model of a Mercedes-Benz lends elegance to its American driver; in Germany, many models are taxicabs. The public considers vehicles for hire on public streets as trouble free and reliable, but less expensive lines also offer such dependability. Daimler-Benz spent considerable time and money persuading Americans to see the Mercedes as a conveyance of distinction. The concept hardly befits a brand used as a common cab.

Advertising and Public Relations

To accomplish these feats of imagery, today's automobile industry relies heavily on advertising. But marketing is far more than the "glitz and glamour" consumers see. Each business generates its own advertising requirements. Most require some publicity. Exceptionally talented public relations firms and ad agencies can be adept at pinpointing useful ideas, and devising clever ways to communicate them. Nonetheless, the high fees charged by the most gifted firms preclude their employment by most businesses.

It doesn't matter whether your goods call for minimal or extensive advertising. You still need to identify, for yourself, how your company actually helps customers now, and can offer additional help in the future. Armed with this understanding, you can make *your business* mean something to your customers. If your firm does not mean anything to them, they will drift away.

The Art and Science of Marketing

Before we return to the automobile industry and its flamboyant behavior, let's examine the reasons some people liken marketing to both an art *and* a science.

It's like a science because it requires the patience to gather accurate data, and the ability to analyze it. These are the primary tools large companies employ. It resembles an art because it requires insight and creativity. Smaller companies favor these because they carry no expense tag. For continual success, a blend of both is usually essential.

Some major U.S. corporations have fallen into the habit of allotting huge sums to market research. The same data often becomes the justification for unwise decisions. Mid-sized and large companies that give their expensive research too much respect are subject to invest in invalid plans. Executives can bury themselves under piles of paper. By so doing, they ignore creativity and gut feelings, and thereby miss a lot of fine opportunities . . . or invest in poor ones.

Smaller companies go with appealing ideas that suddenly occur to management. These inspirations can prove profitable . . . until the time comes when one fails. Then owners have to throw the plan for a whole investment out with the trash. They frequently watch the business go with it. The officers of small firms hesitate to spend their limited time and money on information and analysis. Hence, they trust, too much, on their insight and instinct. Such misplaced frugality encourages people to believe their decisions are absolutely right . . . when they are disastrously wrong.

Technology Leadership

Now we're ready to scan the history that led up to an automobile campaign of the late 1980s. Our study will allow you to see an elaborate plan put into action by a clever and determined marketer.

When the United States dominated the automobile industry, it was a technology led business. The Detroit manufacturers of the 1930s and 1940s consistently offered the technical advances that promised to yield the most profit. Each year they introduced their new models, with the same message: "Here's what we made. Go buy it." They did some gimmicky advertising, like the "merry Oldsmobile" limerick. That ditty bore no resemblance to a concept, and simply was a way to keep the Oldsmobile name in the public's mind.

During those years and into the 1950s and '60s, car manufacturers concentrated on selling their products. However, General Motors, along with the other major auto makers, also had clearly defined niches for their different models. In effect, these served as an excellent marketing tool. Consumers like to differentiate products in the marketplace. The niches allowed an Oldsmobile buyer to know his car's value in relation to a Cadillac and a Chevrolet.

After the Second World War, the public realized something new was happening. Throughout the industry, parts for a company's variously priced vehicles were coming from the same production line. The more car owners thought about this, the more uncertain they became. They were no longer sure of the difference between a merry Oldsmobile and their Cadillac . . . other than the price they'd paid. Some finally decided there were no important differences. Marketing had been sacrificed for the sake of an easy solution to cost-efficient manufacturing.

To the public's misfortune, our car manufacturers had always fed on dazzling success and insignificant competition. It's a rich diet that nourishes arrogance. The long-reigning Emperors of Detroit imperiously ignored all questions about the intermingling of the hoi-poloi with the hoity-toity, in terms of parts. Their silence left their customers feeling cheated and resentful.

Meanwhile, the Japanese were watching with interest. In time, they not only outstripped U.S. manufacturers in their quality and price, but they also identified another element that would become crucial to success in the industry . . . and that was *marketing*.

The Cimarron

U.S. automobile manufacturers are just beginning to return to thoughtful marketing. For example, in 1982, Cadillac put its name on what consumers saw as a Chevrolet. The company called it a Cimarron. By offering a low-end model alongside their high-end models, Cadillac was trying to be all things to all people. The audience watched this parody of marketing, unsure of what they were seeing. When the curtain came down, many consumers dismissed the whole Cadillac brand. They could no longer think of the Cadillac as a car of an unmistakably elevated class. Despite recent improvements, it has yet to regain the majestic position it once held in the marketplace. Cadillac would do well to consider buying up all of the remaining Cimarrons on the road, and crushing them, to remove this continuing misguided image from the public's mind.

The $40,000 Datsun

By 1989, the American public had become well acquainted with the worthiness of some Japanese products. Nevertheless, Nissan startled many car-conscious consumers when the company introduced a "$40,000 Datsun." The automobile was actually a Nissan Infiniti, but the manufacturer's name still brought to mind their inexpensive, unimpressive Datsun. That car had been a perfect example of a transportation vehicle. The only image reflected by it was of a conveyance for a person who wanted to get from point A to point B.

The company eventually dropped the Datsun brand. Nissan, as a brand name, replaced it. When the Infiniti came out, the Nissan 280Z, the mid-priced sports car, had only been in the marketplace a little more than ten years. That was too short a time to erase the memory of the manufacturer's original low-end product.

My disparaging reference to a "$40,000 Datsun" typifies the problem the Nissan Corporation faced, and they knew it. Some people wondered whether the world needed another expensive car. Others questioned whether anyone would pay $40,000 for a Japanese brand. None of it mattered. The manufacturer had decided the United States would buy their concept, and they acted accordingly.

Nissan designed the Infiniti to go after a portion of the Mercedes, BMW, and Jaguar market, and others of their ilk.

Mercedes and Jaguar alone have between them a history of more than 150 years of producing elite motorcars. When the Datsun came to the United States in 1958, it sold for $1,616.

American auto makers had been smiling smugly at Japan's automobile industry for more than thirty years. In 1990, a GMC spokesman, interviewed on television, was still smiling and still appeared smug. Despite his show-business performance, the statistics were available to anyone who wanted to note them. According to *The New York Times*, GMC was selling almost 1.5 million fewer cars per year than they had sold in the previous decade. Others described the loss in stark business terms: the giant had lost ten market share points. If the Japanese could do this to General Motors, they could devour BMW's minuscule share of the market.

Infiniti Takes on BMW, Mercedes, and Others

Although many of their competitors were indulging in self-deception, Nissan knew better than to expect the Infiniti to be an immediate success. They adopted the long view because they had a new concept to market. It began like this: "Japanese luxury is not a showy badge or a symbol of accomplishments." Since the firm lacked a 100 year history of producing prestige cars, it behooved them to scorn the thought of earned credit. In its stead, they proposed a daring idea: "You don't have to be so obvious, so pretentious, so brand name conscious." They were offering us ". . . an experience of ownership based on long lasting quality." I doubt if anyone in the United States, through the 1950s, dreamed that any Japanese manufacturer would ever make such a statement. It would have been even more unthinkable that anyone would take such words seriously.

The Nissan Motor Corporation wanted consumers to question the importance of familiar names, and related values. They told us we no longer needed to pay $80,000 for quality, augmented by an old, distinguished nameplate. They were giving us the opportunity to pay half that price for quality they represented as the same or better. The company knew it could take a long time for this new point of view to catch on. They had plenty of money and abundant patience. These are the same two indispensable ingredients the Gallo brothers needed to possess.

Approaching a New Market

Gallo was also trying to upgrade their products and company image, but there's a major difference in their approach. The winery wanted to become known as a producer of premium quality beverages while they continued to use a name associated with jug wine. This requires liquor stores to stock $3.98 bottles of fermented juice, and comparatively expensive vintage wines, all bearing the same brand.

The Nissan Corporation gave their creation its own unique name, and arranged to open separate dealerships. They had also prepared to differentiate their car, conceptually, from other high priced automobiles. They did everything considered necessary to make their project profitable, and to identify the company as a producer of great cars.

Japan Listens

The Japanese have become masters of both the scientific and artistic sides of marketing. The first cars they brought to the United States in the 1950s were conspicuously inferior. After they recognized their mistake, they labored to improve their workmanship. They also studiously asked American consumers a classic marketing question: "What do you want?"

During those years, our nation's automobile manufacturers were doing business as usual . . . without marketing. They offered no remedy for our concern about gas mileage, and scorned the need for low-priced, entry-level vehicles. Compared to those major issues, the unanswered questions about the intermingling of production line parts had become an almost forgotten subject. Undoubtedly, the Big Three had expected the subject to fade from our minds, and they ignored the widespread resentment their silence fostered. It's even possible they were unaware of our feelings. They had long ago stopped paying much attention to us, the mere consumers, and didn't think they needed to start.

After a while, the Japanese believed they had produced a vehicle matching the needs specified by their research. They came back with an improved model, and took a tiny market share away from their amused competitors, who failed to imagine then that Japan's share would continue to grow for more than thirty years!

Japan's Artistry

The Wall Street Journal article, quoted at the beginning of this chapter, included an account of the artistic side of the Infiniti's development.

Takashi Oka was the engineer in charge of the Infiniti project. While searching for innovations to include in his product, he realized that women with long fingernails would have trouble using the vehicle's interior switches. Later, to make certain they could gracefully use a newly developed switch, he meticulously tested it by taping long fake nails on his own fingers.

Additionally, ". . . the leather on both the steering wheel and the gearshift in each car will come from the hide of the same individual animal! . . . because anything else would wreck the car's 'unified tactile sense.'" Obviously, the company had not targeted animal-rights activists for customers!

Mr. Oka also gave his attention to the door handles. He astutely discerned that the handle is usually the first physical contact a person has with a car. He chose large, die-cast metal handles instead of plastic ones. His intention was to make them feel welcoming, like the door to one's home, yet cool to the touch.

Dealerships as Museums

The *Wall Street Journal* article covered another aspect of the artistry involved. "Such cars, of course, couldn't possibly be sold from a typical grungy mega-lot, with strings of yellow plastic triangles flapping along the entrance from the interstate." Nissan described Infiniti showrooms as "The New Museum of Contemporary Art."

A dealer had to invest several million dollars to build his "museum." That was before purchasing inventory. When the first advertisements for the car appeared, many dealers grew noticeably nervous.

Breaking the Rules

There has always been an unwritten rule in the United States: all automobile advertising should include a picture of the product. Nissan broke the rule. For better or worse, they did not even offer a suggestion of the new concept's appearance. Instead, their advertisements imparted a sense of serenity. They featured such scenes as a peaceful sunset, a placid lake, a clear sky, or a tranquil pine tree. "Infiniti isn't just a new car," each ad intoned, "but a new philosophy." Nissan was inviting us to have "a new significant man-car relationship." For $40,000, they knew they should offer us some kind of relationship!

In reality, the car was not yet really available, and their other Japanese competitor, Toyota's Lexus, was. This exigency pressured them into creating an ad campaign that would build an expectant showroom reception when the car did appear. It worked . . . the public couldn't wait to see a car they had only imagined take shape before their eyes!

Marketing Wars

Nissan's pronouncements served as the first salvo of another battle in a marketing war. Periodically, businesspeople discuss how our competitors help "to keep us on our toes." We say our competition makes us "stronger and better." In truth, after they've performed all these good services for us, we wouldn't mind if they quietly moved into the background.

William Davidow, in his book, *Marketing High Technology,* describes marketing as "civilized warfare." Marketing does translate itself into a war between competitors for the public's favor. We can think of it as "civilized" because its ends are not deadly . . . though a few industries may want to challenge that statement. Even without physical violence, certain individuals and corporations callously employ tactics that wreak profound havoc. Their narrow view often leaves scores of people without the means to feed their families.

As the Infiniti's battlefield strategy unfolded, a picture of the "new philosophy" finally appeared, but the dealers' fears lingered on. Their anxiety did not stem from doubts about the product's eventual success. Many were simply beginning to realize it could be five to seven years before they achieved their initial goals. They had anticipated possibly three years. We know now their fears were unfounded. At that time they did not have our 20-20 hindsight. And they did have several million dollars invested!

Shortcuts

Two Infiniti models went on display. Some reviewers quickly crowned the four-door Q45 a success. They saw it as a new vehicle, built from the ground up. They dismissed the two-door M30 as a repackaged Nissan.

Manufacturers sometimes use models with widely different prices to coax the maximum number of people into showrooms, but a ploy of this nature can also backfire. The M30, like its pampered sibling, bears the same brand. A passerby, examining a parked M30 coupe, could think, "It's just a Nissan Maxima with a new name and a higher price. If that's an Infiniti, who needs it?" This unimpressive introduction to a brand name could have tarnished the luxury sedan. Fortunately, follow-on products came quickly . . . allowing the M30 to fade away.

Though the Q45 held allure, consumers did not rush to trade in their BMWs. This, in itself, did not portend failure. Companies need to remind their customers, continually, of all that a familiar product means to them. Otherwise, eventually, they'll stop buying the old to try something new. Recognizing this truth, BMW promptly counterattacked. Their advertisements admonished consumers not to buy an imitation BMW when they could buy the real thing, in the same price range.

If all the Infiniti's competitors had taken the assault on their customer base as seriously, the "man-car relationship" could have found itself in real trouble. From the outset, Nissan offered monetary incentives to their burdened dealers. Those who had their museum/showroom ready on time received large bonuses. They could also gain a sizable reward by earning a high rating in the customer satisfaction index. Still, if the Infiniti's incubation period had stretched over too many years, dealers would have required appreciably increased subsidies.

This completes our overview of business as seen through the eyes of marketing. We're now ready to dismantle the subject of marketing, and examine its many parts. If, for the present, you only perceive a hazy picture, that is sufficient. The whole picture will acquire a sharper focus as it develops.

PART

A Look at Who Is Offered What

Customers and Common Sense

...simple truth miscall'd simplicity...

William Shakespeare,
Sonnets

A ll marketing departments, regardless of size, have to visualize something their company can offer. They have to decide who will want it, where they will expect to find it, and how much they will pay for it. Such matters may sound too elementary to mention, but in a moment, you'll read how they undid an experienced company.

Regardless of what your firm sells, or to whom, there's one comment you never want a customer to make later: "I knew something wasn't making sense. I should have listened to myself, instead of that salesperson."

Making Sense

As a marketer, you want everything related to your product or service to fit together, sensibly. This means that from the outset, everything a potential customer sees and hears must agree with her idea of what she's buying. Otherwise, your business will be like most of its competitors. Remember, prospective customers need reasons to trade with your firm, instead of with others.

"Making sense" in the marketplace sounds like a comparatively easy assignment, but it requires the resolution of numerous questions. Therefore, it is actually a complex task, but there is a simple way to start getting acquainted with it. You only have to watch what happens when a company's offering proves to be nonsense.

Because American automobile manufacturers ceased practicing marketing, as I define it, I'm going to use the industry for one more story. The Cadillac Allante is a consummate example of a product that made no sense within its market.

The Allante

From the start, the Allante was going to be a limited edition. General Motors hired the award winning Italian firm, Pininfarina, to design and build the body. The economics of the industry required it. GM had equipped their factories to build 200,000 cars of the same model. For years, our major auto makers considered that number to be optimal for maximizing the return on capital investment. When GM wanted substantially fewer cars, they hired an outside firm to build them.

The Allante was a handsome, two passenger convertible, loaded with electronics. It was the first Cadillac to approach, and then exceed, the $50,000 class. The car received favorable reviews, containing the standard complaint. Reviewers monotonously tell us a car handles well, but it needs a bigger engine. Give a car a bigger engine, and they religiously say it suffers poor fuel economy. The reviews also mentioned a problem with the convertible top . . . and the company corrected it.

Cadillac's goal, for the Allante, was the delivery and sale of 7,000 vehicles per year. In spite of such modest expectations, after three years, they had sold only a few thousand, and in early 1993 they canceled the car. What had happened?

An Umbrella Product

There were two schools of thought concerning the most profitable way to use the car. One group saw it as an "umbrella product." They wanted to place it in showrooms across the nation, so its attractive and expensive appearance could reflect on the whole line. They believed this would reincarnate the prestige of the Cadillac brand, which the Cimarron's low price and quality had tarnished. If used as an umbrella, actual sales would become of secondary importance. Companies are glad to simply break even on such products.

Auto makers sponsor race cars for their umbrella effect. The way many consumers see it, if a vehicle wins the Monte Carlo, everything the factory produces must be worth buying. Honda has consistently profited from this cherished supposition. Mercedes-Benz employed a more conventional umbrella tactic in the 1950s, when they still offered comparatively moderate-priced cars. They regularly introduced limited editions of costlier models. Gradually, the brand came to be synonymous with "expensive and exclusive."

A New Line

Others at GM believed the Allante needed its own showrooms. They wanted to establish it in a separate class that future models could join. Presented in this way, the car would still serve to upgrade the line, but actual sales would become more important. Shoppers would not see the model in every Cadillac showroom; hence, it needed to be out on the streets, where the public could notice it. This plan contained two irreversible flaws.

Marketing had chosen to make the car a convertible, which limited its strongest sales to certain climates. Moreover, a total production schedule of only 7,000 vehicles per year could not support its own franchise. In reality, the company had little choice. They offered the model to all Cadillac dealerships. Some dealers undoubtedly believed they could sell it. Others saw it as a lure and an umbrella. This approach contained its own grave weakness.

The Dealership

A potential buyer of anything inordinately expensive—be it a gourmet dinner or a diamond necklace—expects to find certain amenities in the place of purchase. Among them is a luxurious setting. In addition, the staff that presents such merchandise traditionally blends a deferential attitude with a tinge of superiority.

I doubt if there has ever been a Mercedes/Isuzu or a Jaguar/Subaru dealer anywhere in the nation. No one I know has ever seen one. (Perhaps there has been one in Los Angeles, where a person can see almost anything.) Following the Cimarron fiasco, some Cadillac dealers found themselves financially compelled to take on less expensive GM products. Cadillac/Chevrolet and Cadillac/Pontiac dealerships became commonplace. As foreign made, low-end cars grew popular, even more surprising combinations, like Cadillac/Daihatsu dealerships, appeared in certain areas. Many of these establishments served as early showplaces for the $47,000 Allante.

An extensive advertising campaign ushered in the Italian-made beauty. Now imagine this scene. A husband and wife, who regularly buy a new luxury car every two years, enter a Cadillac/Daihatsu showroom. Advertising has finally had its desired effect . . . it always takes longer than we think it will, and they are ready to consider the new high-end Cadillac. The salesman who approaches them has just finished selling a

$9,367 transportation vehicle. He must now try to sell a $50,000 concept.

The odds are against even the most capable and well trained sales force. In actual practice, the staff must switch, at any moment, from selling expensive luxuries to bargain basement necessities. Rarely can anyone successfully sell both kinds of merchandise, on the same day, in the same place. The showroom itself cannot play two such contrasting roles. It comes down to which setting the dealer believes will yield the largest profit. If he prepares an elegant room to serve the wealthy, the more numerous shoppers for his lower priced brand will feel conspicuous and uncomfortable. Therefore, our hypothetical couple find themselves in a room that befits a Daihatsu buyer.

While the salesman struggles to find the right words, his customers take a good look at his product. The plastic dashboard is impressive with its profusion of electronics. Still, a little voice inside them whispers, "Where's the wood?" Every luxurious vehicle they have owned, or seen, contains real wood. The shoppers become acutely aware of the $9,000 cars, with plastic interiors, which the dealer also offers. They mention the absence of wood to the salesman. His attempt to dismiss the lack as irrelevant sounds as impromptu as it actually was. Although other Cadillac models share the floor, their presence does nothing to influence the couple. The brand suggests an uneven degree of quality, akin to the unevenness they now see and hear in the showroom. Something about this automobile does not feel right.

When shoppers do not *feel* that a product is worth $47,000, they have no reason to believe that it is. The couple say they'll think about it, and go on to visit other dealers. Inevitably, they come upon an elite motorcar, in a setting compatible with its price. A salesman wearing a custom-made suit serves them. His manner and conversation harmonize with the prevailing elegance, and the car's inevitable imperfections fade into the showroom's impeccable woodwork.

20-20 Hindsight

The image reflected by showrooms offering any mixture of brands drastically decreased the Allante's mystique. In turn, this also affected sales in single line dealerships. Cadillac says they tried to advise some dealers against the car, but they could not deny anyone a model that was available to all others. Nor, according to their contract, could they forbid franchisees the right to sell other brands.

In retrospect, Cadillac believes the convertible needed its own showrooms. As they presented it, the surroundings did not fit the price, and the sales approach did not fit the product or the price. In truth, nothing about their program fit except the result . . . it was next to nothing.

The damage was done, and the public rejected the concept. It did not generate sales, and failed as an umbrella. Cadillac cites production figures of 3,000 cars per year, at most, and the car was finally canceled despite its 1993 Northstar engine upgrade.

General Motors could survive in spite of such waste; most businesses could not. Marketing has to know, precisely, who may want to buy what, and where they'll want to find it. A plan must contain this basic information, and much more, before a company invests in it. Otherwise, no one can profit from the unfinished work.

Contrast the Allante story with a description of the Infiniti's showroom that appeared in one of their early advertisements. "A small pond, a bridge, a greeting place, four private meeting areas, four cars carefully lit, on four separate platforms." In an "art museum," people expect their purchases to be costly. It would not make sense if they were cheap.

Understanding Customers

Marketers have to understand their customers before anyone can successfully serve them. "Understanding customers" implies you recognize their needs. "Serving them" means you provide for their needs. General Motors was the leader of the national automobile market. As the decades rolled by, they increasingly ignored their customers. Ford and Chrysler, instead of keeping GM "on their toes," chose to play "follow the leader."

In the latter half of the 1980s, the Big Three finally began to face reality. They conceded that their market position had diminished, somewhat. Their numerous former factory workers could not indulge in such a wishful evaluation. They'd long since become painfully aware of what was happening. The auto workers, however, built the cars; they didn't design them. Therefore, the United Auto Workers blamed management, foreign competition, and Government for their problems. Management blamed foreign competition, Government, and perhaps, most of all, the workers, for endlessly demanding increased compensation during a difficult period. No one wanted to admit that in the free enterprise system, nothing can adequately compensate for the lack of competitive goods . . . no matter the importance of other factors.

The Emperors of Detroit finally stopped looking for someone to blame, and began to make positive responses. GM started developing the Saturn. They hoped that someday it would successfully challenge the foreign monopoly of small car sales. They also designed their Buick/Reatta plant to produce 25,000 vehicles, and dispensed with the moving assembly line. This allowed them to drastically reduce capital costs. Ford and Chrysler made aggressive moves of their own.

Fundamentals

Observers often wonder how General Motors, with its awesome success story, could have made so many obvious mistakes, and then taken so long to acknowledge any of them. All three auto makers like to cite complex conditions, beyond their control. This line of thought is self-defeating; it tempts people to ignore their own errors. The Big Three made their first mistake the moment they began to neglect fundamentals. Later blunders were bound to follow.

There are certain basic skills we must acquire before we can perform complicated tasks. As our knowledge increases, we forget about the subjects we originally studied. We think of them as second nature to us. For instance, we no longer concentrate on how to speak a language once we gain a command of its vocabulary and grammar. We concern ourselves with the subjects under discussion. Nevertheless, if we do not hear or read a language for too long, words slip away from us. With time, we may no longer possess even an elementary vocabulary. In like manner, a firm that ignores its customers, the fountainhead of business, can easily lose its sense of direction. When their competitors follow suit, no one has to acknowledge mistakes. Sooner or later, serious competition moves into the marketplace. Then the neglect becomes obvious.

You may believe this oversimplifies the problem. Consider the error Avon committed when they bought Tiffany & Co. They forgot which customers they understood. They also misjudged their employees' ability to adapt to the new clientele, another fundamental role of marketing.

Large and prosperous firms are the most vulnerable. They can easily forget the basics. Their problems have become too complex to include elementary matters. The majority of small businesses never learn the fundamentals. As the owners close their doors, most remain unaware of what they never knew. Mid-size firms eventually stand at a crossroads. Their initial struggle for survival is over. They turn their attention to perpetuating their growth. The actions they acknowledged as essential, in their early years, can readily become the ones they disregard.

What Business Are You In?

There is a process you can follow to reinforce your understanding of the people who compose your market. It begins with a simple definition. Start by expressing the overall help your business offers customers in six words or less. Your definition is not precise enough until it reveals the basic benefit customers gain from your kind of product or service.

For example, I heard a venture capitalist say he "helps good people build businesses." An insurance broker said he "protects people from adversity." Make certain you speak of what you do for your customers. Reciting the benefits stockholders can gain will be of no help.

The railroad magnates in the 1800s could have said "we transport people and their goods." Instead, each sought "to build a financial empire." (The handful of men who astutely managed the Pennsylvania Railroad, for a time, stand out as exceptions.)

The railroad "empire builders" were speaking accurately when they described themselves in such terms, or inspired others to do so. Each concentrated on his own goal, not his company's. Consequently, the men fought each other in ways wholly opposed to their customers' needs.

Some issued unauthorized stock, employed political chicanery, and engaged in harassing litigation. One group became more interested in the gold market than its railways, and its schemes caused the Black Friday panic of 1869. Many conspired to acquire unsound financing, and by so doing, contributed to a series of depressions. All of this stretched over decades, and destroyed the livelihoods of countless individuals. We may fault them, but there are more "empire builders" in the United States today than there were in the 19th century and they're employing identical tactics.

If businesspeople choose to, they can focus on far more diverse aims than the single-minded pursuit of their own and their stockholders gains. Some famous American scholars assert that a business exists for only one reason: to make a profit. They also suggest that anyone who does not agree is not being honest with himself. Although I reject the premise, I am not negating the need or disparaging the desire for profit. I simply belong to another school of thought. A company can seek and make a profit, without the owners considering it the primary reason for their business to exist. In fact, the pursuit of profit, strictly for itself, becomes increasingly compulsive and proportionately less satisfying.

Conducting business can sometimes provide a feeling of satisfaction, for owners and employees, on a minute by minute basis. The root of such satisfaction rests in the six words that tell you how you serve others. Simultaneously, the better your company serves the needs of others, the richer everyone involved can become.

Everybody works for his or her own gain. That is a fact no one even has to try to remember. The question is whether you seek to gain at the expense of others, or by serving their needs. Everyone who works for a living has to decide which course to follow.

If you can't compose the tight, six word description, you may not know the help your business actually provides. Companies squander their capital because they lack this basic understanding. Without it, owners and employees, consciously or unconsciously, behave as though the business exists to support them. They can avoid acknowledging their feelings to themselves, but they can't prevent their customers from sensing it. A recent study shows that 32 percent of retail or industrial customers who stop trading with a company, do so for competitive or unavoidable reasons. They have found goods they prefer, gone out of business, moved, or died. The other 68 percent leave because of what they perceive as indifference by the people who are alleging to serve them.

Your Customers

After you define the help your product or service provides, you're ready to examine your actual market. You're looking for key information about the people who need whatever you offer. There are seven questions that can help you. Before we consider them, you have to know who you are talking about. Who is any company's customer?

The *end-user* of a product or service is your *actual customer*. This is true even if your firm manufactures parts that go into another company's product. Many companies may handle the part you produce, before the finished goods reach the user. You will see how it can be profitable to perceive that unseen person as your customer.

There are innumerable products and services that someone other than the user always buys. If yours is among them, you probably need to focus much of your attention on the literal buyer. She can adequately serve as your customer's surrogate. You can even refer to her as your customer, which I often do throughout the book. It remains a marketer's obligation to remember that his goods must ultimately satisfy the end-user.

Subcontractors have an additional problem. Even your customer's surrogate can change from one job to the next. At different times, a roofer may need to court the general contractor, the architect, or the owner of the building under construction. Ordinarily, customers, and their surrogates, once identified, remain constant until their needs change.

Studying customers can reveal additional products or services you can offer. Conversely, studying a product or service can provide knowledge about those who use it. For now, let's look at the seven questions related to the people who compose your market. The questions refer to consumers of all wares. My comments are only meant to make the broad questions somewhat specific. You need to find the answers that fit *your* own clientele.

Seven Questions

1) Who uses what you offer? Identify, as precisely as you can, the people who are, or could be, your customers. If you work with retirement homes, do not settle for an easy answer, like "elderly people." It can't help you understand them. You know the minimum age, physical condition, and personal income your facilities require. These factors immediately limit your market. No doubt you, and your competitors, have studiously avoided certain problems common to retirees. If you solved any of them, would you materially increase the size of your market? You may know that resolving them would be unprofitable, but don't let that stop you from listing them. Enumerating your customers' needs can give birth to useful concepts, if not today—tomorrow.

2) Why do people even want your kind of product or service, and why should they think of your company in relation to it? When you recognize the "something else" they're actually buying, you'll know why they buy it from you. One sure way to link your firm with your goods is to prove to customers you know their reason for wanting whatever you offer. In later chapters, you'll find out ways to convey your knowledge, in unmistakable terms.

3) Why does anyone trade with you now? Maybe your firm really does offer the best help available, or possibly only as good as most. Your patrons may be following their parents' example, or their company's policy. Perhaps your closest competitor is too far away.

4) How do people want, or need, to buy from you? Your salespeople may have to call on them, or customers may have to go to a wholesale or retail distribution outlet. Some could shop from their office or home, by using the telephone, the mail, the Internet or a fax machine. Do they have to pay cash, or will you accept their check, or a credit card? Do you need to offer specially constructed terms? Throughout Asia, you can ask for a letter of credit, but if you try it in Singapore, you may insult—and lose—your customer.

5) When do people need your kind of goods? They could want it anytime of the year, or only as the seasons change. There may be certain days of the week, or hours of the day or night. Usually, there's a correlation between the time people use something and when they buy it.

6) Who decides it's time to buy something, and exactly which out of many competing products to buy? It's not always the user, or the person who pays for it. It could be whoever orders it, or comes to get it. Or it may be more than one person! Your accurate answer will tell you whether you have to understand a surrogate, as well as the end-user.

7) How much money can you persuade people to pay for your goods? On what basis do you now think customers judge your product's value? You might believe they measure it against what other companies ask for comparable wares. Or, you could think they value its dependability, or the savings it provides over the long term. There's a way to determine the right price for your goods that most businesses do not employ—as we'll see later.

Discussing the many facets of these questions, and their answers, will take us far afield. As we travel down side roads and by-paths, keep in mind that you want your company to serve customers better than the competition does. Therefore, it's not enough to understand the people you serve. You also have to understand the competitors with whom you compete for the public's favor.

Goods That Make Sense—
And Some That Don't

*Nothing astonishes men so much
as common-sense and plain dealing.*

Ralph Waldo Emerson,
Essays, Art

The way customers first learn about your product, contributes to their important initial impression of it. Of course, most of us know our first impression of anything can be deceiving. Too often it promises too much.

How many times have you paid top dollar to see an extravagantly advertised movie, only to have it disappoint you? Later, you may have thought you could have enjoyed it more—if advertisements had permitted you to expect less.

Many industries now employ "show biz hype" to promote themselves or their goods. These firms remain unconscious of, or unconcerned with, the public's distaste for their exaggerations. Our auto industry proved that it doesn't pay to ignore your customers' feelings. It took many years, but their customers were finally able to rebel. As a result, every industry related to American automobile production suffered.

The groundwork for more rebellion is already in place and apparent to anyone who wants to pay attention. The majority of retail consumers no longer expect to receive the actual service, or product, a business says it will deliver. A survey just a few years back revealed that the public now thinks businesspeople deceive them *more than half the time!*

AARP Survey

The American Association of Retired Persons ordered a survey of adults between the ages of 25 and 85, and a 1990 *AARP Bulletin* published the views of the participants: ". . . almost two-thirds (62 percent) of those under age 65 believe that businesses try to mislead consumers at least half the time. Less than half of those 65 and older (44 percent) share that view." The article's intention was to inform naive older consumers of the deceit in today's marketplace.

Not all older consumers are naive, however. The report went on to say, ". . . 43 percent . . . under 65 say they feel misled as a consumer at least half the time while only 28 percent of those 65 and older feel the same way."

I believe there is another reason . . . the opposite of naiveté . . . that enables older consumers to feel that few businesses actually mislead them. Most of these experienced shoppers quickly recognize the nonsense of an offer and move on.

In answer to any reader who questions the capability of our nation's elders, I offer this statement from an article appearing in *Newsweek* magazine: "What needs changing most of all is the image the image makers have of aging. Whistler's Mother may have represented older women in the 1800s, but today's grandmothers are more likely to be sitting on the city council than in a rocking chair."

The Senior Market

In 1989, *The New York Times* reported that people between the ages of 50 and 70 held seventy-seven percent of the money in the United States. The same group controlled more than 50 percent of the discretionary spending. We all know that age group has grown even larger, yet the majority of industries continue to cater to the 18-to-34 year old shoppers.

Further research revealed the reason businesses persistently court the young. They mistakenly believe they can't lure older persons away from familiar brands, and other buying habits. Although their presumption is basically erroneous, in one respect it's accurate. Businesses cannot lure older consumers by using bait laced with nonsense.

Cynicism

The above statistics could serve as useful incentives to various industries. They lead to one all-encompassing conclusion. No matter the age group a business serves, it is playing to an audience of cynics. The business person who courts the cynics is equally cynical. The seller of one product or service is the consumer of others. Knowing the deceitfulness in his own industry, he doubts the promises of others. He would be wise to give his customers credit for perception at least equal to his own, and serve them differently.

Our government officials travel extensively, and entertain grandly, because they "serve the public." They're only the most highly visible objects of our cynicism. The vast majority of the poorly served public now suspects everyone who serves them. This includes the butcher, the baker, and the candlestick maker. People speak with equal disdain of some doctors, most lawyers, and the whole insurance industry.

Cynical customers are never loyal, no matter how long they've traded with a firm. Tomorrow they'll flee, en masse, to any company that *under-promises and over-delivers*. The Big

Three of Detroit finally had to acknowledge this truth; other industries have yet to believe it.

An understatement can make sense, even to cynics. A product that is better than expected takes younger people by surprise, and they spread the word. Older consumers—the ones with the real buying power—are more familiar with understatement. They recall when simplicity in the marketplace was more prevalent than exaggeration.

Credibility

The help promised in the marketplace comes in an infinite number of forms. Frequently, as the AARP survey revealed, it doesn't come as promised. A company that consistently delivers on all promises, proves itself credible. A firm that lacks credibility cannot win their customers' loyalty. Sooner or later, the business must fail.

As a marketer, you need to identify what the public is *actually buying*, or wants to buy. A handful of people can instinctively perceive such matters. Most of us have to develop the insight, by studying the achievements of others. The following tales can begin to acquaint you with the needed vision.

While you look for ways to serve your customers, remember the need for credibility. It's an indispensable yardstick by which you can measure the worth of your ideas. If you realize your firm can't "deliver the goods," discard your idea, quickly. The business will lose the time and money you spent on the project. Were you to continue, you'd lose far more.

Federal Express

Federal Express is an outstanding example of a firm that identified something their market lacked. They translated their recognition into action, proved themselves credible, and achieved an astounding success. Obviously, customers wanted the help. More than half of the market now calls the company whenever they need a package delivered "absolutely, positively overnight."

Through the latter half of the 1980s, Federal Express satisfactorily delivered packages at least 97 percent of the time. That's a performance worth bragging about, but we should also note the statistics of the United States Postal Service. During the same years, they delivered overnight express mail, as promised, between 93 and 96 percent of the time, and for less money.

The Post Office did not offer express delivery to all the areas Federal Express served. Still, wherever they went, during those years, their performance was often close on the heels of the leader. Regardless of their good work, the Postal Service didn't worry anyone in the package delivery business. Had the government lowered its rate, for express delivery, to five dollars, Federal Express wouldn't have needed to lower their price. The Post Office was not a competitor because the public didn't consider them credible—and for valid reasons. By 1990, their performance had already deteriorated. Therefore, unless and until the Post Office, as a business, gains credibility, even if they improve in the future, they will pose no threat, and Federal Express can ignore them.

UPS

No one should dismiss the United Parcel Service, however. UPS has always enjoyed a good reputation, but they had a weakness. Everybody who used the service had recognized it, but nobody improved it.

For years, UPS routinely promised delivery within five to ten days, through their standard service. When they sometimes neglected to deliver a package I sent, I could always rely on the following sequence of events. If I called them on the tenth day, they told me to wait until it had been eleven days. The next day, all they could say about the missing package was, "We'll put a tracer on it." After another two to four weeks, I learned whether they had found it, or given it up for lost.

Federal Express had meanwhile introduced a bar-code system, with related procedures. This now enables them to tell you, at any given moment, if your package is on an airplane flying over Arkansas. It makes the company credible. If they fail to deliver a package, they can quickly locate it. UPS now offers a similar air-express service and tracking system, but they were too slow getting out of the starting gate to fully retrieve their reputation.

Also, because UPS's air and ground package services operate with different systems, they don't offer a consistent level of service to the customer thus further impacting their credibility.

Raising the bar even further, Federal Express has established a World Wide Web site that allows customers to get up-to-date information on their shipments any time with just an airbill number.

Additional Service Benefits

Actually, statistics prove that many packages "get lost" on the receiver's shipping dock. If Sally doesn't get something you sent her, you can call Federal Express, and learn that Sam signed for it at 10:15. You tell Sally, and she says, "Sam never delivers my stuff!" Federal Express has again proven their credibility. They can instantly tell you who signed for what, and when they did it.

The company promises to deliver packages by a certain time of the morning or afternoon. If not, they refund their customer's money, unless the receiver agrees to a late delivery. Some drivers call to ask if a brief delay is acceptable. The receiver says it makes no difference and hangs up the phone. In an incredulous tone, she announces, "The Federal Express guy just called to say he'll be 20 minutes late. I can't believe he'd bother. I've never seen such service. Why don't we use them?" By being up-front, the company turns a small failure into an advantage.

The sender is satisfied because the receiver was satisfied. Federal Express gets paid, though they were late. This also allows them to cite their high percentage of satisfactory delivery. They may also gain a new customer. Everybody wins.

A Tale of Two Retailers

Consider the behavior of two hypothetical retailers. They both sell the same ladies wristwatch in an assortment of high-fashion colors. They buy them for $3 each from a supplier in Hong Kong, and they sell them for $19.95. The watches will last for up to 18 months. As long as they work, they will keep time perfectly. Both firms offer a one year, money back, guarantee.

One store advertises the watch as a fashion accessory. They want women to think of their watches as they do their scarves. For $19.95, they can afford a different color for every outfit. When a watch stops running in a year or so, they can throw it away and buy a new one.

The other describes the watch as an inexpensive, but reliable, timepiece. New technology allows accurate time keeping, with a fashionable appearance, at a low cost. Customers can see it as an example of the company's promise to offer good merchandise at a fair price.

The life of the "throw away," fashion accessory watch may exceed its one year guarantee by six months. If some only work for a year, it makes no difference. Customers still received the short-term fashion accessory they believed they were buying. The firm's message was credible.

The other business finds itself facing resentment. They marketed the watch as technologically sound. Customers do not expect a real watch to stop working in 14 months, regardless of its low cost or brief guarantee. Their child's watch can last longer than that. For months to come, they will be telling their friends about the store that cheated them.

The first company's marketing department searched for, and found, a reason for women to want the product in spite of its short life span. They did not allow their customers to expect more than they were going to get. The other firm did not accomplish anything . . . except to bring themselves closer to going out of business. Their message was not credible, and they should have realized it before they employed it.

TV Dinners—The Proof of the Product

Most of us have had the dubious pleasure of eating frozen dinners. Producers admit that these products do not taste the way their contents suggest they will. The industry lacks the technology needed to improve the process. Thus, when someone cooks four food groups together, like ground sirloin, mashed potatoes, peas, and an apple turnover, each cannot maintain its proper flavor. Single items have a chance, but a full course meal doesn't.

This knowledge, coupled with the importance of credibility, makes the following events inevitable. Years ago, a company introduced a line of frozen dinners, and employed the word *gourmet* in their brand name. Because they used that imposing word, they priced their product higher than the competition's. The higher price made the name appear credible, but the flavor could not satisfy heightened expectations. So the company sold one to everybody and two to almost nobody. In the early 1990's, a different brand, The Budget Gourmet, sold very well. Their dishes were adequately original, and the price allowed the name to be credible.

The benefit consumers gain from frozen meals rests in the convenience they offer at a modest price. Marketers realized that hurried, weight conscious Americans were ready for more help. Diet frozen dinners became an instant success. In effect, the marketers had made a sensible suggestion to consumers. If they had to eat the stuff anyway, they might as well not get fat doing it!

Video Tape

Each person has to decide for himself whether one frozen dinner is worth even a dollar more than whatever it was he ate last time. When the public judges the quality of video or audio tapes, their decision is even more subjective. One listener to taped music could have a "twenty-five cent ear." Another may visibly wince at the slightest musical infraction. One viewer will not notice the occasional imperfections of recorded scenes. Another gets angry over a moment's fault.

Years ago, marketed concepts ("Is it live, or is it Memorex?") taught the public to value tape for its faithful reproduction, or for its lack of glitches. At present, some consumers are questioning the advantages attributed to higher priced video tape. If too many decide the claims are no longer credible, manufacturers will have to offer new reasons for buying it . . . or lower their price. Even then, the question is whether there are enough discriminating users to spare marketers the problem.

Discount Stockbrokers

The Charles Schwab Company introduced discount brokerage service. At that time, they could have said, subtly or bluntly, "We are going to charge smaller commission fees because the other brokers have been ripping you off." If they had done so, traders would have had to decide for themselves how the company could afford to offer such a generous benefit. Some may have thought: "Maybe my trades won't get executed promptly because the service is cheap."

Instead, Charles Schwab had recognized something many consumers needed . . . and did not need. The firm explained, through their advertising, that a broker's commission supports a company's research department, along with everything else. Customers who do their own investigations and pick their own stocks shouldn't have to pay for a service they don't use. Charles Schwab didn't maintain a research department; consequently, they could charge less. The offer was credible and desirable. Later, Schwab introduced a "new" service to provide research for those customers who need it.

A Japanese Department Store

The following is a version of a true story that appeared in a 1985 *Wall Street Journal*. It relates, once again, to the nation that learned, the hard way, to prefer marketing warfare to the real kind.

Some of Japan's marketing practices appear excessive to us, and therefore undesirable. Many of ours appear careless to them, and therefore unacceptable. Beyond question, this tale carries the whole idea of help and credibility to their outer limits. Nevertheless, as you read it, recall the serious financial troubles that have plagued most of our major department stores. You may come to agree with me on two points. When we are consumers, excessive consumption, of food or anything else, usually proves undesirable. When we are providers, it is wiser to err on the side of excess.

An American of Japanese descent took his wife to Japan to visit his parents, with whom they were going to stay. While in Tokyo, the couple decided to buy a compact disc player as a souvenir of their trip. The whole transaction required seven minutes. That included the time it took them to find the right department. The clerk used one minute to rewrite the charge slip because he had misspelled their name.

The next morning, the parents asked their son to demonstrate the player. He tried, but it didn't work. After fiddling with it for awhile, he opened it, and discovered it was a mockup, devoid of electronics. He had to wait until 10 o'clock, when the store opened, to call and vent his anger.

Instead, a minute before opening time, someone called him. The caller announced that the vice-president of the store was bringing him a new player. Fifty minutes later, the executive, accompanied by his assistant, arrived in a taxi. They entered the house, bearing a disc player, along with gifts of towels, cakes, and a Chopin disc. The assistant carefully explained what had transpired throughout the previous night.

Within minutes after the couple left his department, the clerk realized he had given them the hollow floor model. He promptly alerted the security guards, hoping to catch them before they left the building, but it was too late. The salesman, knowing his customers were from the United States, then called 32 hotels in and around the Tokyo area. After that failed, the store contacted American Express—the charge card the man had used—and asked for the couple's home telephone number. Fortunately, the woman's parents were housesitting. They provided the information that resulted in the precisely timed morning call and visit.

We may think all this effort was more than enough, but an epilogue was yet to come. As the men were reentering their waiting cab, the vice-president suddenly turned and ran back to the house. He had forgotten to apologize for the delay the couple had experienced in the store because of the misspelling of their name on the sales slip.

A U.S. Department Store

Not long ago, I went shopping in the men's department of a prominent U.S. store. An adequate number of salespeople were present, but all appeared busy with something other than helping customers. I finally interrupted two salesmen, talking to each other, and asked where I could find a particular brand of jeans. One looked annoyed at the intrusion, while the other casually pointed toward a general area. I searched for at least five minutes, through racks of clothing, until a fellow customer informed me the store no longer carried the brand.

I drove a considerable distance to a shop I knew provided the service for which they charged. On my way, I recalled my grandfather sternly asking: "Who's watching the store?"

For large department store chains, the question requires different phrasing. A person needs to ask, "Where are the people who are in charge of the executives, who are in charge of the managers, who are in charge of the clerks, who are not watching the store?" I suspect they are in big rooms, around big tables, discussing investments in other industries.

Department Stores vs. Malls

Aside from the marketing missteps afflicting them, U.S. department stores are also under attack from another direction . . . malls. A mall is a collection of retailers under one roof who do not interact with each other except to the extent that they're under the same roof. Buying from each retailer in the mall is an independent transaction for the consumer. Any knowledge that one store may have regarding complementary merchandise sold by another is accidental. Purchases at one store must be made independently from purchases made at any other store. Sounds just like a typical department store today!

The benefit the mall retailers have is that they don't even pretend to integrate their merchandise or thinking with the other stores. Therefore each retailer must survive by providing goods and services of value to their target consumers. No one expects the mall stores to have any real interaction.

On the contrary, department stores could offer the consumer a real difference. They could have the departments interact, they could cross-merchandise, they could provide the consumer an integrated shopping experience. Some do. The rest are just under-stocked, under-differentiated malls.

Their empty spaces seem to echo too many people's thoughts: Who needs them?

Department Stores vs. Discount Stores

When department stores were young, even the lower priced chains provided the real service patrons need. Salespeople stayed with their women customers in dressing rooms. They helped them try on clothes and make selections. They fetched other sizes and additional outfits, and promptly removed unwanted garments. Such services relieved customers of the need to dress, and undress, each time they wanted to try a different size or color. It also discouraged them from dressing and leaving. Of especial importance, it prevented theft more reliably than the insulting electronic devices later fastened onto clothing. Actually, women welcomed those cumbersome contraptions. They were preferable to the "unseen eyes" of "unseen spies," watching them in dressing rooms.

Droves of women avoided the spies, spoken of in posted notices, by taking their business to discount shops. If someone was going to watch them, they may as well be in a communal dressing room. Many had spurned such establishments, until they realized they were paying for the privacy and service that had ceased to exist in most department stores.

Any capable marketer should have foreseen that response. They also should have feared the invitation they were extending to their competitors. Instead, department stores added burgeoning discount houses to the list of "uncontrollable events" that have ruined their business.

Business Procedures That Make Sense— And Some That Don't

By different methods different men excel;
But where is he who can do all things well?

Charles Churchill,
Epistle to William Hogarth

Salespeople have to at least appear to make sense when they talk to customers. Anyone who can't adhere to that basic tenet, can't earn a living by selling. Of course, a deceptive offer can't be sensible. It can only appear so . . . as long as no one asks the right questions.

A single salesperson can enhance or diminish the value of any product or service. The impression conveyed can reach far beyond individual customers, to include their friends, relatives, and business associates.

The Sales Army

Some people compare a sales force to an army. The correlation makes sense. They're the persons who fight the daily battles for market share. We all know soldiers fight better when they believe their cause is just. An army also fights better when they have an excellent plan, dependable weapons, sufficient ammunition, and skillful tactical support. A capable marketing department provides their sales department with these crucial supplies. When marketers mentally manufacture high quality provisions, they equip their salespeople better than most.

Not all marketers think of the sales force as their company's army. In practice, some marketing departments believe the goal is to make selling superfluous. They admit it can never really happen, but they continue to speak of the idea as though it has merit. They contend that when marketing is "done right," no one needs to sell anything. From that predication grand predictions grow. A marketer will say, "This burglar alarm is the greatest. Just put it on the shelves, and it'll sell itself."

Once in a while, the mere announcement of a new product or service is all that it takes to sell it. Distributors and customers line up to buy it. Such easy success can become the prelude to disaster. An inexperienced manufacturer could decide that marketing's creativity actually decreases the need for sales skills. If she anticipates a repeat performance with future merchandise, her lack of preparation to sell her goods can launch the company's downfall.

Other marketers believe it's their duty to challenge the sales department. A manufacturer would never consider going onto the factory floor, to "uncalibrate" machinery, to give production a challenge. Yet, it's common to hear marketing tell management, "We don't want to make things too easy for sales. They have to have a challenge to keep them on their toes." While you concentrate on keeping your sales force "on their toes," your competitors will be sending your *former* customers home "dancing a jig."

Make It Easy to Sell

When marketing is "done right," it makes selling as easy as possible. Thus, the firm gains an exceptionally productive sales force. Salespeople do not dash home to watch television the minute they reach their quota. On the contrary, the easier it is for them to sell something, the more they try to do it. Give them credible wares, and an understanding of the plan, and they'll be out there selling, all day . . . every day. That's how good salespeople like to make their living. Usually, the more they can sell, the better living they make. Consequently, they have no reason to quit early, unless they discover they are offering something few people want—at least among those they approach.

Marketing's work provides something to sell—to a specific market. Whatever you planned in the past, the sales staff is offering in the present. If your program lacked substance, their sales volume is probably no better.

A successful idea often takes root during your conversations with customers, and potential customers. This never-failing source of information allows you to hear needs, expressed by different people, in various ways. As your understanding grows, potential solutions come to mind. You verify your instinct and insight with research, and reach conclusions on a myriad of subjects. As time passes, you begin to share your understanding with sales, and add their knowledge to yours. They, in turn, will sow the concepts, and sell the goods you conceived.

Reconnaissance

If a sales department is the infantry, then a marketing department provides the reconnaissance. They study the enemy to learn their strong and weak points, and pass the information on to the soldiers in the field. When no one tells salespeople where to attack, they'll fight wherever they think it's interesting. That's usually wherever they see action. Action suggests adversaries, many of whom could know more about your goods than your own army knows about yours. A sales force that has to fend for itself on the battlefield will rarely win.

Promising the World

A manufacturer of a new line of office furniture listened to his employee "promising the world" to a potential dealer at a trade show. The salesman was comparing his desk with a competitor's. The more he talked, the further he strayed from reality. Finally, the owner stepped in. "I have to remind you," he said to the dealer, "that we aren't somebody else. Our desk is not the same as theirs. It's similar, but it's also different in these ways. . . ."

By having to reign in his salesman, the manufacturer recognized an elementary procedure he had neglected to practice with regularity. After that experience, he religiously met with his staff to provide the latest market information. He had done so only haphazardly in the past. Though he hadn't verbalized his expectations, he'd thought they'd collect needed data for themselves. Some salespeople do; most don't; few investigate thoroughly. In reality, they don't study a market; they try to capture it, by persuading customers to buy their goods. A firm that expects their sales force to do all of its own reconnaissance can go through employees faster than they move their merchandise.

Sometimes, a salesperson will try to persuade her customer to buy whatever she's selling, though her product lacks a specifically requested feature. She'll depreciate the need for a missing attribute, or flatly state that it's not available anywhere. Such statements aren't always as deliberately deceptive as they appear. The salesperson could be unaware of important differences between competing lines. Or, she may simply not know how her product or service compensates for a missing quality. Mediocre salespeople have become excellent, given the right training. Their training comes from the sales manager; but much of the vital information imparted comes from marketers. A highly productive sales department usually indicates a company that is holding a strong hand. A knowledgeable and imaginative marketing department is their ace in the hole.

Mapping the Plan

A marketing plan is the foundation of a sales plan. Marketers need a clear picture of their job. Without it, the planning process can resemble a cramming session for a final exam. A few people go into a room each day, lock the door, and periodically call out for coffee and pizza. As the days drag on, the company loses precious time. At long last, marketing presents its tome to the sales department.

The soldiers of the sales force anticipate reading about new products to offer old customers. They look for new geographic areas where they can introduce existing products. They expect to find original concepts for new or old goods. In essence, they look for a map upon which they can lay out their plan of attack. Instead, they study the marketing plan, and groan. Someone expresses the feelings of all, in one question. "Which idiots thought this up?"

Sales Feedback

Salespeople quickly recognize "pie-in-the-sky" presumptions, or missing ingredients, simply because they know the information they need out in the field. By consulting with sales periodically while you develop your plan, they can pinpoint essential details you're overlooking. Whenever marketing and sales regularly work together, the productivity of both departments increases. Sales can also suggest the advertising, brochures, demonstrations, and promotions that will provide the most helpful tactical support.

Some years ago, the management of a major American semiconductor company provided data books for their salespeople to give to customers. Marketing looked at the books, and decided they were too expensive. They were sure other sales support tools would prove more cost effective, so they gradually reduced the budget for the data books. Then management did a survey. They asked each salesperson to rate the effectiveness of the tools. The data books got a 97 percent rating, higher than any other tool.

It's so easy to identify useful tools that it's sheer nonsense to complicate the process. Just ask the people who use them. Competent salespeople wield tools in ways others can't. They have unique skills. Armed with the necessary information, they know how to differentiate their goods, their company, and themselves, from the competition.

When a CEO receives a marketing plan, he'll talk to the head of sales about it. They go to lunch, and the CEO says, "Marketing wants us to hold on where we are, and start moving into this other area. What do you think?"

If the sales executive says, "I don't know how they can imagine we'll succeed over there," everybody has a problem. If, instead, the answer is, "Yes, we discussed it. I was skeptical, but now I see how it could work. I figure we'll do this first, and follow up with that." Then the CEO has to think, "Okay, they've tied sales into the plan. Let's get moving."

Remember, if you ask your sales force what else to sell, they'll tell you what customers want *today*. Anything they say about the market will usually relate to current events. Sometimes you can make good use of such information. When you are preparing for a future market, you need to do your own research and analysis. Then consult with sales, frequently. Explain your thinking, seriously consider their comments, and respect their knowledge of *how* to sell.

Kenneth Blanchard and Robert Lorber, in their book, *The One Minute Manager,* expressed the idea cleverly. The authors were referring to all aspects of business, when they put a new twist on an old advertising slogan. They told us, "Feedback is the breakfast of champions."

A Common Goal

Marketing and sales are pursuing a mutual goal. They are simply trying to develop and sell something customers want. The marketing department, after completing their research, and consulting with the sales department, decides where they should place the goods. Sales strives to get them there. They have to do this ahead of the competition, or in spite of them, if competitors got there first.

Distributors Are Not Customers

Wholesale and retail distributors, though they may buy the goods they're going to sell, are only types of sales organizations. They are never their suppliers' customers. (Most people think of distribution solely in relation to products. When we return to the subject, in Chapter 12, we'll examine distribution's part in all kinds of industries.) The basic function of any distributor is to make products or services available to those who'll use them.

Over the years, successful manufacturers usually sell their products to the same outlets. Decades of repetition can cause them to forget that these distributors are not, and never were, their customers. Gradually, the factory loses the ability to prepare for the future, by losing contact with their *real* customers. Unless an enthusiastic marketer comes in, the company is on its way out.

New businesses are subject to commit a variation of the same error. They desperately need desirable outlets. When they finally get some, they immediately think and speak of them as "their customers." Their distributors' requirements become a chief topic of conversation. In short order, they've stopped concentrating on their targeted clientele.

A factory that sells directly to end-users serves a market that allows them do so. Otherwise, a product may require any number of intermediate sales organizations; but none are customers in the true sense of the word.

All manufacturers need to treat their wholesale and retail distributors respectfully. Without them, it's difficult to survive . . . much less grow. Nevertheless, they're not the market you serve. If they take your goods on consignment, they are your business partners. If they buy your goods, they're also your banking partners.

Distributors As Marketers

On the other hand, a distributor's position is akin to a franchisee. Theoretically, they should only have to develop a sales plan to sell the products they carry. Their own marketing program will concern itself with differentiating their company from their competitors. It should also define other goods they could profitably handle.

In theory, the distributor's salespeople will sell products to other companies, or retail customers, by using the concepts manufacturers have conceived. The problem is that too many factories ignore marketing. They develop "me too" products for existing markets; they don't think about original concepts. With time, a distributor can find itself saddled with goods that appear identical to a half dozen other brands. Now it has to figure out how to differentiate the goods—or sell them at a cut-rate—in order to unload them.

Many domestic, and even foreign, manufacturers view distributors as a necessary nuisance. Necessary, but overrated in importance. They fail to recognize what these essential links in the chain do to earn their way. Manufacturers really believe their splendid merchandise would sell itself . . . if the distributor persuaded enough people to notice it. The distributor knows it's a factory's responsibility to generate interest in their own goods. But the manufacturers prefer to blame a lack of traffic in the distributor's warehouse, or outlet, for their slow sales.

When a manufacturer's marketing program creates considerable customer traffic, their product commands a distributor's attention, goodwill, and help. This happens even if people don't buy the goods they came to see.

Combining Marketing and Sales

By now you may be wondering about that person in your firm . . . possibly yourself . . . who carries a card introducing him as the "Vice-President of Marketing and Sales." It is rare to find someone who is *outstanding* in both these jobs. Few people take their inspiration from immediate results, while also contemplating the future value of imaginary products or services. (Management may even ask marketing to see ten years into the future which often translates into asking the impossible.)

I suspect some readers, who are CEO's, just muttered, "Great! Now this guy is saying I need another high-salaried employee. What else is he going to tell me that I can't afford to do?"

I appreciate the problem, so here's a suggestion that works. If you, as the CEO, can't afford a person to head each department, take a long look at yourself in the mirror. Decide which job you do best, and hire someone to fill the other position. Since your object is profitable growth, you have to nourish the business with the essential talent it requires. I would prefer that you hire a manager of sales and you retain the marketing function, but if you truly are a much better sales manager, then go with your strength.

Beware of assuming that a person who has held both titles for another firm, must be capable of doing both jobs. We all know there can be a conspicuous difference between holding a title and doing the work. Given extraordinary luck, you may find someone with proven skill in both arenas. If so, hire this prodigy quickly. Realize, however, that (s)he is probably on the way to starting his or her own business.

Those CEOs who are already wearing both sales and marketing hats, and can't afford to hire anyone else, must hope to possess exceptional ability. There's a short term alternative to doing both jobs, explained at the end of the book. You'll also find a summary of traits to look for in a capable marketer.

Get Everyone Involved

A CEO who doubles as the head of sales, still cannot afford to ignore marketing. David Packard, of Hewlett-Packard, said that marketing is too important to leave to the marketing department! His blunt statement holds a dual meaning. First, management has to remain aware of marketing's intentions and progress. Second, the whole company needs to understand the program.

People resist change—and they resent exclusion. The better they understand a firm's actions, the more involved they become in the business. Unexplained orders "from above" often appear excessive or senseless to the uninitiated. Blind obedience becomes boring. It lulls employees into a semiconscious condition that gets them through their work days. When this happens, management starts complaining about slow sales, lost orders, mislabeled products, and misused machinery.

IBM and General Mills, among many other large and small companies, are now turning many of their operations over to their formerly bored employees. A worker at a Goodyear plant, said, "It's nothing like a factory. You're actually in on everything—from making it to sending it out the door." A General Mills' worker put it another way. "You feel like you're going to your own business, not like you're going to do something for somebody else."

An understanding of what the business is trying to accomplish can elicit help from unexpected sources. A company that encourages participation and input stimulates people to think. Later in the book, you'll see what happens in climates where ideas can flourish.

The Need for Marketing

Manufacturers, distributors, and retailers of a given product are all courting the same people—the ultimate customer. A marketing department conceived of the goods these customers could want. Obviously, a concept is worthless until the product or service it relates to is available to those who'll use it.

Goods get where they need to be through the efforts of salespeople. Salespeople get where they need to be, more often and quicker, through the efforts of marketing.

Were you to develop a marketing plan for something you didn't intend to sell, your behavior would rate as absurd. Yet most businesses fail to recognize the absurdity of trying to sell something without first planning how to market it. You could liken it to sending forth a battery of expert marksmen with the following marching orders:

"The enemy is all around us. Take our word for it, we've given you the finest weapon. Pick whatever hill you think you can capture. Collect your ammunition whenever you need it, wherever you can find it. You call yourselves soldiers, let's see you prove it."

Promises That Make Sense—
And Some That Don't

*The louder he talked of his honour,
the faster we counted our spoons.*

Ralph Waldo Emerson,
Conduct of Life

Salespeople may know their offer is everything they say it is. Customers can still wonder which salesperson says what he means, and means what he says . . . as the March Hare and Alice discussed. These days, companies offer a monotonous parade of elaborate claims and promises.

A carefully constructed guarantee of satisfaction bestows credibility on a product or service. Well managed, it immediately differentiates a company from the majority of its competitors. All kinds of businesses claim to stand behind whatever they sell. In reality, most do not even comprehend the real purpose of a guarantee.

When Price Is Not the Issue

Before enlarging on this, we need to look at a dreadful scenario that occurs too frequently these days. A woman has just learned that she has a potentially fatal illness. The doctor, who delivered the news, immediately starts talking about a treatment, available through a local hospital's out-patient clinic. Gradually, the patient starts asking questions about the program, but her first question is not, "How much does it cost?" She wants to know about the treatment, its duration, and the promise it holds. At the end of the consultation, she may ask the price. Or, she may leave without asking . . . whether she has insurance or not. For the moment, she's not thinking about whether she can afford the care; she only wants to know if it can save her life.

The scene exemplifies the intense single-mindedness that can overtake us, at times. We may also suffer this reaction in situations that aren't a matter of life or death. When something threatens to destroy the business we depend on for our livelihoods, even highly improbable ways to save it can completely absorb our attention for a while. The problem becomes even more horrendous if many of our assets are in jeopardy.

Al Burger

Now, we can change to a much lighter subject and use the scene's point. We shall examine the adventures of Al "Bugs" Burger. He started a small business, and became one of the largest pest exterminators in the United States. That, in itself, is an accomplishment, but he did it while charging up to ten times more than his competitors. If any company I've worked with increased their prices by a factor of ten, the deed would have destroyed them. I believe most of you would say the same. This being the case, how did Al Burger do it?

Years ago, he spoke at a pest exterminators convention in Florida. Before he could finish his speech, the audience made it plain they had heard enough. They invited him to leave the stage, and he complied.

In essence, he had been talking about their dirty business. He was not referring to the pests they pursued, but their lack of self-regulation. The industry was doing a poor job, had a deservedly bad reputation, and needed to enforce higher standards—for everybody's sake. After the audience showed him what they thought of his opinion, he quit the Association. He decided to apply his ideas to his own company.

It's easy to understand the chemistry that destroys cockroaches, and other undesirable creatures. The application of the process is far from consistent, however. Burger was sure his firm could do a thorough job, built on the basis of well trained and well paid employees, who gave each job the needed time. This presupposed customers who would be willing to pay more for the service. That is how the "life or death" factor comes into play.

If we were having dinner in a restaurant, and my wife found a cockroach among her vegetables, she wouldn't whisper, "There's a bug on my plate." She'd scream, "Mitch, there's a roach in my food!" I'm certain everyone around us, and throughout the restaurant would hear her. Or, they would hear me on our way out. During the following weeks, we'd tell our friends and relatives about our experience. Carol might speak of it to people at work. I might mention it to some business associates. Some of these people would pass the tale on to others.

How much do you think that one roach could cost the restaurant? Consider the monetary damage to a country club, a hotel, or a caterer. The price they would pay, in future business, might exceed any amount of money they'd have spent to prevent it. Because of this fact, Al Burger knew he could charge more than the going rate—if he could reliably prevent the disaster.

Exterminators routinely claimed they could reduce pests "to an acceptable level." That's a catchy little phrase.

Unfortunately, it will not save the life of a neighborhood coffee shop that serves one roach in a piece of pie. What does "acceptable" mean? Al Burger said the only acceptable level was no pests at all. So, what he promised was what many wanted to hear.

Before he would sign a contract, he did an on-site survey. He made plain how the client had to store their food, and clean their premises, in order to fulfill their side of the bargain. At times, he insisted on minor building alterations, but his demands were always reasonable. For his part, he promised that his skilled employees would do a thorough job. The process should eradicate all pests, and no one had to pay for the service until they believed their premises were clean. If, however, it were to happen that a customer spotted a bug later, Burger adhered to a preset procedure.

He immediately sent a personal letter of apology to the patron, on his own letterhead. He paid for another meal or night's lodging for the customer, to encourage all members of the party to return. His own customer received up to a full year's refund of the service fee. Additionally, Burger paid for them to have one year's extermination service from the company of their choice. The guarantee also acknowledged that a city might close a business because of insects or rodents. In that event, Bugs Burger Bug Killers would pay all fines, replace all lost profits, and pay their customer an extra $5,000. Not surprisingly, the occasional client who became entitled to a year's free service from any company, usually chose to remain with Bugs Burger's firm.

In 1986, BBBK did $33 million in sales, and paid $120,000 in claims. With time, some of his competitors began to copy him. BBBK's charges were no longer ten times higher than others, because competitors had to raise their prices—not because Al lowered his. Occasionally, some of his customers left him, to try a less expensive service. Many came back. They decided the higher fee still gave them more for their money.

Burger had recognized the "something else" his clients were buying. There was more than one additional feature, and his guarantee precisely expressed all of them. Thereby, he proved his thorough understanding of his customers' needs. His employees made an honest and skillful effort to deliver as promised. A claim against the guarantee immediately informed management that the company's performance needed improvement. These policies portray marketing at its finest.

Not Everyone Should Be Your Customer

There are two key points to Al's story. One relates to the customers you serve, and the other, to the guarantee you offer them.

Al Burger refused to do business with certain firms. He only accepted those who convinced him they would comply with his standards of cleanliness. He did this for his own sake: to make his business a success.

Everyone who walks through a company's door is not necessarily a potential customer. A business should try to restrict their trade to those persons they believe they can satisfactorily serve. Through the years, the practice pays off. The trick is to survive while you learn whom you can please, and which ones you should politely send to your competitors!

Executive Search Warranty

A friend of mine owned an executive search business. For years, it remained a modest sized firm, serving a select group of customers. He conducted a limited number of searches, but each assignment produced a sizable fee. He received 33% of an employee's yearly salary. His proportion of the six figure salaries his clients offered provided him with a comfortable income.

One evening, he was complaining about a client he could not satisfy. I suggested a money-back policy. He replied, "I'll replace anybody they don't like. It's written in bold print in every contract." I argued that his offer was not a worthy substitute, and posed the following example.

A business buying from his firm asks for an outstanding employee. They want someone much better than good. If, after hiring, they realize the person is capable, but certainly not excellent, they didn't get what they expected. They invested time and money in the process. If they then decide to settle for a lesser talent, the search service should settle for a lesser fee. A client's only recourse shouldn't require firing the person and starting over.

My friend considered my idea ludicrous. He added that the industry's association might expel him for conducting contingent searches. I insisted the policy was simply a guarantee of satisfaction.

His "failure" rate was around five percent. He admitted that his business could still survive even if he gave every one of those clients full refunds. He also conceded something more. If he offered such terms, he'd probably have to beat potential clients off with a stick.

During the following months, he thought about our conversation. He finally decided to test the policy, cautiously. He knew his success would depend on his ability to practice selectivity in client acquisition, a skill he slowly improved. To guarantee his ability to make a great match between client and prospective employee, and assure he only dealt with clients he understood well enough to guarantee that match, he had to become even more selective in choosing clients. His business became more successful and profitable, with even more satisfied customers.

A Guarantee's Purpose

The more important point of the "Bugs" Burger story relates to the guarantee, itself. A guarantee's primary purpose is *not* to satisfy customers. Its real aim is to enable a company to *improve performance*. A business needs to structure its guarantee so it can know, as quickly as possible, when it's not living up to the promise. Anything else reduces it to the mediocrity most companies offer.

Some years ago, a restaurant chain in California advertised a typically inept guarantee. It could have been useful, but the way they applied it reduced it to nonsense.

The restaurant was among the first to promise a quick lunch. They had paid attention to their customers, statewide, and realized many would welcome it. The company invested in expensive advertising to announce their new policy. They would serve lunch within a given number of minutes . . . or there'd be no charge.

A business associate of mine, whose time was important to him, got his meal a full five minutes late. The waitress, when told of it, replied, "Oh, you don't understand. It's not from the time you give me the order. It's from the time I give it to the cook."

While he ate his lunch, he thought about the answer, and became genuinely annoyed. How could diners in a large restaurant know when an order gets to the cook? Since they couldn't, how would they know when they could collect on the guarantee? When he paid the check, he decided to mention the lateness of the meal again. The cashier's reply began with the same fatuous words: "You don't understand. . . ."

That sentence immediately places the blame squarely on the customer. The guarantee program could have furnished helpful feedback, while it increased business. Instead, it only guaranteed that some patrons would become too angry to return.

Denny's Restaurants, a national chain, proved they had paid attention to the mistakes of others. They promised to serve breakfast and lunch within ten minutes. After taking an order, each waitperson left a stop watch on the table.

Get Complaints

If your guarantee is easy to collect on, people will tell you when something is wrong. If you make it complicated or tedious, you'll annoy your patrons, who may then speak badly of your business to others. If you offer nothing, you'll lose customers without learning how to improve your performance.

No business can always satisfy everybody they serve. A displeased customer who isn't complaining *to* you, is complaining *about* you to somebody else. Statistics show that anyone who feels mistreated by a company will tell a lot of other people. You need to encourage your patrons to vent their displeasure on someone inside the firm.

If a company representative just listens patiently, the business has a 50/50 chance of holding on to the customer. In addition to listening, an employee who tries to help, often nullifies the problem. The complainant is as likely to remain with the firm after the incident as before it. If someone actually resolves the issue, the offended person will frequently turn into an enthusiastic and vocal supporter.

Plumbing Service

The owner of a large plumbing concern recalls his first year in business, serving only commercial establishments. His unplanned reaction to an unforeseen event established a policy he has never regretted.

One day, he learned his answering service had neglected to convey a message left a few days earlier. He immediately telephoned the customer. The manager coldly informed him that someone else had come to their rescue. The plumber explained the reason for his tardiness, but his explanation met with silence. In that moment, acting on instinct, he offered to refund his competitor's charge. He asked the manager to accept the payment as his apology for failing to be there when he was needed. That company is still his customer—along with many of the other businesses in the area.

What They Buy Is What You Guarantee

As a skillful marketer, you must know the "something else" your customers want to buy. Any one, or all, of the additional components can usually become the basis of your guarantee. A promise that precisely expresses your customers' needs, proves you understand them. The company that shows it is paying attention to its clientele will get their money.

Skillful marketing also means that a business recognizes its own limitations. They offer and guarantee products and services they can actually deliver. Whenever necessary, and without argument, the firm refunds all or part of the charges.

It would be wonderful if this practice were always as simple as it sounds. In relation to some occupations, it takes considerable determination and ingenuity to construct a workable promise of satisfaction.

Pereira & Luckman

After Charles Luckman left Lever Brothers, he returned to his boyhood love, architecture. He and his partner rented small offices on the third floor of a walk-up building. They employed only a very few people.

Luckman's business experience made him acutely aware of the curious way architects computed their fees. A while later, he had an opportunity to speak to a chapter of the American Institute of Architects. He used the occasion to voice his strong disapproval of the industry's percentage fee system. Traditionally, architects received a percentage of the cost of constructing a building they designed. When a project ran over budget, the architect earned a larger fee. Conversely, a firm that was frugal with their client's money, earned a smaller fee for their effort. Luckman's implication was plain, and his fellow professionals were angry with him for publicly expressing his views.

He had to answer for his words to the AIA's Ethics Committee. In his book, *Twice In A Lifetime*, he told of his reply. "To them I said that an architect should be paid a lump-sum fee for his work on any project, and an extra bonus for coming in *under* budget, not over."

Luckman, with his partner Pereira, decided to apply the principle in their own practice. At first, it upset their assistants, and some threatened to quit. Nevertheless, after six months, Luckman says his designers found it ". . . more challenging and satisfying to be creative within the limits set by a client's budget." Their employees helped the men build an enormously successful business. Within a comparatively short time, the firm moved to a bronze-and-glass high-rise of its own.

Pereira and Luckman did not refund fees. Their promise worked in reverse. It guaranteed their company a reward for considerate as well as excellent performance. They had to stay within a set budget. Anytime they could reduce costs, while still meeting specifications, they earned a bonus. The concept eventually changed the rules of the whole architectural marketplace. For industries that can apply this formula, Luckman has proven its value.

Self Esteem . . . Guaranteed

Nathaniel Branden is a psychotherapist and clinical psychologist. He is also a prolific author. His main interest revolves around the critically important subject of self-esteem.

During a speech to some businesspeople, Dr. Branden revealed the confidence he had in a method he had developed. Under certain conditions, he promised to return his fee to dissatisfied clients. To my knowledge, this is unprecedented in his profession. The uniqueness of his offer reflects his equally unique and successful approach to helping people help themselves.

Before Dr. Branden will give his guarantee, his client and he decide *exactly* what they'll consider success. One manufacturer of custom automobiles employs a mirror image of the same idea. It gets its customers to decide *exactly* what will satisfy them, by refusing to guarantee their satisfaction!

What Is Satisfaction?

Patrons frequently come to this manufacturer with requirements for a car that could equally become either a Mercedes or a Hyundai. Their words and their stipulations don't match. Unwittingly, they are expecting the finished product to comply with their mental image of it.

This manufacturer knew he couldn't guarantee delivery of an illusive image. Still, he wanted to satisfy his customers. To do so, he had to know exactly what they wanted. This meant he needed to force them to think in specific terms . . . a task they had unconsciously avoided. By refusing to guarantee their satisfaction, he convinced them they had better start talking, or go elsewhere. In turn, the doubts he raised in their minds concerning satisfaction made them dubious of less forthright firms. Most agreed to talk.

After a lengthy conversation, his customers had to sign a plainly worded agreement. It listed all specifications, in precise terms. Each client knew exactly what his car would contain. It then became the factory's responsibility to build according to the agreement. Through a strongly emphasized absence of a guarantee, the policy that replaced it actually provided for the customer's satisfaction.

A Guaranteed Audit

If an accountant knew she would only have to return one $10,000 fee a year, she would gladly guarantee her book-keeping, tax returns, or financial guidance. The publicity would more than make up for it. In real life, the uncertainty of the amount she may have to refund stops her. She needs the data that can help her reduce her uncertainty to a calculated risk. Unfortunately, there's no all-encompassing formula. Each firm has to apply the idea as it relates to the service they offer their clientele. Gradually, as they work the policy into their practice, they'll learn the real costs involved.

Customers don't want to negotiate a guarantee. You need to set your terms and live with them. As you acquire knowledge, you can change your future agreements . . . if necessary.

When an accountant does an audit, she can easily have a conflict of interest. Usually, she's auditing her client's business. She could think, "This guy wants me to say his mushy, moldy fruit still has a monetary value. If I don't buy his argument, I won't get his account next year. If I do, I run the risk of having a bad audit." This arrangement can't work. An honest audit represents an unqualified opinion. Someone's future opinion can hardly lend itself to a guarantee.

Accountants need to know they'll still have a client, even when they have to reject certain reasoning. What, then, can they guarantee? What does management want—other than an opinion that agrees with their own? Ordinarily, it's work done within a given time and budget. An accountant can promise she will complete her audit by a month from Tuesday, and it will cost no more than $10,000. If she's late, she must reduce her fee according to the agreement. If the cost runs higher, she has to eat the difference. Some firms now use a different approach. They contract to do an establishment's books for a year, and toss in the audit.

Domino's

Tom Monaghan, and his brother, bought a small pizza store bordering the Eastern Michigan University campus. The shop was open from late afternoon until midnight, and the brothers each worked a half shift. The hours allowed Tom to remain in college, and his brother to keep his job at the post office. Eight months later, Tom's brother wanted to get out of the partnership. Tom couldn't operate the business by himself and continue his studies. He had to decide whether he wanted to sell pizzas or earn a college degree. If he had opted for the degree, today he might be just another poor college graduate, instead of the wealthy franchiser of Domino's Pizza.

The store only had room for two tiny tables for in-house dining, so Monaghan had to rely on take-out and delivery trade. From that beginning, he built the nation's most successful pizza delivery business. In his book, *Pizza Tiger*, he explains how his famous thirty minute delivery guarantee came into existence.

Most people order home-delivered food when they are already hungry; it follows that quick delivery is important to them. Delivering a quality product was of equal importance to Monaghan, so he used what he considered to be the choicest ingredients. In spite of his insistence on excellence, however, pizza is most flavorful when served at a particular temperature. Therefore, he knew he had to work out how to deliver hot pizza, promptly and consistently. He adopted a time limit of thirty minutes as his goal. He had major problems to solve, before he could make a delivery guarantee part of his company's policy.

He needed a better heat-retaining carton than the standard box used by the industry. It took time to find a manufacturer who was willing and able to develop one. He also needed improved kitchen equipment, which would permit quick preparation and reliable cooking, during the busiest hours. He embarked on a search for the most efficient equipment, an aim the company continues to pursue. Eventually, Monaghan could promise that an order would arrive within thirty minutes—or there was no charge.

Later, management changed the terms to three dollars off the purchase price. They discovered too many customers wouldn't accept a free pizza when it was only a few minutes late. Without realizing it, these fair-minded persons had prevented the company from tracking delivery performance. Because management was paying attention . . . and wanted a successful feedback system . . . they changed to the more readily accepted discount.

A footnote to the story concerns some college students who took refuge in the original guarantee. Thanks to Domino's policy, they found a way to eat while conserving their limited budgets. They ordered pizzas from their own, hard-to-find, locations, and got their food free every time!

After their game became known, the company did not drop the program because a few people had cheated them. On the contrary, Phil Bressler, an owner of 18 Domino franchises, put the incident in its proper perspective. He said, "They'll be Domino's customers for life, those kids." So will their friends. It was some of the most desirable publicity the chain could get.

Unfortunately, as 1993 came to a close, Domino's was forced to drop its delivery time guarantee. An accident involving a Domino's driver caused the company to pay a tremendous penalty as the result of a lawsuit. While driving safely should never be compromised, the loss of the warranty's feedback will make it more difficult for Domino's to monitor their service quality.

Feedback

When push comes to shove, the company that wins will have a tested and proven feedback system in place. Management will know as soon as something goes wrong, so they can fix it promptly. Without feedback, a company may not realize they have a problem, until they've lost a noticeable quantity of customers. Then, they'll have to try to figure out what they're doing wrong.

Frequently, a guarantee spells out the service that management expects their employees to provide their customers. Workers appreciate these guidelines, and respect their employers because of them. People who are proud of their firm's policies take pride in their work.

It Won't Work in *My* Business

Only certain businesses have to create specialized terms. Most will benefit from a guarantee that's easy to collect on, and as all-encompassing as possible. Consumers consider many problems not worth mentioning, unless a business stresses a guarantee of satisfaction. Annoyed patrons just go away . . . and never bother to come back.

Many people believe a money-back, easy to collect on, guarantee is an invitation to bankruptcy. You may think, "Guarantees can work for pizzas, but not in my business, with my customers!" You may be right. But before you dismiss the idea, there are some other factors to consider.

First, if someone repeatedly demands a refund, you can suggest they trade elsewhere. Obviously, your company can't satisfy them. Second, if you deal with a clientele you sincerely believe will misuse a guarantee of satisfaction, you can still establish limited terms. In some industries, a guaranteed delivery time can be a powerful tool. Third, instead of shaking your head against the whole concept, try shaking yourself loose from your preoccupation with people who are out to cheat everybody.

Sears

For decades, Sears was famous for guaranteeing satisfaction. They offered the ultimate promise. To return something, a person simply had to say, "I'm not satisfied." There was another facet of their guarantee, and a story from my youth exemplifies it.

For my sixteenth birthday, I got my first car. It was old enough to need a lot of repairs, and I learned I would never be an auto mechanic. I also discovered how easily a careless novice, with a torque wrench, can cross thread a head bolt. I went to Sears, ruined socket in hand. I'd brought it with me to make sure I got the right replacement. The salesman took one look at it, and handed me a new one. I asked the price. "There's no charge," he said. "It shouldn't have broken."

He took me by such surprise, I blurted out, "But you don't know what I did to it!"

He smiled, and said, "It doesn't matter. It broke, and the store guarantees it won't. So don't argue, just take it."

Although they were extremely lenient, Sears had learned years before that a small percentage of their patrons would bring back their purchases. Furthermore, only a tiny percentage of them were actually cheating. Management decided to ignore that insignificant percentage.

Some years later, Sears changed most of their policies. There are conflicting stories about their internal affairs, but our concern is only with the customers' point of view. Suddenly, the store's highly praised appliance repair service became a source of constant suspicion and aggravation. Simultaneously, the chain's satisfaction guarantee vanished— as far as customers could tell. A request for an exchange, not to mention a refund, evoked a bitter argument. Numberless families, representing generations of loyal patrons, scurried to other firms.

Sears' business plummeted. After more time passed, publicity suggested that the company had returned to some of their former ways. Still, many of their ex-customers, who tried them again, decided it wasn't true.

A few of the concessionaires and subcontractors, who operated through Sears' stores, offered poor quality merchandise, or inferior workmanship. The owners or employees of these concessions rudely dismissed complaints, and refused all requests for refunds. Many of the returning customers believed they were hearing the store's policy, so they didn't complain to the business office. They simply went away again, and may never come back.

In fact, Sears' customer service department gave refunds, from all departments, without an argument. It often required a long wait, in a long line, however. A few clerks had to handle an assortment of services. The chain's all-encompassing guarantee was alive—but not well. It was no longer easy to collect, and it did not include the goods of their concessionaires and subcontractors.

In the public's eyes, Sears had become like too many businesses. Granted, Sears management did not behave as though customers were cheating them. But that was little solace to patrons, who often felt abused, if not cheated.

Regardless of Sears' experience, if cheaters still worry you, consider Michael Leven's observation. Drawing on his experience as a hotel executive, he identified a trait common to management. They usually worry most about only one percent of their customers: the percentage that might cheat. Translate his observation into action, and you can see the danger in the practice. By establishing policies to protect your company from the one percent who might cheat, you are mistreating the ninety-nine percent who are honest.

Prices That Make Sense—
And Some That Don't

*Money speaks sense in a language
all nations understand.*

Aphra Behn,
The Rover

When a company prices its goods, its survival demands that it gets back more than the cost of offering them. Customers don't talk about making a profit. Nonetheless, everyone likes to do better than break even in the marketplace. We willingly trade with firms that give us whatever the market says is our "money's worth." We prefer to trade wherever we feel we get "more for our money."

An engineer will buy injection molding services from a particular supplier because she prefers their workmanship. Or maybe she appreciates their terms, prompt delivery, or helpful personnel. That evening, she chooses to spend her own money in one restaurant, instead of another, for similar reasons.

Retail consumers expect a business to make a profit, but they don't think of themselves as paying the firm its cost-plus.

Our federal government venerates those words. They pay actual cost-plus, when something they need is hard to make. They pay negotiated cost-plus, if the item is more readily producible.

Government Buying Practices

Government purchasing agents don't spend their own money in the evening in the same way they spend tax dollars all day. Rules and tradition require them to determine needs, publish specifications, and accept the lowest bid. Private enterprise may claim a low bid will win, but more often than not they are using the idea for leverage.

The government lists the exact requirements for practically everything it buys. When a project requires hammers, every hammer must pass specific tests, as stated in the contract. The tool may cost $5, but the paperwork attached to prove its worthiness could cost $395. In spite of those individual and costly pedigrees, some may break when used for hammering. We all know that hammers are a benign example of tragic irregularities.

It's impossible for any government agency to make a profit. This prevents "corruption by the profit motive." The government's buying habits lack prudence and all the participants in the charade know it. The persons who could change the procedure are the same ones who frequently benefit from it. Few human beings voluntarily surrender their personal advantages.

Anyone who constantly spends far more than is necessary eventually must get smarter or go broke. The same rule applies to a government. Even our public servants have begun to fear the consequences of their buying habits. Bureaucrats have started paying attention to business strategies for buying right. By listening, at least they're finally acknowledging the importance of something other than just the cost. And maybe their attempts to "level the playing field" between all players is unnatural and anti-competitive.

Cost vs. Price

In the competitive marketplace, only the motion picture industry broadcasts how much money it invests in a production. According to its singular accounting system, it rarely makes a net profit. Still, customers never judge the worth of anything—including a movie—by the amount of money a business was willing to invest in it. There's only one important connection between cost and selling price. It determines whether a firm gets to stay in business.

A supplier sets the original price of its goods, but it doesn't have the last word. The amount of money customers are actually willing to pay settles all questions about the dollar value of everything. Consumers accept an opening price . . . or reject it and force it lower. When the yuppies upscaled Corona beer, as discussed earlier, they provided the exception that accompanies every rule.

While you are deciding how much to ask for your goods, keep a simple truth in mind. Something you find interesting to offer may not be worth as much as you think. Customers pay more for what they consider necessary, or exceptionally well done.

Regardless of persuasive advertising, people eventually decide for themselves how much they want something. They also pass final judgment on its quality. Your quality control department may insist your goods are superior to the competition's, but the customer's opinion is all that counts. Quality and its sister, monetary worth, are whatever consumers perceive them to be. Their verdict does not emerge from a mysterious or unpredictable realm. It accurately reflects how closely a product matches the user's idea of what she's getting.

Real estate salespeople are reminded daily of the way clients predetermine what they should get for their money. A first time home buyer, or seller, often expects too much. Those experienced in buying and selling homes have learned they aren't going to get a perfect house, or receive the highest price. A newcomer in the real estate market personifies the trouble accompanying "great expectations."

Perdue Farms—The Loss of a Gain

Your customers need to know what they should expect for their money, and it's up to you to create their expectations. Frank Perdue, of Perdue Farms, successfully charged more than the going rate for his poultry. He said, "Customers will go out of their way to buy a superior product, and you can charge them a toll for the trip."

Perdue consistently delivered high-quality poultry. He also wanted to differentiate his wares, in a way shoppers could easily recognize. He had learned that most people judged chickens by their color. The more yellow they were, the better. So he fed his poultry marigolds to enhance their hue!

The company offered consistent quality and color. In response, many people willingly paid a few cents more per pound. Buyers felt they were getting more than the extra change was worth in their pockets. If Frank Purdue could do that with dead chickens, consider what you can do with whatever you offer.

However, in 1990, Perdue Farms came under fire for allowing unsafe conditions in the work place, and for other undesirable practices. Groups reporting behavior they consider unfair to humans, animals, and the environment are here to stay. When their charges are sensible and persistent, the public begins to pay attention. Companies that view activists as naive and unreasonable have not been talking to their customers. In today's marketplace, any firm that proves itself socially irresponsible will watch its profit turn to chicken feed.

The Importance of Price

In Chapter 4, there were seven questions concerning the persons who comprise your market. The subject of price was last on the list. It was not there by chance. Price is usually one of the last subjects on a potential buyer's mind. Shoppers examine a product or service and ask about the matters that concern them before they decide they may want to buy it. Then they ask the price. If the figure does not make sense to them, they may reject the goods for that reason alone. Whenever feasible, they will try to negotiate better terms.

A business uses a sophisticated calculator and an internal rate of return calculation, when they contemplate a major purchase. Retail shoppers do the calculating in their heads. Even a child does a return on investment calculation before she selects a candy bar. Which will give her the most for her money, according to her needs of the moment? If she has to share the candy with someone else, she may choose a different candy from one she would buy for herself.

What a firm tries to do when it sets a price consists of two parts. First, is the need to make enough profit to allow plans to proceed. Second, is the necessity for a dollar figure per unit that will allow potential customers to believe they can get at least their money's worth. Ideally, customers will discover they got more than their money's worth. That's just another way of saying they got more than they initially expected—or more than others offered. The word spreads. The most cost-effective advertising will always be word of mouth. Give your clientele something good to say about your business or its wares, and they'll say it. By under-promising and over-delivering, you invite consumer satisfaction with quality and price.

Many businesspeople believe they must keep prices low to make customers feel they can get their money's worth. A low price can sometimes work against a product or service. Shoppers are seldom aware of all the differences between competing goods, so they may assume a price reflects the value of given merchandise.

Costco—Proving Its Worth

Some firms make low prices the sole benefit they offer. Even then, their whole operation has to make sense. Costco knew it was not enough to provide goods at a discount. They also needed the proper setting. In their stores, patrons meet with the same indifferent sales clerks, and the same tedious delays they encounter in higher priced shops. But otherwise impatient shoppers willingly tolerate the inconveniences, because they believe they are saving money. In fact, studies show there must be long lines in discount houses, or people become concerned they may not be getting a "good" deal. They require social proof there are valuable bargains that others also desire.

Costco's marketing message is simple. In essence, it says, "We won't give you service, and we'll put you in a warehouse. That way you'll feel like you're getting a good deal." Customers expect the drab setting they find. They know that unpainted concrete floors and walls allow lower prices. Everything they see and hear appears so convincing that not *all* of the merchandise has to provide actual savings!

Price vs. Value

Consumers, including discount store shoppers, examine different goods until they find what they want. Then they look for a way to justify the price to themselves, and, when necessary, to their company controller, their friends, or their mother. A person who wants an $80,000 automobile knows that no car, in itself, can be worth that much money. If she can justify its price in her own mind she'll buy it. Her personal perception of value determines the final decision.

The question is *not* whether a business can cost-justify the price it sets on its goods. The crucial question is *whether customers can justify the price.* Marketers help them do it. Nevertheless, few firms consider pricing in that light. Most depend on a traditional formula. They add up the money invested to acquire or produce a product or service, and multiply the sum by a "standard" accounting factor. The result becomes the asking price. Customers often are left to find their own justification for paying it.

A business needs to determine *the highest price* it can *sensibly* ask that bespeaks respect for their customers' good judgment. Sometimes, marketers can ask how much someone would be willing to pay for certain goods. Plainly, this procedure works better with custom production than with standard goods.

A standard product, for multiple uses, ordinarily will only support a price in keeping with its lowest valued utilization. The manufacturer of a small motor may sell it to various companies producing motorized equipment. The finished products containing the motor may range from cheap to expensive. The motor's selling price will generally be in keeping with the lowest value assigned it by the whole market.

The rule does not always reign, however. Construction software is a standard product with multiple uses. IBM historically set the price of its software in accordance with the computer it runs on. If a company has a $2 million computer, the software is worth more to them than a firm with a $2,000 machine. One business will be developing skyscrapers, while the other remodels houses. Networks of PCs in large corporations caused the rethinking of this pricing policy.

Before you produce an item for one specific use, such as an improved sewing needle, ask your potential customers what it would be worth to them. Many will give you a truthful answer, if they've bothered to think about it. You'll probably have to pose the questions that will help them decide. Usually, you have to prod people to think about how much time and material they could save with a better tool.

Automobile Pricing and Value

Consumers buy many products and services simply because they have no choice. One is as good as another. In these markets, any substantial improvement, regardless of its higher price, will quickly persuade people to try it. In the United States, the slogan has been, "If it ain't broke, don't fix it." In Japan, the prevailing attitude became "If it's not perfect, keep working on it."

Who's Who in America describes William Edwards Deming as a statistics educator and consultant. He held an incredible assortment of college degrees, and wrote numerous books. He taught the Japanese to value quality above everything else. He had first tried to teach our nation the same lesson, but most of our major corporate executives refused to listen to him. The Japanese listened and learned. They now annually honor him—an American—for their industrial success. One of his axioms was: "Improve continuously forever."

In the mid-1980s, Lee Iacocca said he needed an exchange rate of 150 yen to the dollar to beat the Japanese automobile industry. He got better than he asked for, but even at 125 yen to the dollar he was still losing market share. The price of Japanese cars has never been the primary reason for their popularity. When their quality was inferior, their low prices did not help their sales. Many American cars are now cheaper than comparable Japanese brands. For a long time, the public has seriously questioned the quality of American automobiles. While that question remained, lower prices made no difference. As real and perceived U.S. car quality has improved, so have sales.

Someone strongly attached to a particular product will scrutinize competing goods, with the intention of finding fault. General Motors finally got the message. They delayed delivering their new Saturn line to dealers. The factory would not release the model until they believed it consistently performed as promised.

When marketing initiates a campaign that promises more than their firm will deliver, it destroys their company's credibility. In essence, it forces customers to find the product's quality disappointing, which means whatever they paid for it was too much.

Guarantees

To be sure, a guarantee erases risk, but no one wants to collect on a warranty. A television set that stops working once a month is not going to satisfy anybody, even if the manufacturer, or the dealer, fixes it promptly. Remember, a guarantee's *main purpose* is to help your firm *gauge, then improve its performance.*

A guarantee also speaks for the quality of your goods, but this does not mean you only have to promise something a little better than your competitors offer. A small improvement might give you a small edge in a marketplace. Your product or service still has to become as good as the end-users want it to be. If not, someone, somewhere, will eventually provide what's lacking.

Common Sense and Nonsense

You may consider that much of this should be obvious to anyone with common sense. Regrettably, in this nation that enables people to become wealthy by using their own judgment, we no longer commonly practice common sense. Too many people have become too wealthy to bother with it. Although we call it "common sense," it is usually too common for those who need it most. After becoming financially comfortable, some people quickly embrace nonsense. This truth has an up-side, however. Anyone who wants to conduct a business sensibly can find room in the marketplace. A competitive market rewards sensible behavior.

Not every successful firm or person succumbs to nonsense. There are many prosperous enterprises guided by people who have never lost sight of sensible business procedures. Francis "Buck" Rodgers, IBM's former Vice-President of Marketing, touched upon a reason for his firm's previous remarkable achievements. Actually, he was not praising his own company, or comparing it to others. He was lamenting a nationwide lack. "It's a shame." he said, "that, in so many companies, whenever you get good service, it's an exception."

Nordstrom

For years, Nordstrom department stores have enjoyed an exceptionally loyal patronage, in spite of the industry's troubles. Signs near their cash registers declare they will not be undersold. Of course, they are referring to the better than average merchandise they carry. In truth, shoppers usually ignore the policy. It's not how much the chain charges for what they sell, but the way they sell it, that has created their steadfast customer base.

My wife was unfamiliar with the firm, until a friend took her to our local store. They each bought a blouse. The saleswoman noticed loose buttons on one of the garments, and she could not replace it. She asked the women if they had other shopping to do. When they said they were through, she gave them complimentary passes to the restaurant, while she had the buttons securely fastened. The lunches cost almost as much as the blouses, but the store gained my family as new customers.

The company's founding concept was that shopping in their stores should be easy and pleasant. They used a variety of tactics to translate the idea into actions. For one, management authorized every salesperson to accept returned goods. There was none of the aggravating rigmarole other retailers impose on their clientele.

In 1990, some Nordstrom's sales personnel accused management of placing too much pressure on them. The company announced they would take immediate steps to rectify the situation. Apparently, they had begun to expect more from their staff than was reasonable. Probably customers did, too. I recall the one time I had to wait about two minutes for a salesperson. I actually thought, "The place must be slipping!"

The complaints about excessive pressure suggest that management and marketing had stopped effectively communicating with sales. These situations usually develop over a long period. The sales staff had undoubtedly voiced their problems—more than once before they were heard.

Regardless of the errors that slipped into their program, the firm's history remains to their credit. Through the years, everybody has profited—customers, employees, and stockholders—because of Nordstom's consistently excellent marketing techniques.

The Whole Picture

It never fails to surprise me how many companies don't respect their customers enough to credit them with good judgment. If I found an interior designer in a low rent neighborhood, in a decrepit building, nothing she said or showed me would persuade me to believe she deserved a top fee. I simply could not see her as a highly talented woman, prudently saving her money! On the other hand, if her office were in a building that charges five dollars for every ten minutes of parking, she shouldn't try to convince me that I would be dealing with a cost effective, competitively priced, design firm. I'd have considerable difficulty believing her!

The message a business believes it is conveying by its location, sales force, guarantee, and price, may not resemble the impression it actually conveys. Remember, it's a marketer's never-ending job to see the company through the customers' eyes. If you don't respect your clientele, your vision will fail you.

Efficiency and Good Management

There are all kinds of "easy" ways to make a profit. Anyone who sells illegal drugs knows this. There are even questions about the profits earned by some legal drug manufacturers. This book is not speaking of businesses that prosper by taking unscrupulous advantage of their clientele's problems.

A profit earned by serving others proves marketing's program is sensible. The marketing people envision something certain people need and want. The sales force learns where and how to present it. The concepts accompanying it encourage customers to believe that it is what they want. It carries a price that conveys a respect for the consumer's good judgment. Moreover, whenever it does not live up to its promise, the supplier willingly compensates the buyer.

A profit also proves that all departments operate efficiently. When sales volume is noticeably less than marketing predicted, but still provides a profit, then the efficiency of others probably made up for marketing's errors. Conversely, sales volume can be high, but inefficiency can eat up the profit. Good management can compensate for the occasional errors of individual departments. Nothing can compensate for poor management.

Now we are ready to look closely at how you can accomplish all of this in your business.

PART 3

A Look at How to Offer Anything and a Search for Something Worth Offering

Survival of
the Fittest

*No one can guarantee success in war,
but only deserve it.*

Winston Churchill,
Their Finest Hour

During my college years, I lived in Los Angeles. My friends and I spent much of our leisure time at the beach, and we frequently brought along a popular homemade drink. It consisted of any cheap wine that we mixed with any lemon-lime soda. We surfed, and drank, and dreamed about the future.

For all our dreams, certainly none concerned what we were drinking. It was a commonplace beverage we had learned about from fellow students. Several years later, we had good reason to remember it. Two men in Modesto, California, bottled the concoction, crowned it with the clever name of California Cooler, and swiftly acquired a proverbial fortune.

California Cooler

If you had made the $10,000 initial investment in California Cooler, at its inception in 1980, you would have collected more than $50 million five and one half years later. In September 1985, Brown-Forman, the producers of Jack Daniel whiskey, bought the firm and provided the stunning profit.

The men who built the company, and experienced this dream come true, were smart. They don't deserve this accolade because they thought of bottling a commonplace, homemade drink. In itself, that is not what made them wealthy. It was their understanding of the rules governing every marketplace that actually allowed them to pocket the profit. They recognized when the time came to get out of the business. Otherwise, they would still have been reminiscing about the year they were ". . . riding high in April, and shot down in May." Kay and Gordon told us, "That's life." But these men saw a chance to adopt a different theme song.

Why did they foresee such a bleak future, while others were admiring their fantastic success? Watch what happened!

The Wine Cooler Industry

The public's fancy for wine coolers became obvious when they tasted California Cooler. The extraordinary demand for the novel beverage quickly attracted large and small entrepreneurs.

The wine cooler industry measures the size of the whole market and each producer's share by the number of cases shipped. The measurement year ends in July. The market grew rapidly during its brief infancy, and anyone could make money from it. In the 1986-87 year, sales reached what proved to be their peak. The factories shipped 61 million cases. Of that number Gallo, the makers of Bartles and Jaymes, sold 18 million. Seagram's Wine Cooler held second place by selling 14.5 million. California Cooler shipped 12 million cases, close to 20 percent of the total market. Brown-Forman had bought the firm during the previous fiscal year. Together, the three leaders held more than 70 percent of the market. Numerous other firms split up the leftovers.

By July 1988, the industry had suffered its first down year. The total volume dropped to 51.7 million cases. Of these, Seagram's accounted for 18.5 million, and Gallo sold 15.5 million. The two leaders had switched places. Some people attributed the switch to a change in Gallo's advertising. They may be right, but this doesn't concern us here. The significant point, for our study, is the two leaders' market share. Their combined sales had increased by 1.5 million, in a market that had decreased by 9.3 million. Between them, they served two-thirds of the market.

California Cooler still held third place, but they had sold only 6.7 million cases. Their volume had dropped by close to 50 percent, and their market share to 13 percent. Besides the diminishing demand, there was a new competitor pursuing customers. Miller Brewery, the producers of Matilda Bay, had entered the field during that down year. They sold 3.5 million cases. This left all the previous suppliers, other than the two leaders, sharing a market that had shrunk, for them, by almost 25 percent. Factories closed. In the following year, when the volume fell again, more failed.

California Cooler probably could have remained one of the leading suppliers, had the peak demand been close to 20 million cases. When it started approaching 60 million, the developers of the market realized it was time to get out. Gallo and Seagram's could spill more product than California Cooler produced!

In reality, there was only an unimportant difference in flavor between wine coolers. Therefore, if shoppers did not find the brand they preferred on the grocery shelf, they bought whatever was there. Gallo and Seagram's, with their many product lines, commanded extensive shelf space. California Cooler knew there would soon be little room left for less powerful companies with similar wares. The men proved their real business acumen by realizing the market was getting too big for them. They quit while demand was still growing. Later, Brown-Forman also tried, unsuccessfully, to sell the company.

All Markets Stop Growing!

That story is not meant as a warning to lock your doors and run if giants enter your marketplace. Later in the chapter, you will read of firms that thrive under such conditions. Nor does the story imply that your only hope is for someone to buy your business before demand slows down. It simply exemplifies what occurs whenever a rapidly expanding market becomes a slow growing one or when demand diminishes. When maturity sets in, the rules of survival change.

While a market is growing by leaps and bounds, everyone can make a living. Many people construe this as an opportunity to open a business that can support them for the rest of their lives. They invest their savings, go into debt, and become part of a particular marketplace that is taking form. Markets come in enough sizes to fit anyone. Some people will only enter a national or international arena. Far more people find the promise of a needed revenue within a much smaller framework. They simply seek a marketplace that promises an acceptable return on the investor's money—whatever "acceptable" means to him or her.

There are certain economic conditions that will quickly destroy some companies. A common belief is that most businesses fail in their first few years because they did not start with sufficient capital. That is the most frequent explanation offered by the losers, and occasionally it tells the whole story. To settle for that answer alone, however, often leaves too much untold.

The majority of large companies existing today started with barely enough money. William Procter, of Procter and

Gamble, sold his two horses and wagons and borrowed from friends to raise his share of the initial capital. The men served householders near their small shop in Cincinnati. Without a horse, Procter had to push a heavy wheelbarrow filled with candles and soap along neighborhood streets. A modern day version of that humble beginning still serves as the first step for many successful enterprises.

A new business needs sufficient capital to allow it time to collect enough customers to sustain it. Plenty of start-up companies have enough money, provided they understand what they need to do—and the economic climate does not change too soon.

Sporadically but inevitably, the national economy suffers recession. When that occurs, no one can know how long the downturn will last. A capital twice the size anyone would anticipate needing could disappear before sales pick up again. Between widespread slumps particular markets slow down, nationally or locally, for an indefinite time and for innumerable reasons. During these periods, even firms with the largest sales volume feel the pinch of diminished cash flow. Those with barely enough revenue even in the best of economic times are bound to fail. If one period of slow sales does not topple them, another will.

It's often impossible to see a change coming. Some companies may have just entered the market. Miller Brewery, the second largest beer producer in the nation, entered the wine cooler business in what proved to be its first down year. In addition to recessions and decreasing demand, there are variations on California Cooler's encounter with overpowering competitors.

Video Rental Business

The video rental business provides an example. When the industry first blossomed, every corner shopping center boasted its own store. Each served an inconsequential percentage of their whole city's market, but all could make a living. Then chains appeared. They defined their market as the whole nation—and began their march.

Among the most conspicuous is Blockbuster Video. They opened large outlets, carried a diversified selection, and had numerous copies of each tape. They offered nationwide membership, which allowed members to rent tapes from any of their stores. The chain could restrict the number of outlets, because they knew people would drive a few extra miles to be sure they could get what they wanted.

Small shops which didn't know how to compete couldn't survive. Many owners had relied solely on location. When they lost that advantage to a nearby chain store, they had no idea what they should do. From 1980 to 1990, researchers estimate that 10,000 video rental shops closed. That translates into 50 percent of them nationwide. The day and hour when customers wanted to rent tapes played a major role. Chains were open seven days a week, fourteen hours a day. A mom-and-pop business couldn't work such hours, and many wouldn't afford extra employees.

In some places, the only independent stores still operating serve out-of-the-way, residential neighborhoods—tiny marketplaces unto themselves. The ones that survived near chain outlets lowered their prices and automated their cataloging. Primarily, they personalized their service, which gradually lured many customers back from the impersonal large outlets. Many survivors say the chains helped increase their business—by decreasing the number of their competitors.

Consolidation

Firms that avoid or survive recessions and challenges from much larger enterprises, will eventually watch demand slow down and their market mature. When that happens, each company intensifies its efforts to hold onto customers. Those with the smallest volume seldom get away with it. There will be some companies that want to grow faster than the now slow growing market allows. To do so they must accumulate more customers, and they only have two ways to do it. They can buy a competitor's business, or aggressively pursue their clientele. In short, the faster and smarter buy out the slower and less insightful. More often, they eat them for breakfast when there is nothing else on the platter.

Janitorial Services

Imagine a dozen or more janitorial service companies specializing in offices and industrial buildings. They compete with each other in the thriving downtown business district of their rapidly growing city. Through the years, national and local recessions of various intensity come and go. Each time the economy stagnates, some firms start cleaning their own premises, temporarily. Others go out of business. During these slumps, the janitorial firms serving the most customers can withstand losing some. The ones with the fewest can't stand losing any, and close.

Gradually, growth in the downtown district slows. No large industries move in, but no major employers leave, either. In the coming years, there will be a modest amount of new construction, and moderate real estate and business turnover. Six of our original companies will survive to serve this mature marketplace, by which time the rules of survival have changed.

When we look in on them, the leading janitorial service holds contracts that account for 35 percent of the market's total revenue. It's not a big city, so their revenue is not big, but the firm's success has a solid foundation. They have the largest sales volume and they operate efficiently, which makes them profitable. Since they are not competing in Chicago, they have no need to compare their size with that huge city's leaders.

Another firm holds 25 percent of the market, and also enjoys a comfortable profit. Both leaders have been happy with their growth rate.

The four smaller companies have only 40 percent of the downtown market to divide between them. If they had equal shares of 10 percent, and could hold onto that percentage while operating and living frugally, they might survive indefinitely. However, we find their shares more realistically and unevenly divided. One holds 17 percent, and three are struggling to pay their bills. Of course, they have been pursuing business outside the area but everywhere they go they encounter entrenched competition.

The third placed firm, with 17 percent of the market, is making a profit. Still, a serious mistake committed by any employee could cost them clients they can't afford to lose. Of more importance, the leader's 35 percent share is twice as large as theirs. Translated into money, the leader takes in two dollars for every one dollar the lesser firm collects. With twice as much income and an efficient operation, the front runner can compete far more aggressively.

Changing the Game

We only have to alter the competitive nature of our janitorial companies, to see a different picture. From the beginning in this scenario, none of the owners were skillful or intense competitors. Recessions still knocked the smallest firms out of business, but the six survivors were content to live and let live. Consequently, instead of two firms pulling far ahead, each settled for a more equal share of their maturing marketplace. Through careful business management and modest living, they all survived.

The vital ingredient in this division is its equality. No one grew at a much faster rate than the others. This meant that no one could afford to increase his advertising, upgrade his machinery, or take any aggressive measure the others could not also afford. All the participants simply conducted "business as usual." They competed for new customers, but they did not deliberately pursue their competitors' patrons. Or if they did, they didn't succeed! Nor did any one appreciably differentiate his service from the others.

The day comes when an owner dies. An heir takes over, who doesn't want to settle for his father's modest business. He starts talking to his own and his competitors' customers. What do they want? What do they need? What have they been putting up with all these years because they had no choice? He decides to take a smaller salary than his dad had drawn, go into debt, and buy modern equipment. He gets up early, and checks every job. He promises his employees they'll benefit by helping him build the business . . . and he means it. He says he will not tolerate slipshod work, and he means that too. His competitors soon find themselves losing enough customers to threaten their survival, because someone changed the rules of their mature marketplace.

Once the war for market share begins in earnest, all will have to compete more diligently. When the battle subsides, two or three firms will dominate. The rest will wonder if it is worth remaining in the area. There won't be just one survivor, because the public wants a choice of suppliers. There will rarely be more than three significant firms, because each wants at least a quarter of the market. A lesser share would readily allow someone to grow twice as large as they, and overpower them.

Set Your Sights

As consumers, we always want more than one source for anything we buy. We know that competition forces prices down. Competitors also hasten product and service improvements, and police each other's claims. Intellectually, most of us understand the fault with monopolies. Still, every time we try to place a long distance call from the "wrong" public telephone, we may well wonder if we really gained more than we lost.

When long distance telephone service became competitive, the result was typical of a mature marketplace. A number of small companies attempted to enter the market. Finally as things settled down, three major companies now serve the national market, AT&T, MCI, and Sprint). The demand for long distance service continues to grow, but it is not a rapidly increasing, unpredictable growth.

Research has revealed that a business needs to hold the largest or second largest share of a mature market, or it will close its doors during its owner's lifetime. A third place supplier can also survive, if its share of the market is within close range of the second firm's.

Thus, research actually warns us to get ready for the future from the time we begin. When your market starts to mature, you have to be one of the two or three leading companies. Otherwise, the leaders' greater resources will enable them to pursue your customers relentlessly. At such a time, if you cannot sell the business, you should be prepared to close its doors in your lifetime. You may think, "That's okay. I'm not trying to build something to outlast me." Unfortunately, a business usually closes because the investors have spent all the money they can afford just trying to stay open. As a result, when it closes, the participants are seldom financially in a position to retire.

Most owners and marketers of small businesses believe they must not aim "too high." I am urging you to aim for one of the leading positions in the market of your choice. The trick is to match your capital with the market in which you have a realistic opportunity to become one of the leaders.

Bear a critical fact in mind. Your company does not have to acquire a leading market share in a specific length of time. It just has to gain the needed volume *before you run out of money.* If you linger too long, without gaining a strong position, your competitors will hasten your departure.

A friend of mine owns a cattle ranch in South Dakota. When "city people" meet him, they often think of his business as far different from theirs. But he speaks of it in terms only too familiar. "There were plenty of ranchers in South Dakota. They just ranched until their money ran out." No matter the business, if customers don't buy your goods or services in sufficient quantity, you too ". . . can ranch until the money runs out."

Niches: In Computers

There are only two ways any business, in any marketplace, can compete for a leading share. You have to offer a product or service specialty, or occupy a favorable geographic location. Ideally, you would have both, though that's not a prerequisite.

IBM, HP, and Sun are the American leaders competing in the international computer market. If you're in the computer business, you're a sharecropper in their backyard. This does not mean you have to prepare for a showdown with any of them. You know you couldn't win. Instead, you need a niche that's off their beaten path.

When Apple Computer introduced its first personal computer, it superbly exemplified the principle of product specialization. Apple's marketers were not attempting to compete with IBM across the board. They had developed a single product IBM didn't offer and they ran with it to the goal line.

Because Americans love the underdog, most cheered the success of this upstart firm, but few believed it could last. In 1981, IBM introduced its own personal computer. Onlookers said, "That's it! The party's over for Apple and everybody else." As they predicted, Apple lost ground. Observers commented, "It was inevitable. Nobody can win against a $40 billion corporation."

IBM easily overtook Apple, but not because the giant is invincible. Apple gave their lead away. To be sure, IBM might have eventually overtaken them, but Apple made the job easier. They gave their chief competitor plenty of time to catch up.

IBM didn't develop a personal computer until they decided there was sufficient demand among their own customers. While they did their research and development, Apple spent precious time and money on products nobody needed. The Apple II was an historic success. Nobody wanted the Apple III's improvements, or its unreliable performance. The Lisa I did not offer enough innovations to make its price sensible; the Lisa II repeated the error, and ended the line. By the time IBM introduced their personal computer, they were competing against the old and dated Apple II.

Strong leaders in any market enjoy two major advantages. They don't have to strive to be first with a new product, and their greater resources allow them to survive more mistakes than their competitors can. Whenever they enter a market, they are imposing foes, but they don't always win. The failure of IBM's PC Jr., proves beyond argument that even a giant, competing against much smaller firms, can lose. IBM swallowed their loss and got out. They let Atari, and others, satisfy the needs of home users. But, just to prove that they didn't learn, they tried again with versions of the PS/1. Some companies insist on learning the hard way!

We all know that Apple fought its way back. One of management's first moves, on their comeback trail, was to hire John Sculley to run the company. Sculley had worked for Pepsi-Cola and knew nothing about the computer industry, but he was a masterful marketer. Later, Apple's Macintosh model catapulted them back into combat.

Today, when businesspeople discuss "great companies," someone might mention Apple. I agree with those who say it is too early to call them "great." As I write this, they have only been on the scene a little more than 20 years. If they're still around in another 20 years, no doubt everyone will grant them that title. For the present, there is one tribute they have indisputably earned. They have done an exceptional job of competing on the basis of product specialization.

Niches: In Petroleum Products

Motor oil consists of about 15 percent additives, and transmission fluid contains around 30 percent. Lubrizol is the leading world supplier of the additives. They became the leader in a comparatively brief time. They are now a 1.7 billion dollar corporation, holding close to 40 percent of their huge, specialized market.

Their closest competitor is ExxonMobil Chemical, a widely diversified, two hundred billion dollar enterprise. The super giant holds close to 26 percent of the additive market. Lubrizol is one hundred times smaller than Exxon, but well ahead in market share. They can maintain their lead because they compete with Exxon in only one area. They concentrate, exclusively, on the development of additives for which they can obtain patents.

Niches: In Soft Drinks

Soft drinks constitute approximately a fifty billion dollar a year industry. If you could get just one percent of that market, you would have an annual revenue of $500 million. If the idea entices you, you have missed the main point of this chapter. One percent of any market, no matter how large a revenue it yields, leaves a company dangerously vulnerable.

The soft drink market also exemplifies another basic fact of business life. "A market" is whatever customers make it—not what researchers call it. In some areas, prepackaged meals and fast food stands compete in the same marketplace. One evening, their customers stop at the grocery store to buy a prepackaged dinner. Another day, they pick up some cooked chicken at a fast food outlet.

Soft drinks include colas and non-colas. During 1990, Coca-Cola held 46 percent of the cola market, and Pepsi-Cola held 36 percent. Among the non-colas, 7Up and Sprite were the leading lemon-lime drinks. Officially, Dr. Pepper is also a non-cola, although it resembles a cola in appearance and taste. Hence, the fifty billion dollar soft drink industry is actually several different markets. In turn, they break down into numerous segments, and each can have its own leaders.

Throughout the 1970s, Dr. Pepper was one of the leading soft drinks sold in Texas. The company also held a strong position in other southern States. Their product has a distinctly different flavor, so the company had both a favorable geographic location and a product specialty. It was printing money.

Then, someone in authority grew discontented. The president of the firm announced they were going to make Dr. Pepper one of the leading soft drinks in the nation. He had declared war on the two King-Kongs of the cola market.

Think about the costs involved. Advertising requirements skyrocketed. The number of distributors needing to be supplied adequately and on schedule, soared. Factory and office personnel mushroomed. In short order, the cost of the whole operation became enormous compared to the company's previous experience. The only factor that didn't increase was market share. Dr. Pepper didn't even make a dent in the sales of Coca-Cola and Pepsi-Cola.

A few years later, Dr. Pepper was facing bankruptcy. Different owners came and went. Finally, the firm regained its position as a leading supplier of soft drinks in Texas. Once again, the company was making money by focusing most of its efforts in the geographic area in which it could win. Nobody knows why the drink is popular in the South—it just is.

Vernors has avoided the roller-coaster existence of Dr. Pepper, although they also hold only a minor share of the soft drink market. The beverage might be considered a ginger ale, but its devotees find an important difference in its flavor. They don't go into a store and say, "If you don't have Vernors, I'll take Canada Dry." They know exactly what they want, and they go where they can buy it.

In effect, Vernors has separated itself from the soft drink market. The company does not even compete with other brands for shelf space. Wherever the product is in demand, grocers give it the required space. They know it will sell. When Coke and Pepsi launch wars to increase their market share, they often inflict greater grief on smaller competitors than they do on each other. Their battles have no effect on Vernors' sales. People buy the drink because they prefer its flavor. The firm coins money by offering a unique taste to a segment of the public.

Your business needs to become one of the leaders in its marketplace. To do so, it must accumulate customers while the economy is dancing to jig time. Whenever the music slows to a dirge for a while, the companies with the fewest dance partners will have to leave the floor. Therefore, wherever you are now, aim to win market share. Look to efficiency to increase your profit.

The Trials of Time

Variety's the very spice of life,
That gives it all its flavour.

William Cowper,
The Task

Who, besides George Coakley who did it, would have dreamed that thousands of people would buy a painted rock and take it home to be their pet? The fad lasted as long as quick profit ventures usually last—but it profited somebody, handsomely.

If nothing else, the pet rock business proves one point. Anyone who sincerely believes he knows something the public will buy should offer it. If he can raise the capital, he doesn't need to worry about whether his business or his goods can survive. His objective is to make a quick profit and a swift exit. Many people try, infinitesimally few succeed. When they do, they may never have to concoct another business idea for the rest of their lives.

A company that knows it could easily be here today and gone tomorrow primarily needs salesmanship—plain or embroidered. Oftentimes, management astutely hires ex-carnival hucksters as salespeople. A business that wants a long-lasting position needs a marketer who can weigh the firm's options and reduce its risk.

Most of us dream of owning or working for a business that will support us in a style to which we want to become accustomed. To build such a promising enterprise, your company must become one of the leaders in its market. After you succeed, you get to decide if you want to remain as you are and defend your position, or expand. If you want to open other branches elsewhere, each marketplace you enter has to offer you a real opportunity to become one of the leaders. Of course, it must also be large enough to promise a profit that will make the investment worthwhile, in the investor's opinion. Therefore, the possibilities you see in a marketplace need to spring from proven principles, not just wishful thinking.

It is easy to announce to your family, "I'm going after a profitable niche." Your relatives smile and nod, and have no idea what you are talking about. If you are successful, they brag about you. If you go out of business, they assume the company was under capitalized. In reality, the niche you chose may not have been viable.

For a segment to be viable, the customers who compose it must need the same goods, want it in the same form, and have the same buying habits. For example, many women executives could now say: "I need clothes. I want high quality, fashionable outfits. I have no time to shop, so I buy through catalogues." Neiman-Marcus and Saks Fifth Avenue, among other elite stores, currently serve that customer base.

A segment, or niche, needs all three ingredients, to prosper. In addition, your firm still has to offer a product or service that differentiates it from the competition.

The South Bay Club:
Identifying the Ingredients of a Single Life

Years ago, Ed Broida decided to take a vacation cruise. During the trip, he realized the majority of passengers were enjoying the leisure of their retirement years. He also noticed another group. They were young, single, and eagerly pursuing the possibility of a romance. This started Broida thinking. He was also young, and though no longer single, he could easily recall the feelings of bachelorhood. He knew he would have gladly paid a higher rent if he could have gone home every night to an atmosphere that duplicated a cruise ship.

That was the brainchild that materialized as the South Bay Club Apartments. (In later years, they became the Oakwood Apartments.) They were "singles only" buildings, and they captured the nation's attention. To move in, a person had to be 21 to 35 years old. Every evening and every weekend, something was happening. It could be a dance, dinner, trip, theme party, speaker, or game.

The R & B Development Company spread the concept across the land, and made millions. Their tenants all needed and wanted to live in a certain area, and have ample opportunity to meet their neighbors. They all rented their living quarters, which translates into having the same buying habits. In fact, the tenants frequently proved to have much more in common. The lease stated that anyone who married had to move within six months.

A friend of mine likes to remind me that, "You can't schedule innovation." It comes when it comes. The trick is to recognize a viable segment, and find a way to use it.

Renting Good Neighbors

Ridgewood Properties, based in Atlanta, Georgia, buys and manages apartment buildings that frequently serve a different kind of tenant. They acquired a large complex in Dallas, Texas, located in a low income part of town. The neighborhood had a long-standing history of an 80 percent occupancy rate for residential property. Ridgewood's building averaged between 90 and 95 percent of capacity, while charging 15 percent higher rent.

The complex resembled Disneyland in its meticulous appearance. An excellent maintenance crew kept the landscaping, lighting, plumbing, and all else in perfect condition. The leasing office screened all prospective tenants thoroughly, but not in relation to their race or religion. Minorities constituted most of the neighborhood. The company couldn't have successfully practiced discrimination, even if that had been their intention. The screening process sought to identify an applicant's living habits and attitude toward others. Management could have expressed their intention in six words: "We help tenants have good neighbors."

The firm had recognized something many low-wage earners needed, wanted, and would pay their hard earned money to acquire. It was simply a place to live among people who respected one another's rights. The living quarters were small, and provided only basic amenities. Nevertheless, everyone who moved there was willing to pay a somewhat higher rent. They understood that neat and considerate neighbors and well-kept premises had to carry a higher price tag than three rooms down the street with neighbors who had unpredictable habits and changed at random. The tenants felt they got their money's worth, if not more.

Mass-Market Gourmet Coffee

Gourmet coffee shops, featuring freshly ground, imported coffee beans, became popular some years ago. That was just a variation on another approach, introduced decades earlier. In those years, inexpensive, store brand coffee beans, placed next to an easily operated grinder, were commonplace in grocery stores frequented by budget-minded consumers.

A Washington State businessman put the two concepts together. He persuaded grocers to sell gourmet coffee beans, alongside a grinder, to middle class customers. This largest of all groups does not patronize specialty stores, nor do they only pursue low cost merchandise. Though they regularly shop in ordinary markets, many enjoy gourmet coffee. Still, they don't want it enough, or have the time to travel to a special shop that is often outside their neighborhood.

After his product became available, consumers proved they wanted it. They made it a standard item on their weekly list of needed groceries, as long as they could get it without changing their regular buying habits. The man's company outranked Folger's, in market share, in the state.

Needs and Wants

Most children perceive something they *want* as something they *need*. A typical brief conversation with my ten-year-old son went like this:

"Dad, I *really need* that."

"No, you don't. You just *want* it."

What people need, more often than not, is mandatory. What they want, more often than not, is discretionary. Marketers can help potential customers realize that something they want can actually be something they need. The firm that enables consumers to find both in one product or service gets their business.

Some time ago, I set out to buy a washing machine for our home. There was no question about needing a new one. Before I left the house, I studied *Consumer Reports* to acquaint myself with the top brands. Although I was going to Sears and another prominent store, I wanted to be "an informed shopper."

On my way, I realized I would be passing a Circuit City outlet. I had forgotten about it. In my mind, this was a stereo store, but I remembered, that at that time, it also carried a variety of household appliances. Since I was passing by, I decided to see what it was currently offering.

The store carried three of the four brands I had listed, and the salesman was refreshingly knowledgeable. After he explained the differences to me, I immediately eliminated two brands. Then, he reminded me of the company's policy. "We guarantee the lowest price for 30 days after your purchase. If you see anything you buy from us advertised for less, we'll refund 125 percent of the difference."

His words were just what I wanted to hear, but not because of their monetary promise. I finally had a chance to speak the thought that occurred to me every time I heard that pitch, for any item on television commercials. "Sure you will," I answered. "I only have to find the same unit, with the same serial number."

He smiled, and shook his head. "No, that's not the way it is. In fact, Sears' machine is a lot like this one. If their price is lower, we'll honor the price guarantee."

I couldn't disregard a guarantee that even included similar but not identical merchandise. The cynic who had walked into the store disappeared before the salesman's eyes. Instead, he was dealing with an interested customer.

Before I'd gotten around to questioning the price, he'd removed any suspicion I might have about the store overcharging me. My attention turned to delivery.

It was Saturday, and he said, "How about tomorrow?"

I thought he had forgotten what day it was. "I doubt if you mean that. Tomorrow's Sunday."

"We deliver seven days a week," he countered, "and we'll take away your old appliance, if you want us to." He was indubitably winning our verbal duel, but I could only be glad.

Sunday held an advantage I hadn't considered. My wife worked as a nurse in a hospital. She was on duty that weekend. I realized I could have the machine installed without telling her, and watch her reaction when she discovered it, ready and waiting. That presented a fun angle to the purchase. There was also another benefit. She wouldn't have to stay home on a weekday, from sunrise to sunset, waiting for a delivery that wouldn't happen until she decided to take a shower. It was a convenience I hadn't anticipated, yet I still wanted to check out Sears. The salesman understood and was pleasant about it. Off I went, to Sears.

The saleslady there was also friendly and knowledgeable. She showed me the store's model. It was more expensive than the brand I'd liked at Circuit City, but it had some features that instantly appealed to me. I decided to buy the tried and true, *Consumer Reports* highly rated, Sears' machine.

My first question after that was, "When can I get it?" She said they could deliver it on the coming Wednesday. The answer disappointed me, because Circuit City had raised my expectations, but I decided I could live without my Sunday surprise. After all, I hadn't dreamed of getting next day delivery when I left home.

My next question was, "What about my old washer? It's a Sears' product. Your delivery man will take it away, won't he?"

"No," she replied. "We don't do that, but I'll give you the telephone number of a charity. They'll pick it up."

I had to rethink my decision. In all honesty, I had initially forgotten about disposing of the broken machine. When the Circuit City salesman had mentioned it, my forgetfulness had startled me. Did I really want to wait for a charity to come get it? I knew those organizations came at their own convenience, if they got around to it. We had tried that ostensibly worthy procedure in the past. A couch and chair had sat on our front porch for a month. A sudden downpour virtually ruined them, and my wife had made several phone calls before they finally disappeared. We never did know who took them, we were just glad to see them gone. After I remembered all this, Circuit City's turnkey operation became more valuable than the extra features the Sears' machine offered.

I'd left home needing a washing machine. A store's marketing program had prompted me to want more. I may have still only *wanted* quick installation of my new appliance, but now I *needed* prompt removal of my old one. There was no point in prolonging the process. I went back to buy what I most needed and wanted where I knew I could get it. Six months later, our refrigerator quit. I did not waste my time. I went to Circuit City and bought one.

Winning concepts often appear as conveniences consumers have not previously considered important. Patrons buy from a firm that makes the effort to think of, explain, and offer such help.

Service Segmentation

A business that orders 10,000 blue pens has to be a big company, restocking to supply their personnel. They buy everything in large lots, and are nonchalant about delivery time. Therefore, they can trade with any office supply company that offers them the lowest price.

A supplier who contends with the needs, wants, and buying habits of smaller firms has to deliver small orders promptly. His patrons often want to get what they need the same day they order it, or no later than the next day. Consequently, he has to keep a little of everything on hand. He can't buy anything in volume because he lacks storage space, cash, and the demand. His comparatively small orders to his suppliers cause him to pay more for his merchandise. So he can't depend on sizable discounts as an enticement. He has a viable segment to serve, but he must have the desired goods available to deliver when needed. If he becomes neglectful, he is delivering his customers to a competitor.

Rock Salt Is Rock Salt

Some companies deal in a product they can't differentiate in any way from their competitors' goods. Rock salt fits that description. For the benefit of sun country readers, rock salt is of especial importance to people in snow country. They use it to de-ice roads. When it's not where drivers need it, when they need it, vehicles come to a skidding, lengthy, and sometimes deadly halt.

The problem is that no one can know, from one hour to the next, when roads will need de-icing. However rock salt is rock salt. You can buy it from Dick or Jane, and both will deliver the identical product.

To escape anonymity in that kind of marketplace, a supplier must find some way to differentiate his service, because he can't alter his product. Otherwise, his only recourse is to paint his delivery trucks purple and chartreuse, to make them memorable. (Even that ploy might help.)

A firm operating in the Washington-Baltimore area specializes in seasonal goods, like charcoal, fertilizer, and rock salt. Each time the weather changes, they make money. The company began to examine their products, from the customers' point of view. What did their patrons really need and want, and how did they usually buy it? The study revealed a human trait that enabled the company to become the largest supplier of rock salt in their area. In addition, whenever someone in a company recognizes a habit common to their customers, they often get an extra bonus—they can charge more than the going rate.

The major buyers of rock salt are the personnel in charge of private and public crews, that a whole area depends on. These crews keep roads, parking lots and access open for automobile traffic. Although paved roads can get icy at anytime, it happens in the coldest hours of night more often than the day. Regardless of the hour, the supervisors have to make sure their crews have all the rock salt they need, when they need it. Hence, the supervisors are surrogate customers: they decide when and where to buy the rock salt that benefits others.

This inquisitive company realized that most people who have to make an urgent purchase in the middle of the night will experience similar feelings. How many businesses would you like to call at three o'clock in the morning? If you knew one firm would always solve your problem, no doubt you'd gladly pay a little more for your assurance, and go back to bed.

The company now always keeps an ample supply of rock salt on hand. Their inventory costs are higher than their competitors', but less than the ten percent increase they can add to their selling price.

Their patrons all need the same goods, want to locate it without delay or aggravation, and have no choice but to order it at the last minute. The firm consistently delivers as promised, which earns them credibility—along with a profit.

All Yellow Pages Are Not the Same

All marketers dream of finding a niche so big that their company will make a lot of money—and so small that potential competitors won't notice it. While playing golf one day, I met a woman who has come close to those ideals. Her business sold advertisements in telephone books that compete with local directories.

Had I wanted an idea for a losing business, that would have been it! By now, you surely realize that I have strong opinions. That doesn't mean I'm always right. After she mentioned her product, it kept popping back into my mind. As any golfer can understand, my game suffered from lack of concentration. I admit, my performance annoyed me. It provides the reason, though not an excuse, for my following rudeness.

"I don't see how you can make it in your business," I suddenly announced. "How many people will pay to advertise in an unknown book? I don't know anybody who doesn't use their own phone book's Yellow Pages."

Fortunately, she took my remarks in good humor. "You're right," she said, "but you're thinking about big cities. I've got news for you. In places like Vail, Colorado, I have plenty of customers. The population's small, but the tourists outnumber them. They're the ones who need my books. The telephone company covers a large area, but tourists don't know what's nearby. They want to know what's two blocks away, not 30 miles.

"I show the local merchants that their ad is going into every hotel room and time-share condominium. Believe me, they like the idea. We sell a phenomenal amount of product in that kind of community."

She located potential niches in telephone directories that covered a broad area, and included a popular tourist community. I came to realize there are a remarkable number of them.

I don't know how her rates compared to the telephone company's. It doesn't matter if they were higher, lower, or identical. The important point is that her marketing program addressed tourists' real needs and wants, which enticed advertisers. Visitors may need to locate a luggage repair shop, grocery, cleaners, doctor, dentist, chiropractor, restaurant, clothing store, or you name it. They all want to find what they need quickly, and return to their skiing, or whatever they have come for. Her product enabled them to do it. *That* is marketing to an inconspicuous, but viable segment.

Where to Look
for Winning Goods

. . . Endurance, foresight, strength, and skill . . .

William Wordsworth,
She was a Phantom of Delight

Dentists are seriously talking about running out of patients. They say they can realistically foresee the time when people will no longer have dental problems. We can hope they're right. For now, most of us still see more than we want of a dentist's chair.

Undeniably, dentists already have far fewer cavities to drill and fill than they had in the past. That happy situation came about through an excellent blend of scientific and corporate effort. Procter and Gamble played a lead role in the search for cavity prevention. Finally, they developed Crest. That was the product that changed the dentistry and toothpaste markets.

P&G had invested a fortune in research and development. The American Dental Association acknowledged the firm's achievement in a most unusual way. For the first time in the Association's history, it allowed its Seal of Approval to appear on a product.

Procter and Gamble's marketing coup made Crest the nation's favorite toothpaste. Eventually, other companies earned the right to display the Seal on their packages. Nevertheless, to this day, consumers associate cavity prevention with Crest, whether they use the product or not.

Toothpaste and Shampoo

After the public learned of the Dental Association's endorsement, Crest's competitors scrambled to hang onto their customers. They searched for new ideas in every nook and cranny of our mouths. As a result, we can now choose from a cornucopia of concepts, both new and resurrected. There are cleansers that claim to strengthen our teeth, control tartar, relieve a dry mouth, banish nicotine or caffeine stains, and whiten or brighten our smiles. Whether any of these products are actually better than baking soda, I don't know, but at least toothpaste is creamier and better tasting. To fill that gap, a firm specializing in "natural products" offers us baking soda toothpaste and several others have followed their lead.

We can also buy toothbrushes designed for plaque control, automatic action, and right or left handed people. One brand has three times the number of bristles. Another "reaches," and another "prevents." If any of these products are more helpful than others, most of us cannot say.

The shampoo industry is leading us along a similar path, and again, most of us are unsure its location. We hope we are on the productive soil of Kansas. We know we could be in the ethereal land of Oz. Advertisements soberly advise us to select according to our needs resting assured that there is something for everybody. You can buy help for ordinary or severe dandruff, curly, straight, dry, oily, frizzy, normal, gray, dyed, or permanently waved hair. There is also a special shampoo for bald people.

Products that prove credible will last. The public will gradually stop buying the others.

Defense Can Be the Best Offense

In all industries, businesses strive to be the first to introduce a concept that could catch the public's enthusiastic attention. Many will invest whatever it takes to create a new product that could increase their revenue and their market share. At other times, they are obliged to create something new simply to hold onto their customers.

It's always better to be your own competition. If your customers switch from one of your products to another, at least they're not following a competitor's lure. But the drawback is obvious. It takes a large investment to develop and promote a new item. In return, the goods must attract enough customers to offset the cost. If management doesn't think a purely defensive investment worth the risk, you could lose more revenue than you would have spent in developing a new product. When another firm introduces the product, and captures a sizable market share, you'll also have to spend money trying to replace the customers you lost.

It's almost impossible to attract customers who have become strongly attached to a certain product or service. Conversely, wherever you detect a weakly attached customer base, look for an opportunity to offer something "new and improved." Increased sales derived from exaggerated claims will be here today and gone tomorrow, but not all improvements are intrinsically superficial. As often as not, they're useful refinements of something the marketplace already offers. However, these worthwhile projects sometimes come equipped with their own problems.

During a meeting, you suggest something new. Somebody shouts, "We can't introduce that. It'll kill off our bread and butter product." If she's right, you've discovered what your competition dreams of finding, and you can be sure they will, if you don't do it first. You can also be sure they will not say, "We can't introduce that. It'll kill good old Susan's business."

At such times, your company has a choice. They can get ready to use your new idea, when the time is right. Or they can let a competitor offer it.

Intel and Planned Obsolescence

In the 1970s, Intel invented the world's first erasable electronic memory. It had an 8,000-bit capacity. They patented the invention, and they alone could make it. It was easy for them to sell all they could produce, and they owned 100 percent of the market. Inevitably, others discovered the secrets of the process, and how to get around the existing patents. Intel's market share eroded.

A friend of mine was the product marketing manager for that Intel line. One day, I met him and commiserated over his change of fortune. His market share was dropping, along with the price of the product. "Times must be tough," I said. "What are you going to do?"

He casually replied, "Nothing, right now. I'm waiting till our share drops to 80 percent." After he enjoyed my startled expression, he provided his reason for waiting.

"I'm letting them get a few more points before I introduce our 16K memory. I have a warehouse full of them." As soon as his competitors became heavily invested in manufacturing capacity, he would unveil his "new and improved" version.

Intel had produced and sat on the second generation model, waiting for the right time to introduce it. They could have delayed the development and production of the larger capacity, because it would kill their "bread and butter" product. The delay could also have allowed a competitor time to beat them to the finish line. Or they could have brought out the 16K as soon as it was ready. Either way, they would have lost all the advantages and profit their strategy reaped.

Even in the 1990's we saw Intel still following the proven strategy of letting competitors invest in obsolescent technology. The Pentium microprocessor introduction was delayed. While not stated as a reason, the delay coincided with major competitors' delays in making the earlier 486 series microprocessor. As soon as their production delays were eliminated, the Pentium became available.

DEC

The Digital Equipment Corporation was IBM's closest American competitor in the computer business. They gained that position by specializing in minicomputers and they found most of their customers in the engineering and scientific marketplaces.

Along came Sun Microsystems with something new. They and others created a high-performance microcomputer, known as a workstation. Its price would be lower than minicomputers, which would make it cost effective for many kinds of applications. Many of DEC's customers displayed a lively interest in the new invention, but the company must have questioned the segment's real viability. They didn't rush to enter the market.

Apparently, the firm lacked someone who would or could persuade management of the workstation's worth. Without such a person, there was no one to push development along and argue for adequate resources. DEC produced workstations in a half-hearted manner, but it was some time before they made a serious effort. When they finally offered a complete line, they were late. They were so late that Sun Microsystems went from zero sales to almost four billion dollars' worth in ten years. The majority of Sun's early customers originally belonged to DEC. Ultimately, DEC was acquired by Compaq, who in turn is being acquired by HP.

Under-Served Markets

Marketplaces already provide everything we really need. In fact, before markets existed, human beings had all they needed to survive. Consequently, anyone who views something she creates as "new under the sun" is giving herself undeserved credit. Frozen meals are only another way to prepare and store food. Computer games are another form of recreation. Spacecraft are another means of transportation.

Marketers express the idea in a brief, emphatic sentence: "There are no virgin markets." We do, however, evidence an infinite ability to improve on the old. Because there are *under-served markets*, our human ingenuity has slowly, but at least steadily, made life easier for more people. Ever improving machinery has not only eased farmers' lives, but ensured that more people have all the food they need. Name the subject, and you can find an example.

In the realm of luxuries, we have endless profitable illustrations. The idea of offering an improved product brought us ice cream that now sells for $2.50 a scoop, and not solely because of inflation. Creativity and research have produced a variety of cones that do not get soggy, and enough ice cream flavors to stagger the imagination.

Personalized service businesses will clean and organize your garage or closets, select gifts in your stead, put together your entire wardrobe, or do your grocery shopping. Some clients find they save money by sending professional shoppers to make their selections.

The proliferation of such services enables an ever-increasing number of our citizens to "live like kings." The whole world considers the United States a place where anybody has a chance to get rich. This is true because of our nation's most productive invention: the free enterprise system. It not only helps some people get rich, it enriches the quality of millions of lives.

There are many ways you can help your company "advance to go" and collect $200,000. You may think you have to create something novel, in the tradition of California Cooler. In actual practice, it is far easier to identify poorly served consumers, and add a missing ingredient. Irving Berlin said it perfectly. Just look at your competitors' efforts and think, "Anything you can do, I can do better."

Competitors laughed when Ted Turner decided to offer news, and nothing but news, on his cable television station. The commercial stations soon stopped laughing and changed many aspects of their own news programming. Turner did not think of himself as offering a unique service. On the contrary, he said, "My whole success . . . was coming up with better ways of doing things."

Continuous Improvement

In Calgary, Alberta, a few years ago, there was a handful of firms repairing hospital equipment. A repair job took between two days and two weeks. The owner of a new business developed a different methodology. He could complete all repairs within four to eight hours, cost effectively.

His competitors shook their heads in disbelief. First, they didn't believe he could consistently deliver on his promise, at least not economically. Second, they didn't believe there was a real need for such quick repairs. Obviously, they had not been listening to their customers, or researching improved procedures. The newcomer became the largest supplier in the whole city and surrounding areas.

Later, the successful entrepreneur—almost angry and very disgusted—told me the hospitals now wanted repairs in two to four hours. He said he couldn't do it. Besides that, nobody really needed it. He finally summed up his feelings in one disheartened expression. "They don't remember how bad it used to be."

Customers don't care about bygone troubles. They want solutions for the problems they face today. The outcome of this serial depends on how many hospitals really want the speedier service, and whether it is possible to furnish it profitably. If so, someone will come along with the needed energy and enthusiasm to figure out how to do it.

Full-Service Gas Stations

These days, in many areas, a driver cannot find a gasoline station that offers more than pumps and a cashier in a cage. Some people, especially seniors with money, don't want to measure their tires' air pressure or check under their hood. The whole industry has ignored this customer base, while catering to the young. A few dealers are getting smarter. A station in San Diego has returned to full service in the old-fashioned sense: they even put air in bicycle tires. They report steadily increasing sales. A station must pump a lot of gas to make full service an attractive investment. Yet there are plenty of customers wanting someone to pump gas for them. It's the full service islands that are missing.

A few years ago I learned of a station that successfully introduced a real innovation. They even charge a few cents more, per gallon, than the normal higher price for service, and still attract many new customers. They did it by offering coffee and a newspaper to their patrons. I heard that cars sometimes lined up in the morning hours. This typifies Frank Perdue's observation. To get something superior, "Customers will go out of their way . . . and you can charge them a toll for the trip." (They will go "out of their way," but only for as long as they must. A comparable offer, in a more convenient location, will often capture them.)

The station's patrons need the usual gas, oil, and clean windshields. Most of all, they want someone reliable to monitor their cars. The courteous attendants, in well pressed uniforms, encourage trust. Since personal attention takes time, a cup of coffee and a newspaper helps customers wait patiently. The new and improved service proved worth a little more money to many more customers.

Be sure you are thoroughly familiar with your customers' needs, wants, and buying habits, before you advise management to take on something new. "New" may simply mean products or services your patrons already use. By only selling automobile tires, many dealers discovered they were missing higher margin opportunities. Worse yet, competitors were destroying them by offering related products and services, while selling tires at or below cost. The competitors had studied their invoices, and realized they could still command a good margin based upon the other services they could provide to customers who came to buy tires at the aggressive price.

Filling Voids

Research has revealed two facts that should guide you whenever you look for something new to offer. First, the vast majority of new products fail. Second, much of the time a company selects something new because it fills a void in its line. These results frequently relate to each other.

Cadillac produced the Cimarron to "fill out their line." The new model caused fewer people to look at any part of the line.

Nobody needs or wants to examine an array of merchandise or services, of varying quality and price. That's not in keeping with retail or commercial buying habits. Besides that, people are not even buying products or services. They buy something because of the help it provides. The help may be of a major or minor dimension, critical or frivolous. Whatever they buy, customers seldom, if ever, need something that fills out *your* line. Still, much of the time, companies choose to manufacture or sell another brand extension. They can rightfully describe it as new. Yet this alone is not an auspicious description as most new products fail.

You want to provide goods that make sense to your customers, not a line that appears to make sense to you. Before we move on, try your hand at the following quick quiz. It'll let you test your skill at identifying a group of people who have the same needs, wants, and buying habits. The exercise also demonstrates how a retail business, by studying its customers, can find unexpected items to offer. The goods themselves prove that no one was trying to fill out a product line.

A Market Segment Quiz

To give yourself an A+, you need to name the actual group of people who patronize this large retail chain. In all probability, you don't know the company, so don't waste your time thinking about its identity. Try to recognize the people whose shared interests would cause them to use *all* these products. Your answer has to be more specific than a broad group, such as *men*.

I've listed the goods in the same order the chain introduced them into its outlets, through the years. Only insight and research could have allowed it to offer this unorthodox assortment of wares, under one roof, profitably.

1) Tires
2) Automobile supplies, like spark plugs and motor oil
3) Tools for automotive repairs
4) Standard hardware, like hammers and nails
5) Camping equipment
6) Sporting goods

When I first learned of this unusual inventory, I couldn't see the reasoning behind it. I discovered it contained a valuable lesson in buying habits.

The customers are do-it-yourselfers. The company is Canadian Tire, a chain of retail stores in Canada. They gross over a billion dollars a year. Now, how did they learn it would profit them to offer this mixture of merchandise?

They began by selling tires. In fact, they became the largest tire manufacturer in Canada. (There was no need to identify them as a manufacturer for the purpose of this quiz.) They didn't start to produce their own tires until they had success-fully sold another firm's brand.

It's easy to see how they expanded to take on automobile supplies. With time, they realized that many of their cus-tomers actually repaired their own cars. Carrying the neces-sary tools was the next logical step. Later, they learned that people who work on their cars also do a lot of their own home repairs and improvements. In response, they added general hardware. By then, they knew they were serving do-it-your-selfers, in a larger context than shade tree mechanics.

The real leap came when they discovered a pastime com-mon to people who do their own repair work. The majority regularly go camping. (Someone once commented that camp-ing is a do-it-yourself vacation.) With equal frequency, they actively participate in sports, as opposed to just watching them. (Again, they are engaging in a do-it-yourself activity.) Thus, the company could safely add two highly profitable lines, unrelated to automobiles.

A significant footnote to this story concerns the firm's advertising. Whenever they ran an ad featuring camping or sports equipment, their sales dropped. People don't go to Canadian Tire to buy those products. They buy them because they are already there.

I've asked many Canadians what goods they associate with the company's name. Everyone offered variations of the same answer. "It's a great store for do-it-yourself supplies." When I ask if they ever buy sports or camping gear there, most say, "Sure, all the time." Still, not one of them consciously associ-ates the company with that kind of merchandise. Remember, when we hear "Heinz," we think "ketchup."

Distribution:
The Backbone of Survival

A swarm of bees in May is worth a load of hay;
A swarm of bees in June is worth a silver spoon;
A swarm of bees in July is not worth a fly.

An old rhyme

Nobody likes to fail, and marketers are no exception. To avoid failure, an apprentice marketer can decide to hedge his bets, by trying to make his company good at everything. He could think, "I've got it! I know what it takes to have a great marketing program. We have to create the most differentiated product, go after the largest market share, maintain the lowest costs, establish complete distribution, and provide unbeatable service. That way, we'll have it all covered."

The recipe sounds delicious and every ingredient is important, but few businesses can afford to dine so luxuriously at one sitting. A firm that tries to create the whole dish simultaneously, could wipe out its bank account. A marketer must identify the absolutely essential ingredients for the success of a particular product in its targeted marketplace at that time.

After a while, he can concentrate on other elements. However, if he selects the wrong basics, his business will fail as surely as if he had tried to do everything. The following brief history of one venture typifies a promising concept, misdirected.

Golf Guide

Some years ago three men decided to develop a national golf course guide. It provided addresses, telephone numbers and descriptions of virtually every course in the United States. Gathering all the information took about a year, and a suitcase full of money. But golfers never got to use it. The producers neglected to include a few ingredients, crucial to their product's success until it was too late.

The guide was unquestionably different from anything on the market, so they didn't have to think about competitors or market share. The whole nation was their marketplace, and there was a good possibility of exporting the guide, for use by foreign travelers. The booklet wasn't expected to support a high price, so to make a worthwhile profit, they needed to keep production costs to a minimum. They decided to publish it themselves, to avoid sharing the small profit from each sale with a publisher. Customer service to the end consumer would be minimal.

Therefore, of all the ingredients in their recipe for success, only two required special attention. One was to produce the booklet in an inexpensive form. Of more importance, was skillful distribution across the nation, in places where it would catch the eyes of golfers. Bookstores could not provide outlets as they generally do not carry privately published works that have not proved their worth. Retailers are particular about what fills their limited space.

Most golfers would want to find this kind of information in an easily handled, durable paperback book to keep on a nightstand or in an office desk, and leaf through whenever they want to think about their next vacation. Unfortunately, the compilers had a different perception of their customers. They thought of them as travelers first, and golfers second. They produced their compilation in the style of an airline guide. It became a long, narrow booklet, designed to slide into a male traveler's jacket pocket.

The comprehensiveness of the information could have overcome this marketing disadvantage, but misjudgment of potential customers caused another mistake. The authors had actually created a data book. It contained no pictures of the courses, and did not mention surrounding communities or available amenities. Even avid golfers rarely fly to a location, play a round of golf, and depart on the same day. It was a serious omission, but the contents would still be useful, if seen by enough golfers. Broad distribution became vital to the guide's survival. But two errors proved fatal.

One was the lack of an endorsement from a prominent golf professional. A well known name on the cover would have caught the eye of amateur golfers, and could have offset the other faults. Of greater significance, an endorsement would have enabled distributors to have some confidence in the product's potential. Golfers couldn't buy the booklet unless it was where they could find it, and no one would invest in getting it there. One distributor after another looked at it, and decided it would never yield a desirable return on the required investment. The authors did a little advertising, but they couldn't afford national promotion and distribution. They kept trying various ways to get it into the marketplace until they decided they'd wasted enough money and abandoned the product.

The Digital Watch and the Semiconductor Industry

New, small businesses are not the only ones that fail to identify the needed ingredients for their product's success. The multi-billion dollar electronics industry flunked the same test.

In the early 1970s, the Pulsar, the world's first digital watch, appeared on the *Tonight Show Starring Johnny Carson*. It had a black face and at the push of a button, it displayed the correct time in red digits. The watch caught the public's fancy, but only persons who could afford to pay $1,000 for the latest technology bought it. Although the watch was initially expensive the price was bound to fall and many people foresaw a big demand. Some of them went looking for a way to get into the market.

Semiconductor companies produced electronic chips for the watches. They correctly concluded that their industry could be the predicted low-cost producer of digital watches. Electronics accounted for the principle material costs, cases were comparatively inexpensive.

The semiconductor industry ordinarily manufactures "goes-into" parts for computers and other products that need electronic components. The industry's customers, like all customers, want a choice of suppliers. Consequently, a firm that invents a successful electronic widget either licenses a couple of competitors to make it, or competitors develop their own versions. One way or other, several suppliers start offering an identical widget. Because the followers offer a "me too" product, they also have to offer a "me too" price, somewhat lower than the inventor's asking price. The low cost producer gains an advantage.

Since this is the way much of the semiconductor market works, the semiconductor companies lacked an understanding of markets with entirely different competitive requirements. They believed they'd only have to vie to be the low cost producer. Their reasoning caused the firms to lose, collectively, several hundred million dollars. Not one of them had identified the critical ingredient in the digital watch business. Production cost was a secondary factor. Like the golf guide, success depended primarily on distribution.

In the 1970s, there were two major distribution channels for watches: drugstores and jewelry stores. Drugstores would be superb outlets, for several reasons. They were in every corner of the nation, and they paid for their merchandise in thirty days. They liked to sell watches because they were a popular, profitable item. Although they sold lower-priced merchandise, it was not a problem to price the new electronic watches in their price range. Different watch cases would allow a range of watch prices. Drugstores could carry the low-priced lines.

The electronics industry quickly learned something important about drugstores, however. At that time, Timex had a lock on the channel. It was the only wristwatch drugstores sold, and it had been a profitable arrangement for everyone involved for years. Major chains refused to introduce a competing brand and chance losing Timex.

Jewelry stores would also be excellent outlets. They were as ubiquitous as drugstores, and each could carry watches with cases and prices in keeping with their clientele. Again, there was something the manufacturers didn't know.

Years ago, I noticed a peculiarity common to shopping malls that are going under. While nearly all the businesses are boarding up their windows, the jewelry shops are still open. It made no sense to me, until I discovered a simple explanation. Jewelers can last longer than others, because they don't have to pay for their merchandise for 180 days. Or they can wait 360 days. Or, they simply return the consigned goods all under terms aptly described as "net never." Consequently, to sell through them, a firm must play the role of a bank. (That may explain why the world's premiere watchmakers and banks became headquartered in the same nation!) The financial structure of American semiconductor companies didn't remotely resemble a bank's. Cash flow problems forced every one of them out of the digital watch business.

Texas Instruments (TI) tried a different approach, but they lacked understanding of the public's watch buying habits. TI had previously established retail outlets to sell their consumer-oriented electronic goods, such as children's educational toys and calculators. They lowered the price of their digital watches, and offered them through their own stores.

Regardless what they are buying, consumers prefer to shop where they can compare various brands, unless skillful marketing has convinced them to want a particular name. Since jewelry shops offered a choice, few people bothered to locate and drive to a TI store, to see the TI watch in spite of its lower price.

Timex's Failure to Adapt

Though drugstores finally started to carry digital watches, the events that enabled them to do so typify another easily committed marketing error.

For years, Timex had dominated the low-end watch market. "Success" was their middle name, and we might think they knew the recipe by heart. They may have thought so too, and succumbed to complacency. Yet for some reason, they made little effort to develop a low-priced digital watch.

Japanese manufacturers had the capital needed to successfully sell digital watches through jewelers. The day came when Casio, Seiko, and others, approached the drugstores with their inexpensive electronic watches and two strong arguments. First, consumers wanted them. Second, their watches were not in direct competition with Timex, because Timex was not addressing the digital market. The drugstores began to see the logic of this. There was an obvious and growing demand, which their long-time supplier was not answering. The drug stores decided to carry other brands. If Timex objected . . . too bad!

Timex had a monstrous problem. If there was a viable market for inexpensive electronic wristwatches, they should've been part of it. If there was no real market, why should they object to drugstores offering something that few people wanted, or would want for long? They couldn't argue their way out of the crisis. They had to forfeit their exclusive distribution channel—an advantage they never recouped.

Distribution Defined

A distribution channel is *any sequence of participants* that connects whatever your company makes, or does, with the end-user. Usually, we think of distribution in relation to products. In reality, many service businesses profit by using a sequence of participants to reach their customers.

A printer ordinarily markets his service directly to customers. He can increase his market share by also seeking alliances with graphics designers. Firms often allow the people who do the graphics for their brochures to select the printer they use.

Convalescent homes need a conduit to patients recovering from accidents and serious illnesses so they market their facilities to doctors and hospitals.

In short, anyone who becomes a link to end-users is participating in the distribution of goods. Franchisees serve as distributors for franchisers. They don't fit the traditional definition, but they do the job.

If a factory's marketplace allows it to sell goods directly to end-users, in effect it acts as its own distributor. But this requires vigilance. Self-distribution can invite competitors to use other channels as an effective competitive tactic.

All marketers need to search for off-the-beaten-track links to end-users. You may not want to employ them, but you need to be cognizant of them. First, this gives you a broader choice for your own use. Second, competitors can't easily blind side you by suddenly distributing their goods in a way you hadn't anticipated.

Regardless of other necessary ingredients in the recipe for success, goods need complete distribution. The trap can rest in your interpretation of the word *complete*.

When the 1989 Christmas shopping season began in early November, a novelty appeared in many major department stores. A plastic flower in a pot "danced to music," and sold for around $29.95. Two weeks before Christmas, shoppers saw the items everywhere they turned, but by now it was $9.95. "Everybody" had them, and "everybody" was trying to unload them. The manufacturers had made a deadly mistake.

Distributors consider something over-distributed if anyone carries the line besides themselves. A manufacturer prefers to think that they may be over-distributed only if every distributor in the world carries their product.

Analysis followed by trial and error discloses the ideal number of outlets you need. Bear in mind that it's costly to support a vast distribution network. Proceed cautiously. Aim to be a little under-distributed. If you have too many outlets, your better distributors will lose interest in your wares. They may drop your line, give it less desirable shelf space, or put no effort into selling it. Those are the ultimate signs of over-distribution.

In everyday practice, consumers tend to be more loyal to outlets than they are to specific goods. If a location drops your product, you can no longer count on your customers going someplace else to get it.

One of the interesting aspects of marketing is trying different approaches, and measuring the results against your expectations. As long as you examine an idea thoroughly beforehand, it is unlikely that one bad move will put your company out of business overnight. If you have three outlets in a town, consider adding a fourth. Look for one that offers some real difference that makes it worth trying. No one had sold nylon stockings through grocery stores, until Hanes, the manufacturer of L'eggs Pantyhose tried it. To this day, they dominate this channel and are also the leader in pantyhose.

Whenever you add a new channel, you can be sure your current ones will object. Nevertheless, if wider distribution generates a greater interest in your goods, everybody will make more money. Jay Shelov, a sales consultant and author, strongly encourages all kinds of distribution experiments. He dismisses objections with a modern version of a Biblical admonition. "A forty percent increase in sales will hide a multitude of sins."

Pull vs. Push

In his youth, Charles Luckman went to work in the advertising department of the Colgate-Palmolive-Peet Company. It became the initial step on his journey toward the presidency of Lever Brothers.

His first assignment was to create a brochure that would induce distributors to buy more Palmolive soap. The district manager of sales glanced through Luckman's mock-up, and pronounced his verdict. His exact words were, "It stinks." The quick-tempered youth retorted, "If your salesmen can't sell with that brochure, there's something wrong with them." The manager replied that if Luckman thought his brochure was so helpful, he should try using it. He ordered the impudent young man to report to the sales department the next day. Luckman couldn't afford to quit his job, so he had to comply.

During his first day as a salesman, he sold a pile of soap to five different stores. He returned triumphant to the office, and handed the orders to the manager. That gentleman looked at the size of the orders, and refused to believe they were valid. He immediately sent a supervisor to verify them. The official discovered the orders were legitimate—but all five stores regretted placing them!

Palmolive had been running a special. For every ten gross a distributor ordered, he got one gross free. Luckman hadn't understood they could order less, and still get a proportionate amount free, so he had convinced small stores to buy the whole 10 gross. (The ultimate in product push.) After the remarkably persuasive salesman left, each store owner realized he had bought too much. Luckman's triumph turned into embarrassment, but the sales manager would not let him cancel any part of the orders. He would have to find some other way to make peace with the stores he had oversold.

Before he retraced his steps, he spent a week in training, and then called on a shop owner he had not previously approached. As soon as he identified his company, the retailer told him in plain language to get out. Apparently, the previous salesman had also done a job of overselling. The shopkeeper had eight gross of Palmolive soap bars, and didn't know when he would ever get rid of them. He didn't want to look at another Palmolive salesman, much less hear the word, "reorder."

Luckman, that natural born adman/salesman/marketer-leader, began talking. "I think you do need me, if you've got eight gross of soap in the back room." He set to work, arranging a display for a special promotion. Before he left the store, customers were already proving his tactic a success.

Luckman carried the technique back to the original five stores he had inadvertently oversold. In essence, he had learned a fundamental marketing lesson. Instead of pushing your goods onto distributors, persuade customers to pull your goods off shelves. That is the surest way a factory can get reorders.

Channel Partnerships

Manufacturers hope their wholesale and retail distributors will encourage customers to buy their goods. They can hope for help, but they shouldn't rely on it. If liquor stores were to urge their patrons to try the higher priced Gallo wines, they would immeasurably assist the winery in changing the image of its brand. Gallo knows better than to depend on them. Instead, television commercials depict enthusiastic clerks strongly recommending the new line. Gallo hopes consumers will recall the message the next time they go shopping for wine because they know that few, if any, clerks will duplicate the performance in real life.

When a manufacturer's marketing program persuades enough customers to ask for a specific product, the factory can get any link in the distribution chain they want to carry their product. Conversely, wholesalers or retailers, who want to handle a popular line, have to market backwards. They need to convince a supplier they can move her wares.

Some manufacturers cut out links in the chain on very large orders by selling direct. If someone questions the fairness of this accepted practice, the factory has a packaged reply. "We take care of the *big volume* customers. You get the rest. Everybody plays that way." Everybody doesn't play that way. Auto makers protect their dealerships. If a firm were to order one thousand cars, they would still have to buy through a dealer. Compaq Computers was equally protective of its outlets in its early years.

When I became the president of a high technology company that had always played by the common rules, I was persuaded to change the game. From then on, we referred all old and new customers to our distributors, unless the customer strongly objected. In that case, we still paid the distributor a percentage of his usual margin. At first, our skeptical partners didn't believe we would really support them. When we wrote it into our distribution contract, they began to believe us.

Our sales force worked with potential customers, to show them how they could use our parts in their products. This was a time-consuming procedure. Under the new rules, whenever a sale appeared imminent, the sales rep had to make certain the appropriate distributor had adequate stock on hand. Some cautious companies, before placing an order, call to see how quickly they can actually get the required quantity.

With the new arrangement, our distributors took responsibility for everything related to shipping all orders. They adroitly handled the numerous and tedious chores. This allowed our salespeople to spend far more time working with potential customers, instead of expediting delivery or tracking lost orders. The distributors cooperated fully. They knew that every sale our people made became money in their own pockets. Sales increased, and everybody profited.

Worlds of Wonder

Selecting a channel can be marketing's job. Shipping product to the distributors is beyond Marketing's jurisdiction. Still, we need to look at a common problem related to supplying distributors, because marketers create a demand. Answering that demand is the other half of the equation.

One Christmas shopping season, the Worlds of Wonder Company appeared on the verge of making another fortune. In less than five years, this start-up firm had grown from zero sales into a large company. They passed through mid-sized swiftly. (Small companies, which constitute the majority, start with zero sales and reach $20 million. Mid-sized firms will have sales ranging from $20 million to $200 million. Large companies garner from $200 million to a billion. At that point, a firm stands at the threshold of the land of giants.)

Worlds of Wonder manufactured toys, and their imaginative products were the answers to parents' prayers. Children played with them for hours on end. The manufacturer's success grew out of their extraordinary gift for applying technology to toys and games. They didn't try to invent new playthings. They were simply the first to take old-fashioned items, like teddy bears, and make them talk. Then came the Christmas season that knocked them, like Humpty-Dumpty, off the wall.

Children have probably been playing tag since the first two learned how to run. No doubt, the game has provoked arguments from its inception. Worlds of Wonder invented Lazer Tag. No longer could anyone claim he had tagged someone he hadn't really touched. No longer did parents have to intervene to settle a shouting match.

Advertising, PR, and initial production generated a huge demand for the game. As Christmas approached, parents, aunts, and cousins by the dozen—to borrow loosely from Gilbert and Sullivan—were impatiently waiting to buy the toys for eager youngsters. Most had to settle for something else.

In January, enough games finally arrived to satisfy the December market, but the market had ceased to exist. Tardy delivery had infuriated distributors and the holiday shoppers. Adults didn't even want to hear about the game, so stores lost all interest in it. The factory had invested heavily to meet the demand. They couldn't survive without restructuring, and drastically reducing their whole operation.

The distribution difficulties that undid the firm were not new to them. Their manufacturing plants were in the Far East. Throughout the company's brief history, they had suffered from an inability to master the problems related to foreign production. They didn't pay sufficient attention to the time it took to finalize designs, tool up, purchase and deliver production materials, then manufacture, import, and distribute the goods. The creativity displayed by the firm in product development enabled them to grow like the fairytale beanstalk. Apparently, their phenomenal success lured them away from paying proper attention to their weaknesses. They behaved as though the party would always begin whenever their goods arrived. Most of the time it was true. Christmas, however, waits for no one. Distributors must have all the product they need, on time, or a manufacturer gets shut out.

Competing with the Channel

Some wholesale and retail distributors only employ people who are, in effect, order-takers. Others maintain an excellent sales staff, a bonus for any manufacturer. These distributors frequently discover an interesting phenomenon. Their own sales force knows more about a product than the supplier's salespeople. A manufacturer that allows this to happen usually neglects other important aspects of marketing as well, such as promoting his goods enough to get customers to pull them off shelves. This means the distributor has to spend more of his own time and money to move the product. The added expense cuts into his margin. A competing supplier who realizes its competitor is not supporting the distributors, only has to demonstrate the support her company can provide. By carrying her product, instead, the distributor can increase its margin.

To gain market share, your firm doesn't have to stride into a marketplace with enough money to supply a vast network of distributors. You only have to perceive one weak facet of one competitor's operation. Search diligently. Sooner or later, you'll find a way to approach someone's customer base, either directly or through a link in a chain.

A Big Winner's Power, Privileges, and Problems

This proverb flashes thro' his head,
'The many fail: the one succeeds.

Lord Alfred Tennyson,
The Day-Dream

What should a business expect its marketing program to accomplish? One person might say, "Marketing should persuade our competitors' customers to come to us." Another could reply, "I always thought marketing was supposed to generate greater interest in the kind of goods we offer."

Both answers are right. The pertinent question is, which tack should you follow, to help your firm grow? The answer to that question rests in your answer to two further questions. Do you own your market? Are you in an emerging market?

The wine cooler industry measures market share by the number of cases shipped. More often, we speak of a market's size in dollars. The basis of measurement does not matter. It's the percentage of the market a company holds that counts.

"Owning" the Market

A company that *owns a market* can pursue a course its competitors shouldn't follow. To be "an owner," your business needs two attributes. First, you must collect more than 50 percent of the money spent in your marketplace. Second, your share must be at least twice as large as your closest competitor's. If your firm garners 55 percent of your market's revenue, and your closest competitor only collects 20 percent, you probably "own" the market. However, if you have 50 percent, and another company holds 40 percent, neither of you own it.

Sometimes, when there are many competitors, no one will hold more than half the market. Yet, there may be one company that has a 40 percent share, while the rest are struggling to hold on to their five or ten percent. At those times, the larger firm can *behave* as though it owns the market. Now, what does ownership allow a company to do?

When your business owns its market, you may focus your marketing to generate greater interest in your kind of goods. To be sure, increased interest may also benefit your competitors. However your market position means your firm will collect the vast majority of the new dollars your program attracts. Your competitors can fight for the remainder.

Conversely, if you are just one of many contenders, you don't want to invest your money in making the market grow (except in emerging markets described later). More customers coming into the marketplace means everyone's volume increases. Your competitors' sales will grow at least as fast as yours, but you'll be paying for everyone's feast. So, while your revenue will increase, your profit won't increase as much as your competitors' because of *your* additional expenses. For all that, your share of the enlarged market will remain close to the same . . . or could even shrink.

Emerging Markets

An emerging market is one where there are substantially more customers who could buy than do buy. In this market the opportunity from increasing the total customer base far outweighs the benefit to be gained from fighting for market share. In fact, in some emerging markets, you may be the first, and currently the only supplier.

An emerging market requires special skills of the marketer to gain acceptance of the new product or service in the market. The marketing focus in this category is almost always towards gaining new users who can become loyal customers. Many times a marketer in an emerging market will go to extraordinary efforts to get the "right" early users who can then influence others to try. These "influencers" and "early adopters" are critical to accelerating the success of new products in new markets.

Emerging markets are often misunderstood. Western Union has the distinction of turning down the opportunity for three of the world's greatest inventions because they saw only a limited market opportunity. The first was the typewriter, taken by the Remington rifle company. Second was Alexander Graham Bell's telephone. The third was xerography (which created the Xerox Corporation). Even IBM felt the world market for its early general purpose computers was probably only a dozen machines, or fewer.

Some Markets' Owners

In 1990, Kodak held around 80 percent of the non-instant, color film market. They advertised memories. They wanted us to take pictures—the more the better—because 80 percent of the money we spent would go to them. Fuji kept telling us how superior their film was, and hoping we would believe them.

AT&T reminded us to keep friendships alive through long distance calls. They suggested we "Reach out and touch someone," because 85 percent of us would use their lines. Sprint only held five percent at that time. Their advertisements demonstrated how we could hear a pin drop on their lines.

Unfortunately for AT&T, the market they were serving was changing dramatically and there "ownership" was threatened. They abandoned their market building campaigns in exchange for a more aggressive market share focus as their share dropped from 75% to 60%.

Missed Opportunity

Both Sprint and MCI missed a real opportunity to steal some of AT&T's customers. For the first 24 hours after the 1989 San Francisco earthquake, MCI and Sprint subscribers had less trouble getting through to the affected areas. This continued to be the case long after the earthquake, when AT&T's lines provided a busy signal for hours on end. Possibly the smaller firms feared a backlash from the public if they used the tragedy to promote themselves. Whatever the reason, they didn't seize the moment to let customers know that a smaller company might serve them better, in an emergency. Many of the people who tried to reach the stricken areas compared notes afterward. They learned who got through quickly, while others spent hours re-dialing.

AT&T states, honestly, that their service didn't break down; their lines were just exceptionally busy. The reason for a delay hardly matters to anxious callers. Yet the experience seemed to prove that, even though the customers of a firm that owns its market may experience an occasional disadvantage, that doesn't diminish the power of ownership.

A Strong Defense

Everybody needs to appreciate the strength of a company that owns—or can behave as though it owns—its market. There are many reasons to respect its power, but one, alone, is sufficient. It requires far more money and skill to attack the market owner than it will need to expend in its own defense.

Consider what military planners say about actual warfare. They expect to use three to ten times more of their resources to capture an entrenched position than they'd need to defend one of their own. The same estimate can apply to marketing wars. Anyone who tries to steal customers from a company that's far ahead in market share will find the job difficult and costly. Much of the time, whatever their tactics, they will fail.

Another Missed Opportunity

Procter and Gamble was the first to offer a synthetic laundry detergent. Consumers decided the new chemistry was superior to soap, and Tide became a favorite.

Lever Brothers was slow to enter the synthetic detergent market. The parent company's board of directors delayed committing the needed funds. Eventually, they introduced Breeze without much fanfare, and the public gave it a lukewarm reception.

Charles Luckman was the president of Lever Brothers, during that period. He believed the company had only a short time left to capture a significant share of the new market. He also believed his next detergent, Surf, could do the job, but it would require an exceptionally large investment in advertising. It would be difficult to attract attention away from the firmly entrenched Tide. Once again, the board of directors decided they weren't ready to spend the money. They chose to pay a quarterly dividend to their stockholders, first. Their decision disgusted Luckman. He resigned his presidency, divorced himself from trading in merchandise, and returned to his first love, architecture.

An Unsustained Difference

Tide didn't face a significant challenger until liquid detergents became popular. Liquids were visibly different. An easily recognized difference can be a valuable asset. Moreover, customers perceived liquids as a real improvement, and their opinion is the one that counts. The makers of Wisk, the "ring around the collar" people, repositioned their liquid detergent. Instead of being just a spot removing specialty item, it proved able to challenge the leader. The basis of the war, however, was chemistry that any factory could easily duplicate. Tide responded in liquid form, and retained the crown.

Doing Market Research for the Competition

Royal Crown Cola brought to market the world's first diet soft drink, Diet Rite. The company spent a fortune in time and money developing the beverage. After they introduced it, others recognized the enormous demand for diet drinks that had remained unfulfilled. Coke and Pepsi, without so much as a "thank you for doing our market research," produced their own diet versions. They advertised their new products in the lavish style they could afford, and reduced RC's share to a dribble. RC could argue that the giants grew the diet drink market for everybody. Of course they did, but, by 1990, Royal Crown held only 2.3 percent of the whole cola market.

Apparently, the firm learned nothing from the experience because years later, they did it again. This time they developed and introduced caffeine free cola, RC100. Coke and Pepsi saw the demand and brought out their own brands. RC100 no longer exists.

Royal Crown had introduced two products that held a large, nationwide appeal. They may have thought that being first to supply either segment would assure them a strong position in the specialized niches. They certainly had the right products, in the right market, at the right time. But so did Coca-Cola, and their annual advertising budget could exceed RC's annual profit! In fact, both Coke and Pepsi held far more than five times RC's market share. Neither of the giants actually owns the cola market. Yet Royal Crown couldn't possibly hold onto a sizable share against their concerted attacks, any more than California Cooler could effectively compete against Gallo and Seagram's.

There's also the possibility that RC's marketers didn't recognize the huge demand awaiting the products. They may have anticipated becoming the first supplier of niches too small to command the giants' interest. Whatever their reasoning, they invested considerable time and money developing markets for the leaders — and they did it twice.

Maybe three times? In late 1995, RC was test marketing what was undoubtedly the world's first "draft cola" in Los Angeles. Fortunately, or unfortunately for RC, this idea produced a non-starter. Either way, sometimes old habits die hard.

Ownership Is Relative

"A market owner" doesn't have to be a $50 million company. Your annual revenue may contain only a few zeros, but you could own your city's screen printing market. When you do, you can profit by getting more people interested in screen printing. Your program should aim to acquaint the public with the many applications of the process. Few people know much about it.

As the owner of your market, you could have at least 15 screen printing firms competing against you. The business has a low barrier to entry. There will always be others entering the marketplace and departing. It doesn't matter how many challengers rise up against you. Your large market share, and double the share of number two, gives you the coveted commanding position. Your competitors will find it difficult to unseat you—unless, of course, you make it easy for them.

As the marketer for a successful firm, you may grow restless. It can become boring just sitting on the top of a hill, year in and year out, countering the competitions' endless maneuvers. Pursuing another two percent increase in sales often isn't enough of a challenge. You want to do something different, which will enable your company to experience appreciable growth. This means you have to find a new market. When your thoughts go somewhere else, so can your market leadership.

Taking Your Eye Off the Market

Imagine this situation, a marketer of computer software, used by independently owned hotels. Her business develops the software, and maintains an excellent support staff, to teach clients how to make full use of the program. The company owns the southern half of a popular resort state, containing hundreds of hotels. They have one insignificant competitor, and the leader doesn't want to chase them out of the marketplace. It would open the door to a stranger. Somebody has to play the role of the alternate supplier.

For the marketing manager of this successful company the days are growing monotonous. Her employer doesn't want to invest in challenging the formidable competition in the northern half of the state. So, she starts wondering what the business could do for restaurants. The idea is promising, but it could become a lengthy project. She's the company's only marketer. It will take time to determine the kind of program the restaurants could profitably use, and to learn if enough of them would want it. She'll have to neglect her hotel clients, but the thought doesn't bother her. The support staff takes care of their incidental problems, and the sales force sees them, regularly. She tells her employer, and herself, that the hotels can get along without marketing for a year or so. She's actually saying that she *hopes* they can.

Because of her new preoccupation with the restaurant industry, it takes her a while to hear about a new concept taking root in the hotel industry. Many hotels are beginning to think about instituting a "relationship marketing program," or staying in personal touch with their clientele.

The competing firm learns of the idea when it first surfaces. Its marketer regularly visits the hotels because the company can't afford to quit seeking new ways to serve its own—and the leader's—customers. This marketer asks all kinds of questions. He has to understand, in detail, what the hotels need to do to achieve their individual objectives.

Basically, whenever a previous guest calls for a reservation, the hotel wants to be able to ask pertinent and personalized questions. Does their guest still prefer a room with a king-size bed, facing the park, on a low floor, far from the ice machine? Would she like tickets to a theater or a sporting event, as she did during her last stay? They also want to acquaint her with any new service they've added since her last visit.

The marketer gradually begins to define a software package for his company to develop, that can be tailored by each hotel to fit its own competitive tactics. In reality, he's doing for the hotels exactly what his powerful competitor is now trying to do for the restaurants.

The leader's marketer eventually hears about the growing trend from her sales force or support crew. She catches the drift of the program, but doesn't appreciate the immediate and growing demand. She tells her people "she'll look into it shortly." When she finally gets back to the hotels, she discovers that her insignificant competition has made serious inroads into her customer base.

By the same token, you could've owned your market in Long Island for 30 years, but now, want to expand into Florida because you like the weather better. Go ahead, if it looks promising. Just be certain to leave capable marketing people to attend to your Long Island customers' future needs. Longevity alone will never protect your position.

It's Not Easy Being 4th

A determined effort to gain market share always creates some problems, no matter how strong your starting position. Coors carved out a niche for themselves in Colorado, by supplying a cold-filtered, non-pasteurized beer. They became the top supplier in the eleven western states. They appeared satisfied and well able to defend their position. Somehow, the public learned that passengers on Air Force One were drinking Coors. A national cult emerged, composed of people who wanted to drink the beer that was good enough to be on the President's plane.

Coors was not available east of the Rockies. Under pressure, the brewery agreed to expand, and the cult enabled the firm to achieve a modest degree of success in the new markets. But for all the effort, by 1989 Coors served only nine percent of the national market, a weak fourth position. More importantly, they are no longer the leader in the west!

They decided to acquire the third place Stroh Brewery Company. By so doing, they would hold 19 percent of the national market. That share would let them breathe down the neck of the second ranked firm. Miller held 21.8 percent of the market. The proposed purchase of Stroh's raised some legal questions, and other troubles. Coors didn't acquire them, and the problems they inherited by becoming a small fish in a big pond continue to hound them. To solve the problem Coors has divested many of its non-beer distractions to allow an all out focus on the beer market.

Cannibalizing an Existing Brand

Miller remains the second largest-selling beer in the nation. Originally, they sold Miller High Life. Then, they invented light beer, a brilliant move that significantly increased their market share.

The brewery called their new beverage Lite, and the word became synonymous with the brand. A patron in a bar only had to say "I'll have a light," and he automatically got a Miller. Though it is usually dangerous to extend a brand name, the firm didn't have to worry. They printed the word "Lite" in big letters on the container. A person would have to study the fine print on the can to find out who made it. Besides that, even people who did not like Miller High Life tried the new beverage, because it was unique.

Later, the brewery came out with a cold-filtered, non-pasteurized beer, to compete with Coors. They test-marketed it, using the name, Plank Road. Their advertisements explained that the brewing process produces a flavor closely resembling draft beer. Coors had never helped the public understand the significance of the process. Instead, many people thought of Coors as "non-pasteurized," and the term made some shy away from the brand. Miller's explanation persuaded many consumers to try "draft beer in a bottle." The test-market customers described Plank Road as "fabulous."

The new beer appeared in the national market as Miller Genuine Draft. The name expresses the value of the brewing process, but this time Miller displayed their company name, prominently. They may have decided it would cost too much to promote a new brand, or it was simply unnecessary. The possibility remains that someone who does not like Miller High Life will not even try Miller Genuine Draft. Even among those who like Miller's products, the more they associate it with Genuine Draft, the less they'll remember or buy High Life.

In addition while Miller's Genuine Draft has displaced High Life in the market, several competitors have now introduced their own genuine draft brand eliminating Miller's difference. Recently, at long last, Miller has begun to use the Plank Road name for some of their newer beers in more than just test-markets.

Defense Again

When Coors first sought to buy Stroh to strengthen its position, Anheuser-Busch already held 42 percent of the beer market. The company was a breath away from becoming twice as large as Miller. Currently, Budweiser remains the largest seller in the nation, and the brewery is the market leader. It brought out Bud Light which, though not initially a strong seller, prevented erosion of the customer base. The company has never allowed a large lead to lull them into complacency and has seen Bud Light move to the number one position in light beers.

The owner of a market needs to remember that the second through "nth" companies have nothing to tempt them to become bored or complacent. These smaller competitors spend their time searching for any fort, anyplace, that has been left undefended.

Problems: Ways to Avoid or Survive Them

The better part of valour is discretion.

William Shakespeare,
King Henry IV

To raise capital, some companies market themselves to investment bankers and to the public. Others take their plan to a bank. The rest start talking to venture capitalists, relatives, or friends. No matter who invests in a start-up or expanding company, few investors will bet on a pioneer.

When there is only one company offering a product or service, it is alone for one of two reasons. Either it's the first of many to come, or there's no market. Sometimes it's hard to tell the difference. While you struggle to figure out what is really happening, your investors know too well their money is disappearing. Consequently, most people prefer to back a business that will compete in an established marketplace.

An established marketplace should be easy to recognize. When two or more companies offer a product, it's likely that there's some demand for it. Though the premise sounds sensible, in real life, there can be exceptions.

A Solution Looking for a Problem

Etak, a Silicon Valley company, invented the first electronic mapping system for automobiles. A driver simply typed in his destination, and a detailed map appeared on a screen. While he drove, the map pinpointed his location, plus or minus 10 feet. Every time the car turned a corner, the system self-calibrated with astonishing accuracy.

It took Etak almost two years to develop their first mapping product. That was not much time, compared to how long the company searched for customers. Its original plan was to sell the system through car stereo shops. The marketing theory must have been people would go into a store and say, "I'll take a Blaupunkt and an Etak." It didn't work that way.

Of necessity, the product's price was high. At least, it was higher than average drivers considered sensible for what most perceived as a toy. My mother gets lost easily, and would love to have one. Yet she wouldn't spend over a thousand dollars to play with a digital mapping system in her car. Apparently, most of us felt the same way. Only a few thousand people bought Etak's original product. General Motors licensed it—but they also let it sit on a shelf until 1995.

At first glance, a person could think that fleets would make good use of the system. Their drivers always need directions to unfamiliar addresses. But map books can serve them equally well. Fleet dispatchers, on the other hand, have no way of knowing where their drivers really are. They spend hundreds of hours calling around, trying to determine who is closest to the next job. Etak's product didn't answer the dispatchers' need.

In spite of this serious flaw, Etak didn't remain alone in this non-existent marketplace. Competitors developed and began to offer their own mapping systems. Incredibly, the competitions' products lacked the same indispensable feature. A fortune in time and money invested had failed to produce a product that could help a big volume user. Five years later, Trimble Navigation added what could be the missing piece to the puzzle. Trimble believed its navigational positioning system could be used with Etak's mapping system, to enable dispatchers to track their vehicles. In addition, GM has finally decided to implement systems using Etak's mapping technology. After all these years, the Etak concept may finally become an "over-night" success.

Innovation with a Customer in Mind

In the U.S. high technology industry, Etak's behavior is not uncommon. Most of our high tech companies don't think about what customers are actually buying. They proceed as though people will part with their money for the sheer joy of owning the newest widget. A few people do. But most of us buy not so much the technology as what it does for us, exactly as we buy any other product or service.

The Minnesota Mining and Manufacturing Company (3M) is a firm that concentrates on applying technological achievements to everyday needs. The man who invented 3M's omnipresent sticky note paper was actually looking for a super strong adhesive. He came up with a glue that didn't even remotely resemble his intention. A friend began using it to attach temporary notes in his hymnal book. True to form, the company found the glue too promising to ignore. The firm took the man's technology, which had been a failure as a "super adhesive," and turned into a "super product."

Technology is fun. Using it to ease daily life is an act that makes money. If your concept requires a large investment, and is technology-led, *beware*. As Etak's experience proves, technology is not a consistently reliable leader. A business needs to be driven by customer needs, not just by the offerings of technology.

A Segment Has to Be Reachable

You may know you have something many people would gladly use, but *where* are those people? Customers aren't always where you expect to find them, nor as reachable as they appear. A widespread customer base can deny you a cost-effective method of communication.

Many years ago, out of frustration, I developed a program to keep track of frequent flyer credits. My program was computer data based, and contained all the interactions, partnerships, and awards between airlines, hotels, and car rental agencies. I updated it monthly, for my own use.

When I thought about the millions of people who were frequent flyer members, like myself, I decided I only had to serve one percent of them, and I could soon retire. The defect in my retirement plan gradually became obvious.

It took a few minutes for the multi-million person market to shrink, and my exuberance along with it. First I could only serve travelers with access to computers which, at the time, were less common. That sobering thought was followed by other realizations about traits my potential customers needed to share.

It also occurred to me that countless people sign up for frequent traveler programs, who aren't, in fact, frequent travelers. I'd have to differentiate between true potential customers and the twice-a-year traveler, to keep my advertising budget realistic. A high price for my product with monthly service wouldn't make sense either for myself or for them.

All my thinking became irrelevant when I discovered that airlines won't allow anyone near their frequent flyer lists. It was a major setback.

I turned to travel agencies, only to watch that channel to customers disappear the moment I touched it. Travel agents' computer terminals only linked them to airline reservation systems.

I didn't pick up the idea of frequent flyer software again until personal computers became commonplace in travel agencies. The first fact of life I discovered was that travel agents are extremely busy just serving their customers' immediate needs. My program had to be separate from their reservation system. Switching programs to obtain frequent flyer information would take too much of their time.

I refused to give up. I knew that millions of people were growing increasingly frustrated by the tedium of studying their entitlements. They needed and wanted the help my program offered. Frequent travelers, however, come from infinitely diverse backgrounds. I couldn't find a shared trait among them that allowed me to narrow my focus to a single, *reachable* segment, large enough to promise a profit.

Eventually, through word of mouth and extremely selective and expensive advertising, I acquired some subscribers. But reality eventually won out. Customers will never pay more than they think something is worth. It cost a fortune to tell them about my program, so they chose to live without it!

Pioneering Can Be Futile

It's possible to offer something cost effective and unquestionably useful, and still overlook a problem that can bankrupt your company. Failure awaits anyone who grossly overestimates his ability to produce goods, or his competitions' willingness to allow him to remain in the marketplace. One example stands as an alert to both dangers.

As World War II ended, Preston Tucker was planning a way to serve the automobile-starved public. He knew what people wanted. He also knew what they needed, though many drivers had not even dreamed of the innovations he planned. By the mid-1940s, Tucker was looking for financial backing for his new design. He said it would contain, among other features, a fuel injection system and hydraulic valve lifters. For greater safety, he proposed disc brakes, a rubber crash panel, seat belts, and pop-out, shatter-proof glass. The Big Three,

General Motors, Ford, and Chrysler, would slowly introduce these improvements over the following decades.

Tucker only had to talk about his dream car to create a phenomenal demand. Dealers lined up to invest in his company, but the cars never arrived at the dealerships. People accused Tucker of trading fantasies for cash. They claimed he was unable to produce the promised model and furthermore he knew it was impossible before he sold stock and dealerships. In fact, Tucker did produce a few cars that contained many of the proposed features. They were praised by those who drove them. Tucker claimed the Big Three, through overt and covert actions, prevented him from mass producing them.

To investors, it hardly mattered which story was true. They still got nothing in return for their money. Because Tucker's car contained safety features others didn't offer, he publicly pronounced his verdict. Depending on the story you believe, his words can sound like a statement born of honest outrage, or an outrageous statement. He said, "The entire automobile industry of America is guilty of criminal negligence . . . ," and should be ". . . convicted of manslaughter."

Thinking It Through

Tucker marketed his concept and signed up dealers before he had produced a single working model. The practice is far from unusual. Airlines sign purchase orders for jumbo jets when the planes only exist on drawing boards. Big profits or big losses regularly accompany investments in nonexistent products.

Regardless of whether you plan to blaze a new trail or follow a traditional path, you need to know *who* your big volume buyers will be. Otherwise, you and your potential investors can't know if enough people need your goods. You have to know *where* your customers are. Otherwise, no one can know if the company can reach them cost effectively. You have to know *how* you can circumvent anything that could prevent you from "delivering the goods." Otherwise, astute investors can't consider your plan credible.

There will always be far more opportunities available than your business can afford to undertake. You have to pick the one that best fits your perception of the future. If you find yourself comparing two ventures that appear more or less equal, pursue the one that is quickest to implement. If you're right, the cash flow it generates can fund the other one. If you're wrong, you will have minimized the time and money lost.

Four Paths to Growth

In essence, there is a choice of four highways for a business to travel. There are innumerable side roads too, but all companies have to start down one of the major arteries.

The first highway leads you to seek ways of improving your existing product or service for existing customers. This method can enable you to hold onto your patrons. It's usually the most profitable way to proceed, because it requires the least incremental investment.

The second route leads to investment in new goods to offer your current clientele. You already understand your customers. Hence, your primary investment will be in development or acquisition of the new goods.

Third, you could invest in attracting new customers. There are various ways to do this, such as wider advertising, broadening your sales force's areas, or opening another branch. It usually costs five to ten times more to gain one new customer, than it costs to sell a new product to an existing customer. It takes time and money to attract attention, and more time to win customer loyalty. You may also have to spend time and money seeking a location where the competition is weak enough to suit your purpose. All this isn't meant to discourage, but to alert you to the additional resources required.

There's something else about the high cost of acquiring new customers you need to remember. If, each year, you lose two customers out of every ten, you are losing twenty percent of your customer base. Therefore, to increase your customer base by ten percent, annually, you will first have to replace the twenty percent you lost. Your firm will have to spend enough money to gain thirty new customers to grow by ten! Be sure to put that arithmetic on the scale, when you weigh the worth of a guarantee that can help you hold onto the people you already serve.

The fourth way involves investing in new goods to sell to new customers—the two fundamental ingredients of a new business. Some marketers like to believe that a successful company can add any related product or service. It probably can, as long as it only needs one of the two elements that constitute a new business. This means dealing with either the same goods or the same customers. If both factors are new, the venture usually needs its own name and its own ample funding.

An employment agency famous for supplying efficient security guards could be destroyed by offering another kind of employee under the same company name. The agency may believe its reputation was built on its conscientious attention to client needs. But in all probability, the public identifies it, first and foremost, with the kind of personnel it offers. Consequently, a different expertise for different clients, should be offered under a different business name. Anything else could begin the dangerous process of blurring the agency's established image.

An unwritten law rules new businesses. An enterprise always takes more money and time to get on its feet than anyone anticipates. Lacking first-hand knowledge of the customers and the goods, you have to be in a business for a reasonable period of time before you can know how it *really* works.

The critical factor is what people first think of when they hear your company name. If you see your business as customers actually see it—not as you wish they would—you'll know what course to follow. Nothing you read in this book or any other can tell you everything you should do now or in the future. Your most useful skills are to ask the right questions, listen carefully to the answers, remain aware of crucial aspects, and recognize where trouble customarily resides.

Spotting Profitable Trends

The future can be easy to read for someone who can translate compelling beliefs into practical applications. Years ago, it became obvious that environmentalists would someday demand the recycling of everything conceivable. Today, grocers report an increase in sales of products labeled environmentally safe, or composed of recycled material. Many companies are now scrambling to catch up with competitors who recognized the need, prepared for it, and changed their marketplace.

Sooner or later, animal activists had to demand an end to using animals to test products as frivolous as cosmetics. Before the cause became popular, The Body Shop had already eschewed testing their cosmetics on animals. In one decade, their sales increased by an average of 50 percent a year.

When enough people feel strongly about certain issues, you can safely bet something will change. As long as a group's convictions don't morally conflict with your own or management's, act upon them. Those who see the inevitability of change and get ready for it ahead of time, can profit from it. Those who disregard the beliefs of others will lose by it.

Armand Hammer adhered to that principle. From the time of the Russian Revolution, Hammer never believed that Marxist Communism would work. He made his opinion plain to the new nation's leaders. He believed the system was so inimical to human nature, it would self destruct. Yet he also understood that the people, who had to endure the socioeconomic experiment, sorely needed goods. He saw no reason not to help them survive, while helping his own companies.

Ill-Advised Predictions

Some changes are unforeseeable and unavoidable. I've yet to meet a business person who claims he had prepared for the Berlin wall to come tumbling down, overnight. Most unanticipated occurrences are not as welcome.

In the late 1980s, Genentech, Inc. believed they knew the day the Food and Drug Administration (FDA) would approve one of its newly created drugs. They broadcast the news widely, but the approval didn't materialize on the date they had predicted. The mistake didn't destroy the company; it merely depreciated the stock's value by twenty-five percent! That ill-advised and unexpected prediction affected every biotechnology company. Investors lost confidence in the entire industry, and shied away from their stocks for years.

Al Ries and Jack Trout, in their book, *Marketing Warfare,* express the kind of error Genentech committed, in unmistakable terms. They say, "No military commander in his right mind gives a timetable for victory." Marketers, like all warriors, have to practice such common sense restraint.

Unforeseen Consequences

Although you cannot escape the fall-out from someone else's behavior, sometimes you can apply a life-saving procedure if you act promptly. Ayds Diet Candy had been on the market for fifty years. Suddenly, the company watched thirty percent of its market share vanish, in less than one year. The product had become a victim of AIDS, the disease. Customers didn't run away because they thought there was a connection between the illness and the product. They ran because of their inhibitions. They simply wouldn't ask a drugstore clerk, "Do you carry Ayds?"

The manufacturer turned to experts for urgently needed advice. One told the firm there was no choice: the product's name must be changed. Nobody needs to pay "an expert" to tell them to throw away their fifty-year-old trademark. Another said they should continue using the same name, but invest in educating the public about the disease while promoting the product. Again, nobody needs "an expert" to explain how to go bankrupt, while trying to educate a frightened populace on matters of life and death. This was especially true when the subject had no real connection with the product. The third told them to modify the name by putting some other word in front of it. That suggestion looked hopeful.

The product became Diet-Ayds. Carefully designed packaging made the name visible, without highlighting it. The words appeared in translucent letters, super-imposed on a picture of a man and a woman. The design firm deliberately placed the couple in bright sunlight, and didn't allow them to touch each other. The designers knew that druggists often display diet products on a rack next to condoms. Prophylactic packages frequently portray a man and a woman embracing, as the sun rises or sets behind them. Similar packaging could've led to product confusion.

When the candy was in its prime, it came in a parade of flavors. By 1990, it was only available in chocolate and vanilla. Nevertheless, it survived in spite of the unprecedented trouble that befell the manufacturer.

Leverage from the Inside Out

Companies that deal with goes-into products face a unique set of problems. Most of us don't know and don't care what goes into the products we buy. In this anonymous field, it's a real test of a marketer's ingenuity to elicit customer loyalty. Dolby did it. They marketed their noise reduction part so effectively that many people won't buy stereo equipment unless it has a Dolby component.

The most promising move, for a marketer of a goes-into, is to help the companies that buy the part grow the market for their own goods. The more retail products they sell, the more parts they will buy. Alternatively, the marketer can attempt to grow her own market, as though her company owned it. A glazier may find it impossible to convince end-users to specify her glass in their buildings. She can still find imaginative ways to promote the use of more glass in all buildings.

Because the public has become so health conscious, a food ingredient can now gain an identity comparable to Dolby's. NutraSweet has done it. The public unquestionably prefers it to other artificial sweeteners. Any food manufacturer that uses it gains a profitable advantage. They also gain something else: the NutraSweet logo, which they *must* include on their package.

From the beginning, J. D. Searle, the pharmaceutical house that produced NutraSweet, wanted to make customers aware of their product's name. Searle was looking ahead to the day their patents would expire. By training consumers to look for the NutraSweet logo, they hoped to nullify the onslaught of future imitators. As the patent expiration date approached, people were unquestionably aware of the product. They also learned to look for the logo, but Searle came to realize they had another problem.

Through the years, the firm gained a reputation for arrogance. They'd consistently treated manufacturers as though they should be eternally grateful for the privilege of using NutraSweet. When identical sweeteners became available, the food companies had the option of switching. If too many of them did, consumers could start trying familiar products with a different sweetener. If they were allowed to discover that some familiar foods tasted the same as always, NutraSweet could become just another unnoticed ingredient.

Searle made successful attempts to undo the harm they did themselves, by improving relations with the manufacturers. It appears the mistreated companies have forgiven their supplier and end-users have not been allowed to forget the goes-into.

More Problems—And More Ways to Outlive Them

The man who makes no mistakes
does not usually make anything.

Edward John Phelps

When your company gains a momentous advantage over a competitor, it's not yet time to celebrate. The besieged firm will call upon its last drop of ingenuity, to save its market position. Such a company could resort to doing "the unthinkable," and "the unimaginable." To appreciate the full meaning of those words, we only have to look at what two of our nation's most prominent businesses did to each other.

Pepsi-Cola conducted the "Pepsi Challenge" taste test. The results proved that, in this staged environement, a majority of the public preferred the taste of Pepsi-Cola to Coca-Cola. The winner of this seemingly innocuous but savage competition broadcast the test results to everybody, everywhere.

Doing the "Un-Doable"

Coca-Cola had to do "the unimaginable." Under secrecy as strict as any business or military commander could hope to maintain, it developed New Coke. When the innovative soda was introduced, the nation went into a state resembling shock. Now, it was Coke's turn to perform taste tests. These tests proved, beyond question, that a majority of the public, in this same controlled environment, preferred the flavor of New Coke to Pepsi. The winner promptly broadcast the results to everybody, everywhere, and continued spreading the word until the company was forced to admit the test results were useless. Even though people claimed to prefer the flavor of New Coke, they wouldn't buy it. The public was taking its turn to do the unexpected. Consumers simply refused to accept a substitute for the All-American institution that is Coca-Cola.

The company had backed itself into a corner, and couldn't come out unless it brought the old formula with them. So it was reinstated with a new name: Coca-Cola Classic. This time the company had committed the "the unthinkable." It had associated the Coca-Cola name with two different flavors.

Two flavors soon became three. Cherry Coke and Diet Cherry Coke appeared in stores. The new products consumed more shelf space, and Coke's market share grew accordingly. Pepsi finally discovered it had helped its chief competitor become even more competitive.

Of course, the commotion had also increased Pepsi's market share. Smaller firms, caught between the giants, found themselves squeezed into even smaller slots on store shelves.

The lesson from all this is difficult to master. An attack upon a competitor, in which you might actually overtake it, will call forth its last full measure of inventiveness. Before you attack, you need to imagine everything you'd do, if you were in their place. Beware of dismissing ideas with, "They'd never do that!" Think of Coca-Cola and rethink your supposition. If a company can do something, expect that it will. Have your counter-attack ready, assuming you took the time to think of one.

Novel New Product Positioning

At an earlier time, Pepsi-Cola had decided to enter the lemon-lime market. There were two leaders in that arena, 7Up and Sprite (a Coca-Cola product). The demand for lemon-lime drinks is not large, compared to colas. Still, the total revenue is a few billion dollars, and Pepsi wanted a piece of it. They knew it would be a waste of money to simply stick a new name on another lemon-lime drink. Remember a marketplace of any size, rarely really *needs* more than two suppliers of similar goods.

Pepsi put fruit juice into the basic lemon-lime formula, and called it Slice. This new product had winning traits. First, the fruit juice was a change customers could easily recognize. Second, it gave the drink a distinctly different flavor from anything already in the marketplace. Best of all, the juice made the drink something competitors couldn't readily duplicate.

Fruit juice is more expensive than sugar or corn syrup. This made Slice more costly to produce, but low production cost was not vital to the product's success. In fact, higher costs worked to Pepsi's advantage.

From the outset, Pepsi lowered its anticipated profit margin, and persuaded its bottlers to do the same. By basing the new program on the lower profits, the company conquered cost problems, and made product duplication unlikely. They knew that competitors couldn't add juice to their existing popular beverages. It would change the flavor, which would probably alienate many of their customers. Nor could they simply produce variations of their current drinks; the cost of the fruit juice would consume the profit. Were they to invest in a new brand, they'd only acquire a "me too" product, with an unknown name.

The fruit juice also placed Slice in the realm of "natural food." Although the juice was only a small part of the whole beverage, some parents chose it for their children. It didn't take long for the new beverage to gain a strong third position, and it now comes in assorted flavors.

It's Only a Commodity If You're Looking at What You're Selling

Occasionally, most companies fall into all-out battles with their competitors. Firms selling long-term commodities can get involved in them frequently. A long-term commodity is a product that is identical to others, and unalterable. To be part of a business that deals in such goods is intrinsically difficult.

There have to be long-term commodities. Nevertheless, a company doesn't have to remain a long-term commodity *business*. People who buy commodities, like all customers, are often buying more than the goods delivered to them. Recall the seasonal goods firm that sold rock salt, a long-term commodity. By searching for what was important to some customers, they successfully differentiated themselves from other rock salt suppliers.

A while ago, a company in the sand and gravel business broke out of the commodity mold by altering its delivery service. Of course, they would not reveal the details of the operation, but the procedure is not the important point. The value of the story rests in the kind of help it offered its clientele, over and above the commodity itself.

Concrete firms, among others, buy his goods. They store the gravel in enormous storage hoppers, and supply contractors. Large concrete companies usually maintain two of these immense containers. They cannot afford to run short, for even an hour, so each time they empty a hopper, they promptly reorder.

This company developed a cost effective system, which enabled it to provide consistently prompt delivery from the pits to the yards. The service gave their customers a distinct advantage. They no longer had to tie up their money in a hopper full of extra inventory. The company relieved their customers' cash flow problems, and they, in turn, made it a ten-lengths-ahead leader in this difficult marketplace.

Low-Cost Producers

Competitors, not customers, determine the price of undifferentiated, long-term commodities. Anyone who wants to trade in such goods without differentiating her offer, needs to be cognizant of the true nature of the marketplace. Everybody's asking price has to match the lowest figure any company will accept. To survive, a business must maintain strict control over every expense. The margin can become so narrow that, only the lowest cost producers can survive. That doesn't simply mean the lowest manufacturing costs, which some in the semiconductor industry need to achieve when they produce their "me too" products.

To be a low-cost producer, a company must also maintain rock-bottom overhead, marketing, selling, and distribution costs. In addition, they must be willing to work on the lowest profit margin. All of that is still not sufficient to describe conditions surrounding some long-term commodities.

Many U.S. firms like to conduct business in air-conditioned suites, with thick carpeting and oak doors. The higher echelon executives enjoy working at their beautiful mahogany desks. No sane marketer would ever suggest such a company take on a long-term commodity unless of course you have a monopoly or a price fixing agreement! Their competition could be working six or seven days a week, sitting on orange crates, writing on a chalk board, in an unheated room, with a concrete floor. Their production crews will be working in more primitive conditions, in Third World nations.

Even if a business manufactures its goods in the United States, cutting labor costs won't always help, as it did in the past. Technology has made numerous industries far less labor intensive. Many American manufacturers, of non-commodity products, have labor costs less than three percent of the firm's total expenses. Consequently, when selling a long-term commodity, management has to maintain minimal expenses, in every area, every hour of every day.

This means that, initially, you could view a business as a promising little fifteen percent margin enterprise, to add to your firm's holdings. A brief study may disclose your would-be competitors are happy with three percent. If management doesn't want to conduct such a stringent operation, leave the goods alone until you can find a way to differentiate your offer. Remember the rock salt company, after studying their customers buying habits, successfully charged ten percent more than the "going rate."

Short-Term Commodities

On the other hand, any product or service company can find itself suddenly burdened with a short-term commodity. Trucking will behave like a commodity, whenever supply exceeds demand. While the real estate market is hot, appraisers can charge as much as they can get. As soon as the market turns soft, appraisal fees become extremely competitive— a telltale sign of an emerging commodity.

A product always becomes a short-term commodity when stores grossly overestimate demand for a suddenly popular item. Following the 1989 San Francisco earthquake, merchants throughout California couldn't keep up with requests for any flashlight that contained a built-in radio. A few months later, they were unable to move them off their shelves, even at drastically reduced prices.

Short-term commodities appear so frequently that Windermere Associates, a consulting firm in San Francisco, decided to study them. They concluded that most businesses struggling with a short-term commodity, regardless of their goods, face similar problems that respond to similar solutions. They now specialize in guiding firms through these troublesome times.

In actual practice, short-term commodities often come into existence because many marketers hate research—and stretch the truth! Most people exaggerate, upon occasion. When marketers substitute fancy for fact, they can affect a whole marketplace. To avoid leading your company into a trap of your own making, or one to which you contributed, you need to abstain, religiously, from certain behaviors.

Dangerous exaggerations manifest themselves in simple arithmetic. Ask competing marketers the percentage of a market their company serves, add up their answers, and you can bet the farm the sum will exceed 100 percent. Then, ask them about the growth they anticipate in the next few years, for the whole market and their own company. Their answers will contain the same perilous mixture of optimism, braggadocio, and flagrant deceit. Everybody expects and dismisses such talk in the marketplace. It's irrelevant, except when marketers carry the stories back to their companies' presidents. Imagine the problem facing the executives of the competing firms when each hears that demand will double over the next three years. They study reports, designed to convince them of the need for greater manufacturing, inventory, or service capacity.

I'm not suggesting that a marketer will deliberately lie to her employer. On the contrary, at such times, she doesn't think she's even exaggerating, much less lying. Usually, she's swallowed whole the poor analyses and distortions of others. She's anxious to persuade management to prepare for the promising future. She does a little research, finds enough information to support the conclusion, and allows her overoptimism free rein.

Each president decides she must get ready for the predicted demand, or risk falling behind the competition. They all start building their company's capacity. With time, the market starts growing faster than usual, but it doesn't approach the exaggerated forecast. Supply ends up far outstripping demand, and prices fall. That's the most common and most avoidable way to saddle your company with a short-term commodity.

Give a Little Extra

Any industry, even without widespread exaggeration, can experience excess capacity, from time to time. When it happens, management customarily reacts by focusing its attention on competitors. They want to know everyone's asking price, from one minute to the next. Instead of traveling that crowded road, think of some extra service your business can offer. It takes surprisingly little effort to persuade customers to continue trading with you. A few people will always flee to a company offering a slightly lower price. Most will stay, when nudged to remember their supplier consistently serves them well.

Declining Markets

You need to think carefully before you decide your product or service shows signs of becoming a *short-term* commodity. Sometimes, demand is in permanent decline, whatever is done to try to prevent it.

Shrinking markets can present a unique problem, and an equally unique opportunity. You'll need to weigh your chances of outlasting your competitors. As the last company serving a market, you can reap a profitable harvest—while it lasts. Besides, the demand may never decline to zero.

Your decision to jump out of a dying market, or stay and fight, should rest, largely, on your competitors' attitudes. Another company may also decide to be the last one in the marketplace. One of you is destined to be mistaken. Your success could depend on how accurately you gauge your competitor's willingness to stick it out.

One experienced manufacturer was the last with a product line all others had dropped. He grossed an average of $2.7 million a year in sales, from the line. The goods also generated twice the gross margin derived from everything else he produced. He didn't have to spend money on promotion, or any related matter. He just kept selling the line, knowing the market would probably die in another three to five years. Until it did, he reaped a bountiful profit.

Market Shifts

Other times, a declining demand indicates a permanently changing market. The sooner you realize it, the more time you'll have to take a strong position in the altered marketplace.

Fax machines permanently changed the courier business. The need for couriers to deliver paperwork has practically vanished, but there are numerous industries that require prompt and reliable pick-up and delivery. Hospitals need blood; lawyers need court filings; advertising agencies need spot commercials speedily delivered.

Long before fax machines became widespread in offices, astute couriers were letting their paperwork business slide. Unconscious competitors—there are always some in a busy marketplace—were thrilled with the sudden surge in business they experienced. Instead of looking for the reason, they accepted it, joyfully concocting their own explanations for the windfall. In the meantime, a few firms were cultivating strong ties with other customer bases. By the time paperwork delivery became inconsequential, the far-sighted companies already held a large percentage of their city's reconstituted market. Countless couriers closed their doors and blamed their failure on fax machines!

Technology can now touch most businesses. Marketers need to keep an unblinking eye on the drawing boards of the world.

Brands vs. Private Labels

Little, if anything, exists in a free market that doesn't lend itself to variations. However, alternate offers don't always appear in the form of direct competition. For instance, there are brands and private labels. The two kinds of merchandise can appear as brothers, able to grow and thrive under the same roof. In reality, the economics of each business is different from the other. A marketer for a private labeled product can use the difference to her company's advantage.

A supplier of private labeled canned corn furnishes grocers with cans bearing the retailer's label. One manufacturer may supply many competing outlets with the same product. The grocery stores sell their own line at a lower price than the national brands. This means they must buy for less, so they can mark up their goods and remain under major brand prices.

Therefore, a manufacturer, offering both private label and branded merchandise, is selling the private labeled goods for much less than the branded goods. The former make far less money, but don't have promotion costs, so the profit can be attractive. Simultaneously, the brand has to prosper on its own, to support its needed, extensive promotion.

Some manufacturers perceive private label contracts as a sensible way to keep their factories busy during slow periods. However, grocers know that a dual focused supplier is often unreliable. Whenever the factory has comparatively few orders for its branded product, it will deliver private labeled product, as promised. As soon as orders for the brand pick up again, the factory gives them preference. Everyone else has to wait, because the supplier needs the added margin to keep the brand going.

Retailers do not graciously accept late orders for private labeled goods, which produce important profits. They want to deal with suppliers who consistently deliver on their promises. Therefore, a private label supplier, who's not also trying to support a brand, is in a better position to market the factory's undivided attention—which translates into reliability and credibility.

In the late 1960s, Spreckels Sugar Company discontinued its brand, and became a private label supplier for numerous grocery store chains. Decades later, they considered reviving their brand. The possibility prompted them to research the market. They needed to know how they could improve on their competitors' offers. Their studies disclosed that retailers and consumers had long resented the paper packaging which the industry traditionally used. Large bags of sugar never open properly, and inevitably leak. Spreckels designed their new package in the form of an easily handled, moisture resistant milk carton. It made their reentry into the world of brands a welcome event.

Hard Choices

Sometimes, the decision to produce a brand, instead of private labeled goods, comes from nothing more than a gut feeling. In the late 1950s, Akio Morita came to the United States to sell his transistor radios. A large company offered to buy 100,000 of them. The offer tempted Morita. His factory had never received such a large order; in fact, they only produced 10,000 radios a month.

There was a catch. No one knew Morita's brand, so the outlet wanted to put their own name on the radio. Morita decided he had to turn down the order. He simply believed that thirty years from then, Sony would be as well-known a name as any other. He says that refusing to take that order was one of the smartest decisions of his career.

Exceptions to Every Rule

While urging you to focus your business in only one direction, recognize that exceptions accompany all rules. Gary Neville, a Southern California businessman, bought a 60 year old retirement hotel, overlooking the ocean, in Santa Monica. The city extends three miles from north to south, and two and one half miles from the ocean to its eastern border. When Neville bought the hotel, there were 14 homes for retirees in that tiny area. Los Angeles, and the multiple cities and suburbs surrounding it, swim in retirement homes. The retirement industry serves a rapidly growing market, so everyone, especially in mild climates, can make a living. However, many of the residents live on fixed incomes. That implacable economic fact severely limits a facility's ability to differentiate their service from their innumerable competitors.

Neville didn't know what he wanted to do with the hotel. He'd bought it because he liked the location; he knew nothing about the people the business served. He soon learned that seniors ". . . pay rents on time and aren't party animals." He didn't want to lose such excellent tenants. Still, the property was expensive, and the building needed renovation. As a retirement facility, it couldn't earn a profit in keeping with the millions of dollars he'd have to invest.

He finally decided to follow a wholly unorthodox procedure. He divided his one business into two parts, by assigning half the rooms to retirees, and half to tourists. To succeed, he knew he'd have to maintain two separate marketing programs. One would address persons looking for a permanent residence. The other would appeal to tourists, seeking bed and breakfast accommodations. At the time, he said, "It's a hard message. There's no model to follow. There's nothing to compare it to."

Initially, the retirees were very dubious. They soon discovered they enjoyed the tourists with their varied interests and backgrounds. The satisfied permanent residents provided Neville with a steady income base. This compensated for the inevitable fluctuations of the bed-and-breakfast trade. In turn, the tourists and professionals, who were in town for a month or two, praised the location, the reasonable rates, and the better than average accommodations. In effect, Neville had divorced his retirement facility from its busy but monotonous marketplace.

Hard Reality

In closing this concentrated study of troublesome subjects, I have to mention the worst trouble that can befall any business. Sometimes, problems encircle and close in on a company. Before the firm can solve one, a dozen more develop. Frederick the Great, a remarkably innovative military campaigner, said, "He who attempts to defend everywhere, defends nothing." A capable marketer knows it, and recognizes the signs. He needs to urge management to sell out, while there is still something to sell. A new owner may be willing and able to do what the former could not.

I mention this dismal possibility, because we don't always want to believe we're beating a dead horse. You're reading this book to learn how to market. You may decide you have nothing worth marketing. If so, then make up your mind to divest yourself of the old, and look for something worth doing. While you can still salvage something, get out of a market in which you're too vulnerable, and pick one in which you can win.

Another old wartime adage applies here. "He that fights and runs away, may live to fight another day."

Market Research:
The What and How of It

My favourite, I might say, my only study, is man.

George Borrow,
The Bible in Spain

A lan Anderson, a Professor of Marketing at the University of Illinois, coined a definition of research. His brief sentence tells the whole story in a nutshell. He tells us, "Any reliable information that improves marketing decisions can be considered marketing research." You don't have to buy data to call it research. Nor do you have to spend endless hours pouring over lengthy documents. You simply need a sufficient amount of trustworthy information that helps you reach informed conclusions.

MTV As Market Research

Merry-Go-Round Clothes, a previously successful retail chain, discovered that the tastes of the adolescents they served could change every few months. The firm needed to know, quickly, which fashions their customers would want next. Otherwise they couldn't satisfy them and profit from their inclination to switch styles frequently. They started talking to the youngsters. The research disclosed that most of them were watching the same cable television station. The outfits worn by the entertainers dictated their taste. The company subscribed to MTV and continued their research.

Available Research

There's plenty of professionally compiled research publicly available, but it usually relates to large segments of the market. It's almost impossible to find information about small niches, unless it concerns a shrinking market. Comprehensive studies have to be funded. Big businesses can afford to know about the huge markets they serve. Research firms occasionally fund their own studies, but only when they're convinced there's enough demand to make their work profitable. Consequently, if you uncover a mountain of information about a segment, presume there has been considerable interest in it. That probably means it may be too big and mature for a small or mid-sized company to invade.

There are businesses that sell virtually every available survey. Software for use on personal computers now provides easy access to demographics, derived from the federal census. Diverse businesses choose new locations, according to the average age, income, and marital status of an area's residents. Cable television stations use the data to identify desirable programming for given locales.

In addition to the census, the federal government and individual states keep all kinds of records. They, and private companies, sell much of the information, or make it available to the public. It can sometimes provide all the facts a small business needs.

Atlantic Aviation

Matt Graham, the President of Atlantic Aviation, sold jet airplanes. He believed many CEOs were like himself: he couldn't sit still, peacefully, for longer than two hours! That unique perception prompted him to do some research.

He consulted the FAA records of flight plans. He wanted to identify the executives who regularly flew for more than two hours, in company owned propeller driven planes. When he was through, he had uncovered a small mine of potential customers.

It's difficult to justify the cost of any privately owned airplane, much less a jet. Graham wanted his sales force to approach persons who had already found a reason to own a plane. If his initial premise was accurate, a percentage of the impatient executives would seriously consider the advantages of having a jet. His army invaded—and found the mine full of gold.

The Past Doesn't Always Extrapolate

Research can tell you about the past and the present. *You* have to figure out how the information relates to the future. Studying yesterday and today, to help you decide what will happen tomorrow, is a precise example of an imprecise activity. One person's guess could be as good as another's. As a marketer, if your instincts prove right enough of the time, your firm makes money. If not—you change professions.

An American businessman was considering importing a new line of vodka. He decided to research the idea, before he proceeded with the large investment. More than one analysis of the current market warned him that the public didn't need or want another vodka. Most consumers couldn't tell the difference between the numerous brands already on store shelves. Another offering could only be a loser.

His imported product was going to have a brand name he considered "absolutely clever." In his mind, the many ways he could use the name, in promotions, kept outweighing the dire predictions. He finally decided to go ahead, in spite of the research. Absolut Vodka ultimately became the largest selling brand in the nation.

As he had foreseen, the way the name lent itself to advertisements was primarily responsible for the product's success. Everywhere we looked, we saw pictures depicting an "absolute this" or an "absolute that." In short order, Absolut Vodka became "absolutely vodka." Other brands faded into the background. The company went from zero sales to large, with barely a pause.

Uncertainty into Risk

Obviously, you shouldn't base your actions on research alone, whether the information is negative or positive. That doesn't mean it's necessarily best to save money and time, by skipping research. Facts are the most reliable antidote for uncertainty. They can convert doubt into a calculated risk. It is uncertainty that worries us. Someone who's afraid to take risks doesn't go into business, or become a marketer. By collecting and analyzing enough details, you can decide whether a risk is worth taking.

Professional researchers will study almost any subject, if you can afford to pay for their time and effort. You can also do it yourself.

To learn about the wider aspects of a business, begin by approaching some people who are part of it. They will usually talk to you, if you can convince them you won't become their competitor. Ideally, you should talk to people in a marketplace that is away from your own.

Visit them and ask questions. Anyone you approach will be more cooperative, if you give them some information in return. There may be tactics used in your area that differ from theirs. Even if you have nothing to offer them, most businesspeople enjoy discussing problems connected with the production, distribution, and sale of their goods.

Three dimensional tee-shirts became popular in California before they appeared elsewhere. (The silk screening process puffs out parts of the picture.) The owner of a screen printing firm in Michigan might have gone to California on a vacation. (Vacation or not, marketers always have an eye open for something new to offer.) When she spied the shirts, she could have located the silk screeners and asked some basic questions. How did they do it? How much did the application cost? Who was buying the product? If she knew she could reach a similar customer base, the facts she gleaned might adequately correlate in her own area. The cost of labor and availability of materials might differ, but she could factor the differences into her program. She wouldn't have found such information in a published study. It was too young and too small a segment.

Don't expect anyone to tell you trade secrets, but people will sometimes discuss their mistakes. Collect information from different areas and analyze it, especially as it relates to costs. If you feel something is missing—it probably is. Suspect a secret no one is telling. Stay away from the business, until you learn enough to feel confident.

How Big Is the Market?

Periodically, you may need to determine the precise size of a market. If it appears small, don't expect to find published statistics. Collect them yourself, by studying a few of the most successful firms. From the data you compile, you can extrapolate the needed information. If you know nothing about the companies currently operating in the marketplace, begin with the listings in the phone book's Yellow Pages. Try to identify the ones doing the most business. While not always an exact correlation, note the firms with large advertisements and go see them to get a firsthand impression of their size. Count cars in their parking lot shortly after a work shift begins, to calculate the number of employees. (But remember that many companies now encourage car pools.) Tell an experienced executive approximately how many employees her competitor has, and she can estimate their sales, within 10 to 20 percent. State sales tax records can help you estimate a retail firm's revenue with sufficient accuracy. Publicly owned corporations are required to publish annual reports for stockholders. Different industries have their own ways of inadvertently revealing financial information.

The combined revenue of the two or three obvious leaders will often represent more than 50 percent of the market's total volume. When the companies are operating roughly on par, the lead is up for grabs.

What's the Need?

After you ascertain the size of a market, you need to learn how you can effectively compete against the leaders. Talk to four or five of their big volume customers. If you have no idea who they are, go back to the phone book. Call some of the most prominently advertised companies that would buy the product or service. Contact the purchasing department, and identify yourself as a marketer studying customers' needs. That way, the listener will know he's not contending with a potentially tenacious salesperson. Remember, marketers don't try to sell anything. Your job is to identify problems and find ways to solve them. Many buyers will be glad to tell you, in detail, what they have to put up with from their present supplier.

Begin by asking if they patronize a local firm, and if so which one. Many will name a supplier. You may want to ask if they've ever considered buying from an out-of-town source. Whether the answer is yes or no, ask the reason. You'll begin to understand why they trade locally, or elsewhere.

They might tell you that they buy the best product or service available. That only means it is the best there is—not the best there could be. Or you may hear something more promising: "They tell us we'll have it in three days, but it almost never happens." Inquire about the excuses offered for tardiness. The answer could relate to labor, transportation, or supplies. Further research will tell you if the troubles are real, or a cover-up. From there on, your questions will grow out of the answers you hear. Gradually, you can compose a questionnaire that includes all pertinent subjects.

Wishing Doesn't Make It So

Before you embark on any study, identify exactly what you are trying to find out. You may have a feeling there's a poorly served market for concrete aggregate, in some city. You could be right, but until you can cite supporting facts, your opinion remains an intuition. Intuitive feelings are the offspring of creativity, not research. Research reveals facts, and a fact can be observed and documented. If you perceive feelings as facts, your research will fail you.

You should also beware of relying exclusively on success stories. Other people's failures could also prove your concept may not work in a particular area. Public libraries preserve copies of old newspapers, on microfilm. Websites contain archives. Articles in the business section about local firms, and advertisements from companies that no longer exist, can sometimes divulge priceless information. Keep in mind that conditions existing in the past may have disappeared. Look for differences between yesterday and today.

Research and analysis require honesty and common sense. Someone who has already made up his mind, pays attention to information that supports his position. In truth, research can prove whatever you want it to prove. It's not uncommon for professional researchers to hear clients say, "I need you to confirm this. My job depends on it." For professionals, the request poses an ethical dilemma. Phrasing, alone, can usually make results appear to support any conclusion. Statistics can be presented to prove diverse outcomes. A marketer pursuing long term success seeks positive and negative facts with equal vigor and without prejudice.

Professional Help or Do It Yourself

Fundamental procedures like the collection of facts, opinions and statistics are the domain of professional researchers. You'll probably spend at least a month of chronological time, though not full time, collecting information. Depending on the complexity of the job, approximately a month's effort will yield the elementary data you need. Undeniably, a research firm can be more thorough. Companies will tell professional researchers facts they might never tell an inquisitive stranger. Professional researchers are also better able to extrapolate accurate conclusions from statistics. Moreover, they have knowledge of a variety of industries, for comparative purposes. With persistent effort, you can gain the necessary research skills to learn about the kind of business that interests you.

Building Up Domino's

When Tom Monaghan set out to expand Domino's Pizza, he conscientiously studied his competitors. He spent hours sitting in his car, watching their operation, and imagining ways they could increase their business. By thinking about what they might do, he often identified procedures he could use. When traveling in other states, he went to see some of the most prosperous pizza parlors. The owners frequently shared valuable information with him.

One day, a friend told him about a store that served a much tastier sauce than his. He visited the shop. "To my surprise," he relates in his book, "the owner didn't hesitate to give me the recipe. . . ." Later, he employed blind people as tasters. He knew that blindness usually enhances a person's sense of smell and taste. His tasters' comments led to major improvements in his sauce.

Monaghan began to expand by opening stores near other college campuses. That was the market he meticulously studied, and his research steadily paid off. At first, he had offered pizzas in five sizes. He gradually reduced it to two. Each time he discontinued a size, his efficiency and profit improved. He learned to open stores that complemented one another rather than competing for business.

After the first shop in an area had become successful, he'd aim to open another, within two to three miles of it. A second store, properly placed, always improved business for the first. In his early days, while delivering his pizzas to college dorms, he had realized that soft drinks were a frequent source of order errors. He instructed his stores to carry only one soft drink, instead of a variety, and mistakes noticeably decreased.

Under Monaghan's guidance, Domino's sold a steady stream of prosperous franchises, until the firm tried to add a different customer base. Their new strategy proved to be a financial disaster.

Growth at Any Cost

From the outset, Monaghan had believed pizza would become as popular as it now is. After achieving some success, he decided he needed to expand more rapidly so that he could take the company public. His crew regularly searched for promising college campus locations. They finally reported they had run out of good ones. Management discussed the situation, and concluded they should start serving residential communities. In an initial ten month period, they opened 32 stores, mostly in residential neighborhoods. Few of them did more than $600 a week. The shops catering to college students were bringing in at least $6,000 a week.

The additional cost of advertising in cities, compared to the economical focus of campus publications, proved devastating. Moreover, Monaghan insisted that the residential locations continue to serve nothing but pizza, and focus strictly on delivery. At that time, his long standing policy didn't fit his new customers' buying habits. Most callers laughed and hung up, when they learned that Domino's only sold pizzas. Other shops were offering alternatives, like submarine sandwiches. Besides that, many residential customers preferred to go to a restaurant to eat. Successive failures from its hasty, and ill-advised, expansion reduced the company's strength.

Habitual Thinking

When Domino's first addressed the residential market, the majority of women hadn't yet entered the work force. When families ate at home, they ate home-cooked meals. When they wanted pizza, or any other food for convenience or a special occasion, they went to a restaurant. It took a while for adults to get into the habit of having meals delivered to their homes. A new habit takes time to develop because it usually has to replace some other habit. All of us adopt and unconsciously follow well established thought patterns. We readily accept suggestions that concur with our habitual thinking, and dismiss unfamiliar ideas.

Marketers are as prone as anyone else to follow a familiar train of thought. The habit can readily cause you to overlook unusual opportunities. Whenever you find your thinking in a rut, its important to lift yourself out of it. A version of a story told by Joel Barker, a futurist, could serve as a helpful catalyst. To my mind, it typifies our instinct to think and react out of habit.

A man was driving leisurely in a rural area when an automobile speeded around a curve and headed straight towards him. He slammed on his brakes, but stopping suddenly could not have prevented a collision. At the last moment, the driver swerved away, sped past him, and yelled, "Pig! Pig!" Furious, he shouted after her, "Sow! Sow!" His swift and appropriate response, to her unprovoked insult, delighted him. He drove around the curve—and ran head-on into the pig she was referring to!

You might try developing the habit of saying to yourself, "pig/sow," whenever you reach a habitual conclusion. You can suspect you've done it, if you hear yourself dismissing ideas with snappy expressions like, "Forget it. That can't work." Marketers can't afford to make careless judgments. Anything "can work"—unless you know exactly why it can't. Habitual thinking habitually smothers the notions that might inspire innovation.

Be a Significant Player

Nothing, including a unique, well-researched concept, will save you in a battle with competitors you never should have challenged. You need a segment in which you can become one of the leaders, before you run out of money. Various studies have produced an accepted rule of thumb. A company should enter a market with a goal to achieve a 15 to 20 percent share. A well managed, aggressively marketed business, with sufficient capital, can reasonably expect to acquire 15–20 percent of a market over time.

By that formula, a new company, entering a $200 million marketplace, will need sales totaling $40 million to have a 20 percent share. To most people, the thought of starting with zero sales, while needing a $40 million volume to challenge the real competition, sounds ludicrous. In fact, some start-up companies have done far better than that. Absolut Vodka and Worlds of Wonder sailed past small and mid-sized competitors, barely acknowledging their existence.

Most businesses row down narrower streams at a much slower pace. To become a leader, a company doesn't need sales in the tens of millions. Certain segments must have small firms to serve them. A family owned bakery, specializing in particular pastries, can gain fame and fortune in a city, and last for generations. A mid-sized bakery, supplying grocery stores in the same city wouldn't want to serve the small bakery's market—and probably couldn't.

Imagine a new business, entering a five million dollar segment. It will need sales totaling one million dollars to hold 20 percent of the market. Many efficiently run firms, with innovative marketing techniques, accomplish this in less than a year. With that share, they should be moving close to the leaders. They could start investing part of their profit in improving their goods or offering something new to their existing customers. If they don't become wasteful, or tempted by their swift success into ignoring their weaknesses, they can continue to grow at a healthy pace. When they gain a 30 percent share, it would be a company with $1.5 million in sales. This would make it half again as large as when it first moved into serious contention with the leaders. It may be ready to enter a larger marketplace by expanding the customer base for existing products. For example by investing part of the profit in a branch.

Research each market you enter carefully. Never forget, it's a trap to just pursue a tiny share of a huge market as if this alone made it a segment. Really segment it, geographically or with a product or service specialty. Divide and conquer.

When you encounter intense, skillful competition, it can take years to increase your market share. The trick will be to keep everyone's mind on the company's long range goal, and to invest regularly in tactics to promote growth. Watch your competitors' progress. A company may start to outdistance you significantly, and you'll need to reevaluate your position. Remember, a leader twice anyone else's size can invest in growing a larger market. While its program will increase your income, your own market share could be shrinking. You may need to further segment the marketplace. Or it could be time to sell out at a profit. The increased volume potential makes your business appear desirable to someone who believes she can contend with the far-ahead leader. Maybe she can—but let her business try to beat the odds, rather than yours.

Partnering

Some marketers, after analyzing their company's position, decide that the surest way to gain market share is to form a strategic partnership. Businesspeople usually refer to a "strategic partnership," when theirs is a small company and their partner is much larger—or located in Europe or Asia. If both firms are close to the same size, the union becomes a "joint venture." A partner, by any name, is still a partner.

You could find yourself thinking, "This'll be a piece of cake. They'll do most of the work, and we'll collect the money." If you entertain thoughts even resembling those, beware of uniting. For a joint venture to prosper, whole entities must communicate with each other and coordinate their efforts. Arguments no longer involve someone in the next office, but an entire organization's policies and personnel. Instead of coasting and "collecting the money," the dreamer often starts increasing a law firm's revenue.

Market Research:
The Dollars and Sense of It

Some future day when what is now is not,
When all old faults and follies are forgot.

Arthur Clough,
Some Future Day

Throughout the time you spend deciding upon and researching a plan of action, that plan keeps getting more expensive. Each year, test marketing requires a greater capital investment. Besides that, you may need to file the research results under a Gershwin song title: "It Ain't Necessarily So."

A manufacturer test markets a new product in Rochester, New York. The competition finds out, and quadruples its advertising in the area. More frequently, one company tests while another clones. Technology now allows competitors to quickly copy almost anything. A cheaper clone appears in the marketplace, sometimes ahead of the original. The clone makers didn't invest in research, or in promoting a brand name. They use private labels, and rely on the drawing power of a lower price. They're simply betting there's a market for the goods based upon evidence of sales of the primary product, or the believed marketing skills of the original supplier. Many lose their bets. On the other hand, the benefits of test marketing don't necessarily outweigh the competitive advantage that is sometimes forfeited by delaying until the market is adequately understood.

It's not surprising that all kinds of industries are growing increasingly skeptical of traditional market research procedures. Nevertheless, we can't solve the problem by simply dispensing with all tests.

Failure Fees

Grocery wholesalers and retailers have introduced failure fees, thereby dramatically proving how they feel about unsuccessful products. In 1989, manufacturers introduced more than 12,000 new grocery items, an unprecedented number. Distributors reported that more than 80 percent failed. They blamed the abnormal percentage of failures on what amounted to testing in "live settings." The grocers claimed that traditional test markets ahead of introduction and distribution could have proven that few people needed or wanted most of the products.

Many of the new items were only a copy of another company's success. Or they were brand extensions. A powerful manufacturer may profit by extending its line of household cleansers, even if the new brand is a poor seller. The more shelf space used, the less room is left for competitors' brands. However, increasing the number of available cleansers does not increase the number of customers who buy cleansers. Grocers can't make an extra dime. On the other hand, they can lose money introducing, and then removing, products that don't sell.

In a business where pennies count, the losses prompted some retailers to institute failure fees. Packaged goods companies have to pay a penalty, if a specified amount of product doesn't sell within six months. The penalties provoked a debate. Those who opposed the idea thought it struck at the heart of the free enterprise system. A food company can spend up to $30 million to introduce a product nationwide. If distributors penalize them for failing, this could seriously curtail experimentation . . . the lifeblood of a competitive marketplace.

The fees were initially hard to collect, but they are still legitimately and more widely levied. Retail grocers feel they should not have to bear the cost of research. A General Mills executive, commenting on the penalties, said, "It . . . may no longer be appropriate . . . for a manufacturer to introduce the 35th line extension of pound cake." The fact that he'd make such a statement shows that many manufacturers have replaced common sense with greed. Abuses by some persons and companies always breed counter abuses. The cycle repeats itself, until enough people grow weary of the game and force a change in the rules of the marketplace.

Since the number of new grocery related products introduced in 2000 was greater than that of 1989, and the failure rate just as high, it may be time for manufacturers to recognize the true nature of certain "slotting allowances," which retailers charge. When a producer pays for shelf space to introduce goods, they are actually test marketing in a "live setting." The slotting allowance compensates the retailer for the test. If seen in that light, the resented charges could become a reasonable alternative to other forms of testing.

It could also be time for producers of any goods to develop standard test agreements with retailers. The arrangement could put an end to the growing animosity between manufacturers and their channels of distribution, and save everyone involved some money.

You'll recall that studies have continued to show as many as nine out of ten new products fail to achieve sales levels initially deemed as the minimum acceptable by the supplier. Those that fail during tests kept the manufacturer's losses to a minimum. Conventional test markets have the disadvantage of announcing your arrival, and revealing what you're bringing with you. The imitators hurry to meet you, hoping to share your profit, but there may be no profit to share. The test results could correctly warn you not to proceed.

A cost/benefit analysis can help you decide the fiscally prudent course to follow. It's an application of the cautionary lines: "How much will it *cost*?" "Do you mean, if we buy it? Or if we *don't* buy it?"

The Costs of Research

There are two fundamental costs related to research. One is the time and money you spend conducting a study. The other is the time and money you lose by not selling while waiting for the results. You can adequately predict the cost of the needed research, but it's impossible to ascertain the cost in lost sales while you collect data and analyze it. Therefore, the amount and type of research you conduct ultimately depends on the degree of your or your CEO's uncertainty.

Will People Cooperate?

Market research is a $2.5+ billion a year industry. A St. Louis company that tracks research trends discovered in 1988 that 34 percent of adults asked to take part in a consumer survey refused to be interviewed. The rejection rate was up 15 percent from their 1982 figures.

The Council of American Survey Research Organizations had an equally dismal report. They found that 38 percent of consumers approached by their interviewers refused to cooperate even when asked to spend only two minutes expressing their opinion of a product or service. The level of refusal was significant enough to leave some researchers wondering if the views they gather can accurately represent the majority's opinion.

If, as mentioned in earlier chapters, consumers believe more than half of all businesspeople deceive them, why should they bother to answer questions for people they don't trust or respect? Whatever the reason, many customers, the most reliable source of information for marketers, will no longer talk to researchers.

Alternatives to Traditional Research

What can marketers do when consumers become unwilling to talk about their preferences? Fortunately, there have always been ways to gather information, aside from consumer surveys.

Akio Morita, in his book *Made in Japan*, said, "I do not believe that any amount of market research could have told us that the Sony Walkman would be successful. . . ." When he wrote those words, he must've been thinking only of formal studies. He went on to describe his own observations, which, in fact, provided the reliable information he needed.

The New York retailers first approached by Morita asked him why he was making such tiny radios. They pointed out that Americans have big houses and want big radios. He replied, "There are more than twenty radio stations in New York City alone. . . ." A small radio would allow people to listen to whatever station they wanted ". . . without disturbing or bothering anybody else." Although his viewpoint overturned the conventional wisdom, it made sense to many retailers, and an overwhelming number of American consumers confirmed it.

Lifestyles are an endless source of information, and the way consumers spend their money speaks volumes. (As the beloved baseball philosopher, Yogi Berra, said, "You can observe a lot . . . just by watching.") Moreover, the questions people are willing to answer can tell you as much as the answers themselves. Environmental surveys never lack cooperative respondents. Eighty-six percent of those answering

one survey after Earth Day 1990 said they'd made some eco-
logically induced changes in their purchases.

For years, Heinz had used a particular plastic ketchup bottle. After listening to the public, the company changed to
recyclable material.

Tom's of Maine not only introduced baking soda toothpaste
for the users of "natural products," but also put their paste
into a tube made of recycled material. Tom's is a small firm,
going up against giants in the toothpaste market. They cir-
cumvented the inevitable shelf space problem by initially distributing through select pharmacies. Among their outlets is
the AARP Mail Order Pharmacy Service. A small company
can offer a guaranteed product through mail order, and discover it is all the test marketing they need.

Many AARP members no longer drive and like to shop by
mail, if they can trust the quality of the goods and the service
accompanying it. There are more members of the American
Association of Retired Persons than there are people living in
Canada. The incredible size of the organization proves what a
lucrative customer base people over 50 represent. Volumes of
research exist on this age group, because large companies are
searching for ways to serve them. In this case, a small firm
does well to use the mountain of available information about
a rapidly expanding marketplace. Skillfully segmented, it can
become the birthplace of tomorrow's giants.

The research has revealed numerous taboos, many established through costly experience. Most of the proscribed
behavior fits under one heading: drawing attention to your
customers' age is not the way to succeed. The mere suggestion that any product or service befits "older people" can
make your goods a loser. Age is always a touchy subject. The
young don't like advertisements that single them out either,
and businesses know it. When they want to appeal to pre-
teens and teenagers, they talk only about whatever they offer.
Age is a factor reflected only in the choice of design element
or language, not mentioned overtly. Yet for some reason,

many companies think they have to spell everything out to a more experienced clientele!

Mark Zitter, a California consultant, wanted to emphasize the diversity of a particular age group. He said, "Among people 65 to 70, there are people in wheelchairs and people who run marathons, people in poverty and people who are millionaires." In that one sentence, Zitter has actually encompassed all customers regardless of age. Marketers should always keep in mind the diversity within their target market, as well as what distinguishes it from others.

Focus Groups

No matter what you offer, or to whom, focus groups are a comparatively low cost way to encourage people to talk about your wares. Some research firms specialize in putting these groups together. They select individuals who fit a profile closely resembling your customers. A problem rests in the artificial setting. Participants sit in a room and discuss your product or service. Sometimes they have to express an opinion about something they've never used, because it doesn't yet exist. In spite of the drawbacks, industries have learned that focus groups frequently suggest valuable modifications, or even wholly new products.

SEC Filings

Your competition can unwittingly feed you essential facts. A competitor saved my own business at least a quarter of a million dollars. As a public company, they had to file annual 10K and quarterly 10Q government forms. By studying the information the law required them to reveal, we discovered they'd revealed more than that.

We were preparing to enter a market we perceived as 35 percent government. As the existing market leader, they told us, via their 10K, that it was 65 percent government. We still entered the market, but as a result of their information we applied our resources differently, and saved a small fortune in time and money.

Clipping Services

You can also learn from your competitors by subscribing to a "clipping" service. These companies track virtually everything printed. They will "clip out" every reference to a topic, person, business name, or almost any subject you specify. They charge a few hundred dollars a year, and a modest fee per clipping. The thoroughness of the service can annoy some subscribers. When a business issues a press release, ten publications may print it. A service subscriber may get all ten. This costs a few extra dollars, and the few seconds it takes to recognize duplicates. But it can be well worth your money and time, to learn what a competitor plans to do. New "electronic clipping" services can eliminate the duplication and may be faster and more complete.

Some executives love to talk to the press. Though much that they say is intended to conceal rather than reveal, an occasional statement can reveal their biases. They might also expose what they wish they could do, but can't, thus providing you valuable information for your business. Recognize that you may scan 100 reports and learn nothing and then read one that makes it all worthwhile.

Do not forget about clipping services whenever you speak for publication, even to your neighborhood newspaper. Talk all you want, but be cautious when discussing your own business, or your industry. Lack of vigilance could tell discerning observers more than you want them to know about your company's internal affairs. Look upon the interviewer as your competitor, with whom you would be pleasant but guarded. That way, you won't say anything you wouldn't say to a competitor's face. Remember that someone, somewhere, might find your words in her e-mailbox, neatly 'clipped'.

Two Other Information Sources

There are two other excellent sources of information available to any business that chooses to use them. The first is your easy-to-collect guarantee, designed to alert you to problems. The money spent on refunds buys first-hand knowledge of what customers find wrong with your goods or services.

The second is employees. Their suggestions can help a company improve efficiency as well as goods. Mitsubishi and Canon have historically received between 70 and 100 suggestions from each employee per year. American firms average one suggestion from every seven employees, annually despite various quality improvement and empowerment programs of the 1980s and 1990s.

An Amazing Story

Research, in any of its thousand forms, can repay you a thousand fold, when coupled with insight. In fact, skillful marketing depends on research and creativity more than it will ever depend on money. I don't know of a better story to illustrate that truth than one told by Edward Bernays. Through the years, tales told by other marketers may equal it, but I doubt if any will ever surpass it. (Although the following story may sound impossible in today's complex market, it nevertheless illustrates an important truth.)

In essence, Public Relations firms employ communications professionals who use PR techniques to achieve marketing goals. Bernays was among the most talented of them. In his book, *biography of an idea*, he described one of his challenging experiences.

Lucky Strike cigarettes is a product of the American Tobacco Company. In the 1930s, it was the largest selling brand in the United States. The firm's President, at that time, was George Washington Hill, a fiercely competitive man.

Research had revealed that men smoked Luckys, but women preferred Camels and Chesterfields. Hill hired

Bernays to determine why women weren't buying his brand, and what the company could do about it.

Bernays learned there was a simple and unequivocal reason women preferred other brands. Too often, Lucky's green package didn't harmonize with their clothes. He advised the ill-tempered Hill that it was an easy problem to solve. All the company had to do was change their package to a neutral color. Hill replied, "I've spent millions of dollars advertising the package. Now you ask me to change it. That's lousy advice."

Bernays reminded his client that the firm had little choice. They either had to change the color of the package or dictate the color of fashions. Hill promptly announced, "Change the fashion—that's a good idea. Do it." With that brief statement, Bernays acquired the assignment.

Bernays' thinking, in relation to this uncommon task, grew out of his previous experience with a silk manufacturer. The reasoning he employed followed an exquisitely straight line. I've condensed it into a few questions and answers.

Why do women wear certain colors? They have to buy what the stores sell.

Why do stores focus on different colors each season? They have to take whatever manufacturers offer.

What causes manufacturers to offer particular colors? They can only work with whatever the textile industry produces.

What motivates the textile industry? They must comply with the current fashions.

Who sets the fashions? Paris designers created the originals. Individual manufacturers produced endless versions, of varying quality.

Bernays knew what he had to do. In keeping with his policy, he turned to research to learn how people perceived the color green. He learned that both sexes felt that green conveys the promise of springtime, and promotes a sense of tranquillity. Bernays was off and running.

He went to the chairwoman of an organization that supported the Women's Infirmary of New York. They regularly conducted fund-raising events, on the hospital's behalf. He suggested the group hold a Green Ball, in November. Research proved people liked the color, and it would offset the gray skies of approaching winter. He told her ". . . a nameless sponsor would defray the costs up to $25,000 . . . ," provided green was ". . . the obligatory color of all the gowns worn at the ball." The chairwoman thought it was a terrific idea. The Infirmary would tangibly benefit from the financial help, and it would be fun to have such an unusual theme.

Next, Bernays approached a silk manufacturer, outlined his program, and suggested the man's firm could become the national leader in color. The silk maker decided ". . . to bet on green," and to help himself win his bet, he gave a fashion luncheon. Menus, printed on green paper, listed ". . . green beans, asparagus-tip salad, pistachio mousse glacé, green mints and creme de menthe."

Afterward, the headline of a newspaper article, describing the luncheon, announced, "It Looks Like a Green Winter." Another headline proclaimed a "Green Autumn." The textile industry got the message.

For the rest of the summer, Bernays marketed green in every direction. An emerald nail polish even appeared in the marketplace. His program was so persuasive that Camel cigarettes became its victim. They wanted their advertisements to portray the latest fashion trend. They featured a girl wearing a green dress, trimmed with red . . . the exact colors of their chief competitor's package.

The socialites, and other celebrities, ordered green gowns for the Ball. The Paris designers complied, and the textile industry had the cloth waiting. Manufacturers of ready-made clothes ordered on cue. Soon, department stores throughout the nation were featuring green window displays. Women everywhere . . . whether they liked the color or not . . . had little choice. They bought green dresses, blouses, skirts, and hats . . . and Lucky Strike sales went through the roof.

During the Second World War, the armed services needed green dye for uniforms. The tobacco company proclaimed: "Lucky Strike green has gone to war." Conveniently, the color never returned.

In six months, Bernays had performed a phenomenal piece of work. He had spent only $25,000. Though the money bought far more than it would today, it was an amazingly modest amount, considering the enormity of the assignment.

Bernays described his approach as, "the engineering of consent." In another example of the method, he told of Alfred Reeves, a member of the American Automobile Manufacturers Association.

Reeves successfully developed the market for American automobiles in England. The narrow, curved roads, which spanned the nation, had made large American cars unwieldy and unwelcome. Reeves solved this difficult marketing problem through a public relations program. He ". . . campaigned for wider and straighter roads. The sale of American cars followed."

Marketers—no matter their actual working title—help solve crucial problems as well as frivolous ones. They perceive what people really need, and conceive of a way to provide it. Everyone profits.

Someday, the world may learn to trade goods in a more efficient and fair way. Until then, we need to remember the value implicit in the free enterprise system. The system, despite its imperfections, provides more lucrative, challenging, and satisfying employment, for more people, than any other economic structure devised by man.

PART

A View of the Plan

A Plan's Revelations

Who needs a Marketing Plan? Every business needs one, except those that want to remain a tiny presence in a tiny community. Even they need to remember that someone else could be looking for a way to serve the community better.

On the other hand, many businesses will never have a plan. Of those that do, most won't benefit from whatever they thought was in it. Eventually, someone will say, "Marketing plans are a waste of time. Nobody even uses them."

What is this composition that some people consider vital—and others say isn't worth their time to write or read? Simply put, a well thought out plan states what the company will offer now and in the future. This could include new, old, or improved products or services. The plan speaks of who and where customers are, and outlines ways to reach them.

A Map

Ordinarily, a business creates a new plan once a year, though some like to make mid-year revisions. When a plan is well done, it's not a document that goes into a drawer, to remain there until another replaces it. It's a type of calendar, by which a business can measure its progress against expectations. It's also a map that describes potential roadblocks and delineates emergency detours.

Each year's map will contain a metaphorical arrow saying, "We are here." The arrow points out more than your company's market position. It might mention that revenue has been lower than last year's plan anticipated, because the public has less money to spend. In response, the marketing department may have decided to lower prices, temporarily, and advertise the cut as an answer to their customers' immediate needs. Offering anything extra, while everyone else is cutting back and openly worrying, can immediately differentiate your business in the public's eyes.

On the other hand, your revenue may be lower because your customers have gone to your competitors. The plan should then reveal the cause of their disaffection, and exactly what the company plans to do about it.

The arrow also indicates what lies ahead, as the marketing department sees it. Painful cost increases may appear inevitable, or alternatively the coming year could look promising. The plan cites evidence showing customers are losing or gaining interest in old or new goods. It anticipates increasing or decreasing competition. You may need to explain why the company is jumping out of a shrinking market, instead of fighting to be last in the ring.

None of this requires tedious detail. You can cover each subject in a sentence or a paragraph. If the plan is short, people will read it from cover to cover. If it resembles a college thesis, it will be a disaster.

The plan is the culmination of months of research, analysis, and applied insight, but you can put it together in a few days.

It states the firm's long-term goal, explains the underlying strategy to reach the goal, and the tactics to implement the strategy. The company could have a new goal: to become a twenty-five million dollar business in three years, and the second largest supplier in the marketplace. A strategy grows out of the products or services offered. What is the six word definition of the help your business provides? Usually, you can translate it into a precise expression of your strategy. The strategy gives birth to tactics. Successful tactics produce ongoing orders.

Sears' Misguided Adventures

For generations, Sears' goal was simply to enlarge their lead in the national marketplace. Through the decades, they could have defined the help they offered in the same six words: *providing highly durable, modestly priced merchandise.* Their unchanging strategy consisted of offering a broad range of such goods for everyday use by all age groups. Their customers came from low-to-middle-income households, in urban and rural communities nationwide. To keep the attention of their clientele and lure new patrons, they consistently used only one tactic. Periodically, they held storewide sales on their already low-priced goods.

They veered away from their strategy, and fell into a full-scale war with Wal-Mart Stores, Inc. and Kmart Corp. By 1991, both challengers had moved ahead of Sears in sales, which didn't surprise anyone. Sears had reported their profits declined by 63 percent in the first six months of 1990.

From the customers' point of view, Sears had stopped providing the durable products and dependable services which had made them famous. In effect, they'd also stopped guaranteeing the goods they did offer. The company has yet to express, in word or deed, a new, clearly defined strategy. This omission has caused them to introduce a parade of disjointed tactics for a time. The public could say, "Sears sells everything from socks to stocks." Unfortunately, some of their merchandise has a life span shorter than dime store wares. This may be equally true of their competitors' goods, but it's not what the public expects or will tolerate from Sears.

One of their tactics was an inferior rerun of their old successful performance. They began to advertise "everyday low prices." That failed when too many of their prices proved higher than their competitors', for comparable merchandise. The revelation dealt another blow to their already damaged credibility.

Analysts caution us not to count out the 110-year-old concern too soon. In some locations, they have initiated radical, but promising, changes. They also started allowing department managers to provide refunds at their own discretion. This eliminated the line at the customer service desk, and is reminiscent of their no-questions-asked guarantee. No matter what happens next, their behavior has been an excellent study of a nondescript strategy . . . with matching tactics.

The Cost of Capital

A well thought out strategy and imaginative tactics are useless . . . if not grounded in reality. No business has the funds to pursue every good idea that occurs to them, and borrowing money costs money. The two questions related to capital in any business are, "Can we get it, and how much will it cost?" Al Shugart, former CEO of Seagate Technology, expressed the idea in more explicit terms. He said, "Cash is more important than your mother," and, "Prime plus six is better than no loan at all." Whatever sums you require in capital, you have to build its estimated cost into your program.

Depending on the size and nature of a business, a finished marketing plan could include the costs of production, inventory, distribution, promotion, sales, and capital. The payment terms you offer your customers will directly affect the amount of capital your company needs to raise. A clientele that furnishes letters of credit represent one kind of market. When you have to wait 120 days to get your money, you have a different kind of market to serve, and far different problems to solve.

Occasionally, a firm can secure the needed capital, but at a cost that forces the price of their goods too high to be viable. More often, a company can't raise what they need. A two million dollar business can't usually borrow what a twenty million dollar firm could command. Hence, a plan that suits the larger is useless to the smaller.

Without realism, your planned events will never materialize. People might read a couple of your unrealistic prophecies, but if you bother to write another, it will remain unread. Even worse, bankers dismiss plans that don't demonstrate attention to the details of material reality. They won't bet on a plan based on random guesses, and they know a guess when they hear one. Conversely, a well laid plan can become your own or your CEO's key to the bank door.

Know When to Say When

When someone drills for oil, they'll only drill to a certain depth before quitting. They decide, in advance, when it will be time to move on. No business can always be right in everything they do. A plan enables you to realize if the road you're on isn't what you anticipated. Budget and time limits, built into your program, can keep one project from consuming the company's capital. Without milestones, identified detours, and actual jump off points, your company will go until it hits the wall.

Marketers have to make basic assumptions, and link their assumptions to specific actions. Assumptions will defeat you more than any other factor. If you assumed that building construction would boom in the Spring of 1991, actual events wreaked havoc with your plan. Therefore, knowing this factor was crucial, you needed an alternate route. Planned course corrections can help you avoid having to react to market conditions without enough time to think carefully. By imagining worst-case scenarios, you also make it more difficult for competitors to blind-side you.

Creating an Imaginary Plan

By conjuring up an imaginary embossing company, we can watch some of the planning process in action. The firm embosses plastic cards, such as credit cards, with a name, account number, expiration date, etc. The actual customer for these cards is the end-user. Our imaginary company's customers are the businesses that solicit credit-worthy clients, and then order cards for them, from an embosser. Numerous embossing firms compete in this expanding marketplace.

Go back a few years, and imagine you're a marketer for the embossing company. One day, you ask yourself a question: "Why aren't we mailing the cards directly to the consumers, instead of sending them to our customer for them to mail?" Before you enlarge on the thought, you need to talk to your CEO. He may have a bias against assuming responsibility for individual delivery. A CEO's fundamental role is to ensure that the company doesn't do anything that violates his personal convictions. In this case, there'd be nothing morally or legally troubling about the idea, so he says, "It sounds interesting. Look into it." Now you get to follow the path you've uncovered and see where it leads.

You've thought of something that's different from anything your competitors offer. The service would help your customers, by relieving them of a procedure that must cause them some aggravation. You need to determine if it's a viable market and of a size your firm can serve cost effectively.

You begin with your sales manager. Does she see a problem her staff might encounter in offering the service? Is there any reason the same sales force couldn't offer it? In this case, you can't think of an objection she could raise. Still, you do not presume to know everything the sales department could foresee. You also want their early participation. By helping you develop the idea, they have time to recognize its full potential, and become enthusiastic about the offer.

The sales manager assures you her people will only need a brief training period. She helps you select a few promising customers to approach. You and the salesperson in charge of each account will call on them. You won't go alone for two reasons. First, it would rightfully anger the salesperson, who has worked hard to get the account and is responsible for it. Second, the salesperson's thinking differs from yours. Together, you can collect all the needed information, and answer all the questions which Mr. Department Store or Ms. Oil Company might ask.

The presentation begins: "We have an idea, and we want to see what you think of it. Would it benefit you for us to . . . ?" There are various ways to phrase the question, but the gist of it is, would the idea benefit them? You hear a conditional, "Yes." Your next question: "What is it costing them to send the cards?" The answer includes postage, envelopes, personnel, time. It adds up to a couple of dollars to deliver each card. You ask about the delivery schedule, and learn the card must reach the user no later than 10 days after your company gets the embossing order. You also inquire about their growth projection over the next three years. (For most businesses, three years is a realistic period to predict.)

After consulting with a few additional customers, you're ready to start outlining everything required to provide the service. The main questions concern production. You know how long it ordinarily takes to produce the client's orders. This leaves a certain number of days to put the right card in the right envelope, and send it out, on time. You identify the costs related to extra space, employees, supplies, postage, and billing your customer for the service.

The end-user doesn't care who sends the card to her. Consequently, changing the mailer's identity gives no added value to the product. It only eliminates a step in the issuer's procedure, and possibly gets the card to the user sooner. It also changes a simple step into a more complicated one for your business. This leaves the question of its profitability up in the air.

What would it take to deliver plastic credit cards to their users? Of course, your customer must believe your company is capable of efficient delivery. If you can erase their doubts and, in consultation with the finance department, arrive at a sensible asking price, the customer is likely to agree to try the service. If your price has to be much higher than their cost for delivery, clearly you would not offer a service, they'd inevitably refuse.

In our story, the price looks favorable, so you're ready to present the plan for your CEO's approval. If he were to ask you to express the additional help the company will provide, in six words, you could do it: "We *relieve customers of all delivery problems.*"

You wish you could also tell your CEO, "We'll offer the service to everybody because it's a slam dunk. Every customer I've talked to wants it as soon as possible." Your more likely strategy will be, "We'll pilot it with this one customer, to see how it works. They've agreed to give us 10 percent of their business for three months. If we execute well, they'll give us 25 percent for another three months. Then it's all ours, and we can go after everybody. I've talked to this number of our customers, and we'll have most of them as soon as we're ready. The growth forecast is such and such a percentage over the next three years. We'll need to increase our production capability in such and such a time frame."

The finished plan contains a three year goal, a strategy, tactics, assumptions, and milestones. Now comes the execution. You track the performance record, regularly, to see if everything is progressing according to plan. A few months later, all looks well, and your company is ready to start delivering 25 percent of the cards, on schedule. A week before it should happen, your salesperson goes to visit the customer, and learns the bad news. The executive who had agreed to the project resigned and walked out the previous week. The person who has taken his place never liked the idea, and he won't extend the contract for the rest of the test period.

You have a detour already planned around this roadblock. When you evaluated the responses from other clients, you noted who was most interested, and could best serve as an alternate proving ground. You also decided exactly which procedures you want thoroughly proven, before you can feel comfortable approaching competitors' customers. This means it's too early to speak to anyone other than your own clientele. You not only understand them, you know the volume to expect, so you can protect your company from overextending itself. Your salesperson approaches the firm you recommend, and the test period begins anew.

The opposite scenario could have developed during that first three months. Your company had previously only dealt with bulk deliveries. The process of mailing individual cards on time caused a steady parade of problems. You consulted everybody involved, rearranged, and eliminated, but you couldn't find a way to perform the service at the anticipated cost. The card issuer bills each card holder, monthly. For them, mailing a card is simply an initial or occasional step in the same procedure.

Your company has reached a jump-off point, in time to save its credibility. Your salesperson is told, "The costs are running higher than expected. Tell your customer we appreciate his participation, but, regrettably, we can't execute the program on a cost effective basis, for them or us."

In reality, embossers proved able to provide delivery service, profitably. These days, many of us get our cards directly from them, though we seldom give it any thought. Someone also devised a method to replace lost cards in 24 hours. Some issuers find it a benefit worth offering their clients. Embossers, and related industries, are also trying to grow a larger market, through "the engineering of consent" encouraged by Edward L. Bernays in the last chapter. They steadily lobby Congress, and seek to educate the public, about the inherent advantages of an "all-plastic" society.

Presenting Your Own Plan

Before you can test your own plan, your employer has to decide if all the data is credible, and the tactics acceptable. The promise of profit won't guarantee approval. Remember, she wants tactics in keeping with the company's name. Anyone can lower their nursing home costs—by tying patients to their beds.

Many executives have learned to save time by asking questions before they start reading. Your employer could simply ask how the offer differs from the competitions'. If you say, "It's a lot better," you haven't answered the question. Tell him the difference customers will see. Or she might ask, "Why would anybody buy this *from us*?" That elementary question has left many a marketer stuck for an answer!

Be sure you plan to make good use of employee expertise, and mention it. Also, use a sentence or two to explain your reason for choosing one alternative over another. If you say nothing about options, others could think you didn't consider them. The omission invites tedious discussions. Throughout your plan, use precise wording, which leaves no room for misinterpretations. Keep in mind that all people don't draw the same conclusions from the same words.

Communication

At a marketing and sales meeting, one of my marketers suggested a radical distribution plan. He explained the mechanics, but he failed to mention the implementation procedure, detours, or jump-off points. Everyone walked out of the meeting thinking his idea was a calamity in the making.

Later, he explained to me how he expected to implement the plan in stages. He estimated a six month trial period would prove or disprove it. In his original presentation, he had spoken as though it could not fail. It hadn't occurred to him that anyone would think he was intending to establish the entire program in one swoop. Nor had he thought it necessary to mention a variation he had in mind. It was a very promising idea, so the departments held another meeting. This time he won the needed support and his innovation proved almost as good as he thought it would be.

The Best Laid Plans

No one can positively know if something will work, until it does. Marketers, however, are born optimists, a quality which can cause them to become unrealistic at times. In sanguine moods, they can miscalculate the time it will take for results to materialize. (Recall the previous discussion of Genentech's prediction of an exact date for FDA approval: a catastrophic example of over-optimism.)

Built-in milestones balance enthusiasm. At a designated time, you may discover sales are running at only 60 percent of "realistic" expectations. Now, you have to find out what's happening. Why was your "conservative estimate" that far off? Are the sales and support tools you developed not doing the job? Have you been talking to your distributors and customers, or just listening to your salespeople?

A Weighty Plan

The plan for a small company will fill around twenty to thirty pages. Make it thicker, and the staff will say, "Look at this! We're becoming a *Fortune* 500 bureaucracy except we don't have the perks." Remember, you write a plan for people to read and follow—not weigh and file. To emphasize that admonition, a consultant I know tells the following story . . . but only to his friends. Though the tale may sound too fantastic to believe, it's true.

A firm had hired him to write an Operations Plan for their management information system—a more formal name for the computer department. They told him the department was a mess, and sorely needed a professional's help. The MIS manager was a long-time employee, but in recent years he'd inherited a new superior. Since then, every year, the executive had told the manager that his plan was "inadequate and lacked real substance." In large companies, when a plan fails to win a superior's support, it becomes impossible to get the requested funding. That, in itself, can preordain "a mess."

The consultant immediately went to the new executive's secretary, and asked what he looked for in a plan. She confided that he didn't read any of the plans submitted to him. He weighed them on a scale he kept locked in the lower right hand drawer of his desk. If a plan weighed above a certain amount, he praised it. Otherwise, he berated the author.

The consultant and the department manager worked together, created a polished plan, and put it on the heaviest stock paper they could buy. The executive promptly proclaimed the document the best anyone had ever submitted. It probably was—but I doubt if he had accurately weighed its value.

I'm not recommending heavy paper! Still, if a company has exhausted every avenue for financing, you might consider the idea worth trying. You could encounter someone, with more money than sense, who owns a scale.

Pushing Some Buttons
to Help a Plan Grow

Thou shalt not covet; but tradition
Approves all forms of competition.

Arthur Clough,
The Latest Decalogue

Yesterday, you and your employer parted company. Today, you decided to try to raise the capital to open a competing business. Your former firm is the leader in the marketplace, but you know the flaws in their operation. You've been watching the owner gradually shorten the training period for the new employees he now hires, and reduce the quality of supplies they use. You were told the customers won't know the difference. You know he is relying on the reputation you helped the company build for ten years. You also know customer complaints are starting to increase. What else are they no longer doing that you can use to your advantage?

The value of this exercise is not to prepare you to become your employer's competitor. By conjuring up a company to compete with yours, you may see flaws you've overlooked or ignored. There'll always be marketers watching for your errors of omission and commission—and trying to out-think you. They perceive you as someone who can put them out of business. You view them in the same light. Marketers, by nature, must be competitive people. That doesn't imply they must also be amoral, vindictive, and greedy. They simply have to enjoy matching wits with others—and to win enough matches to make their company profitable. They also have to work as hard to recognize their own blunders as they do at perceiving their competitors' errors.

If You Could Do It Again

Try imagining the answer to another question. If you were to open the same kind of business today, what would you do differently? Or if you were forced to start a new business today to compete with your current business, how would you go about doing it?

It's popular today to consider "re-engineering" the workplace. In many companies that's just a euphemism for lay-offs or downsizing. Trying to do more with less. Or worse, trying to do more of the same with less. An old saying goes "Doing the same thing over and over again and expecting a different result is the definition of insanity." So rather than just "right-size" without any conception of why or what, consider your business from the customers' viewpoint.

Now with this view, if you could do it again from scratch, how would you do it differently? What are you doing today that provides no value to the customer but adds cost? Or, worse yet, what are you doing today that adds not just cost but also is a disservice to the customer?

Start with a spreadsheet, a blank piece of paper, and an open mind. You'll be surprised at your own answers. Now, why not implement some of them today?

Focus and Change

You can also resolve to look squarely at what you've been avoiding. Imagine you're in the hotel business. "We know the day is coming when competitors will invade our resort area, and build modern facilities. We can't afford a remodel to match theirs. Even if we could, we'd be just one of many. What can we do to get ready for private saunas, and sunken bathtubs with Jacuzzis?"

Through the years, most of your guests have brought their children. You decide to serve *families who want separate vacations, together*. Will you want to offer planned activities, for different ages, all day and evening? Or would you prefer to appeal to adults who enjoy vacationing with their children, but would appreciate some hours away from them? The distinction between the two kinds of programs is crucial, for more reasons than just costs and procedures. There are consequential differences in the customers themselves. In most industries, along with precisely identifying *who is* your customer, you must also identify *who is not*.

You decide to offer breakfast and morning activities for children, so parents can sleep until eleven o'clock. Supervised dinners could let the youngsters eat "their kind of food," while the adults enjoy their own dinner date. Divide the dining room with a one-way mirrored wall, and parents can observe their offspring, without having to hear them.

These ideas add up to a new strategy to serve the needs and wants of a large segment of your present market. Join the guests and get to know each one personally. You'll be doing all the research you need, to help you plan variations in activities from season to season. Quarterly newsletters can tell patrons of coming events. But always under-promise, so you can over-deliver.

Most businesses need an assortment of tactics to attract customers, and to keep the competition off balance. While your competitors are scrambling to compensate for your current tactics, you're planning new ones. (That is one of the reasons it's easier to defend than to attack.)

Rethinking the Structure

For a marketing program to succeed, it has to permeate and motivate the whole company. Sometimes that requires a thorough house-cleaning. If you believe reorganization is essential, you'll have to persuade your employer of the need. The most well-conceived marketing plan imaginable can't make a success of an inefficient company.

As the president/marketer of your business, you have to alert yourself to the need for reorganization. Acknowledge it, then act on it. In essence, you'll be saying, "Okay, this is our goal. We're selling this kind of goods. We want to have so many dollars in sales, in this length of time. Now I need a new organization to implement the marketing plan."

Doling out paper clips is not going to materially lower your overhead. On the other hand, making sure everyone understands marketing's purpose can make a noticeable difference. Ask each employee to write, in a few sentences, what they do to help attract and keep customers. Or ask them to say what their job does for customers—those persons who actually pay their salary. The exercise can help everyone relate to the people the business serves, no matter how physically removed they may be. You might discover that someone who distributes the mail, or polishes the floor, helps customers more than a body taking up space in a private office.

On paper, describe the process necessary to serve your customers. Then write down the positions the company needs to efficiently and effectively support the process. Add a sentence about why you need each, so you can weigh the job's actual contribution. After you justify every position, it's time to decide if you have the right people doing the work. Note each employee's brief description of what they do for customers. Evaluate these against your opinion of each employee; you may decide they're more astute than you thought. Then, select the ones you want, and "expand the employment opportunities" of the rest. A few employees might benefit from new assignments, because you took the time to recognize a better use of their talents. The company will benefit too.

The Company's Face to the Outside World

The receptionist's job is often regarded as an entry level position, requiring anyone who has a high school diploma, an acceptable appearance, and the willingness to work for a small salary. The assumption is that the job only involves the ability to show up on time and write an adequately legible message. Such reasoning is common but lacks common sense.

There's an even less sensible way to select a receptionist. Some firms give the job to an employee who doesn't get along with fellow workers. At the front desk, they can work alone. Everyone is glad to be rid of them. Everyone is also too busy to notice how they respond to callers—except the callers. Customers hear, "Who'd jasay yawanna talk to? Oh yeah, I saw her leave. I dunnow when she's comin' back. Nobody tells me." That genre of greeting proves your business can tolerate a querulous attitude or even gross inexperience. It also proves your office procedure leaves the receptionist ignorant of the staff's schedule. None of which promises dependable performance for customers.

A new caller can decide that something doesn't "feel right" about a company that opens business in that manner. Potential customers will fade away almost as fast as your marketing program can attract them. You'll probably never learn the reason you didn't hear from some of the people you approached. If you contact them again, they may be unreceptive believing that everyone at the company has such un-businesslike standards.

Firms that pay their receptionist more than any other secretary often face objections from the other secretarial staff. Offer them the job, and they say, "Are you kidding? I don't want to be a receptionist!" Everybody knows the job carries no prestige. Yet in the majority of offices, the receptionist is the first person who answers callers' questions. If the answer isn't good enough, no one else may get a chance to improve on it.

When their dissatisfied customers are lured away, your competitors probably never knew how their employees, or their procedures, were annoying their patrons. If they had, they might've done something about it. Soliciting anonymous feedback from customers can alert you to mistakes committed by anyone in the firm.

Customer Feedback

The owner of an escrow company composed a questionnaire, printed it on company stationary, and included a stamped, self-addressed envelope. She sent it to every real estate agent, buyer, and seller of property, which her firm had handled in the past year. A surprising number not only returned but also signed it, regardless of what they had to say. She passed the results on to the staff. They had no idea they had pleased—or displeased—so many clients, in small but memorable ways.

The firm's president/marketer also called the people who had expressed dissatisfaction. She explained that she was not trying to solicit their future business; she only wanted to hear anything more they could recall about her company's disappointing performance. Few refused to spend some time talking to her. In addition, she went to see her satisfied clients. She wanted specific information about what her staff did right. Never neglect an opportunity to learn what your business does well, so you can plan to do more of it.

Chaos of Inspiration

Whether you are starting a new business or trying to increase your market share, the process of creating a marketing plan is the same. As the president and chief marketer, you may have dozens of ideas the company could pursue. How much of your thinking should you share with your employees, before you move into the planning stage?

A man bought a small but long established manufacturing firm. He knew they had operated for years under the assumption they could only make precisely what they were making. He hadn't decided what else they should do, but he knew there was an array of interesting opportunities to consider. He believed he should share his thinking with the heads of all departments.

He called a meeting of managers, and threw a bunch of suggestions up in the air. Then sat back and waited to see which ones struck a chord. He'd expected to listen to comments, and get a feel for each person's interests and talent. Instead, he learned a fact of life. When you talk about numerous possibilities to people unfamiliar with marketing, they think you are failing to focus on anything. They don't understand that marketers may have to scan a hundred proposals to find one good one. By sharing too much, he had confused his employees instead of inspiring them.

After a while, he decided to keep his ideas to himself, and hire a marketer to conduct research. In the meantime, everything proceeded as usual. His employees thought he had settled on something, and were noticeably relieved. It was more than a year before the firm was ready to expand.

Employee Feedback

If you, as the president/marketer, have a marketing staff, you have to remember what no one else can forget: you are their employer. Anyone who tries to wear two hats has to become adept at encouraging open discussions and constructive criticism. Each time you assume a marketer's role, let everyone know it. "I'm putting on my marketing manager's hat," you announce at the start of the meeting. The thought is easy to express, but your performance has to match your words. You won't be perfect—but when you play dual roles, you have to try doubly hard.

It's difficult for management to get anyone to criticize peers openly, much less express real dissatisfaction with superiors. This fact, coupled with modern technology, has spawned helpful computer programs. They provide a way to collect anonymous feedback from subordinates, peers, and superiors. The companies that developed the programs do the analysis, explain the results, and offer suggestions. Feedback from employees who don't fear retaliation, can make any firm more productive.

A minor officer of a well known business tried to warn his superior about the effect a new, high-ranking executive was having on the personnel. His opening words brought such a sharp rebuff, he feared dismissal. He kept quiet, and watched the company disintegrate.

He had tried to discuss a scene that transpired every time a customer needed urgent help—a common occurrence in that industry. At such times, the executive openly rejoiced. He always began by announcing, "We've got them now. They're going to pay plenty for this!" Then he delivered a monologue which invariably revealed his contempt for the client. He never recognized the message he was conveying to the staff: "We may spend a fortune advertising how we care about our customers, but don't you believe it! We'll squeeze every dollar out of them, at every chance we get. We're here to make money, not friends. If you want to move up in this company, you'd better remember this." One day, key lower ranked employees submitted their resignations en masse, and went to work for major competitors.

Marketing at Work

A well organized marketing department, at a moderate-sized business, could have between one and four persons marketing its products or services. The manager assigns and coordinates flexible and overlapping work assignments. All members will look for something new to offer, or a different distribution channel for existing goods. Sales support material requires fresh input. Customers and potential customers need personal visits. Someone has to keep an eye on competing offers and pricing. Of course, everybody watches the progress of the current program and looks for ways to improve it.

When the time comes for the department to discuss a new plan, each member will have his or her own opinion. Sometimes, there could be major questions to resolve. Your previous goal may have been to grow your profit to finance a future venture. The market allowed it, and management preferred it to borrowing money or selling stock. At this point, should you prepare to offer new goods, or compete harder with the ones you have? Should you strive to get every last piece of business in Pittsburgh, or guard your position while you move into Philadelphia? Answering such questions is a critical marketing skill.

Staff will have to study all related subjects. The process can be time consuming, and a clear-cut answer can still prove elusive. An impatient member of staff reaching her own conclusion, could say, "We'll just have to move into Philadelphia and see what happens." No matter what you do, you'll have to wait to see what happens. But if you move without a finished plan, you could soon be saying, "Hold everything, we can't make it in Philadelphia." That kind of certainty only wastes more time and money as you redeploy the army.

Thinking About the Future

Most of the time, you'll be looking for ways to improve your product or service. The important question then is: what do your customers wish you'd do for them?

Throughout the year, you have evaluated remarks from clients and distributors. You've been exchanging views about past and present, and conjecturing on the future. What's the competition, the government, or some foreign nation going to do next? By employing insight and creativity, research and analysis, dialogue and discussion, everyone eventually agrees on the course to follow.

Mundane questions will need answers. Who'll actually write the plan, when is it due, and what form should it take? Usually, the manager writes it. Sometimes each person composes a portion, and the manager prepares a coordinated document. Avoid becoming engrossed with procedures—a mistake committed by a surprising number of firms. The plan's *content* is all that's important, whether it moves forward or backward.

To move forward, the plan begins by posing an updated concept of the customers the firm wants to serve. If, for example, the company manufactures, distributes, or retails men's suits which sell for $500 to $600, the staff should know that currently, 21 percent of all men who buy suits select merchandise in this price range. A business dealing with more expensive suits has fewer customers, but more competition.

Your typical customer is a young man who needs a professional appearance. He is earning around $85,000 a year and has children, car payments, and a house mortgage, which limit his discretionary income. He also engages in some formal social activities common to persons with his income and education. By employing research and insight, certain businesses could offer their clientele some unusual and profitable "unrelated goods."

To work backward, the plan asks, "Why will people buy this from us? What is the difference between our company and others?" You may discover the only difference between your firm and the leader in Philadelphia is that they are in Philadelphia! You dismiss the idea of opening a branch there. Then again, the difference between you and the leader can be plain and promising. Your company must offer precise answers to the standard questions all customers, of all products or services, ask themselves. "Is this really what I need and want? When can I get it? Will it work? If it doesn't, what will the supplier do about it?"

Resting on Your Laurels

Some marketers view their company's history as a worthy substitute for detailed planning. They believe their sales force can simply lay proof of performance in front of potential clients. "Look how well we've done. We've only missed two percent of our deliveries in the last 12 months. We've missed those by an average of only three days." The premise is commendable, but it has a dangerous weakness. At any time, a competitor could decide to match your performance, or improve on it. Marketing can't depend solely on a tactic others can readily copy, whenever they recognize its value. It isn't prudent to rely even on something that's difficult to duplicate. That way lies complacency.

Changing the Rules

The Xerox Corporation holds the patents on the basic process of xerography. Originally, it owned the photocopier market. The company knew its patents would protect it for a while, but at the same time it maintained a superb support organization. The quality of its customer service ultimately became the most effective barrier to entry from upstart competitors.

Canon wanted to get into the business. The company found a way around the Xerox patents, but still couldn't afford to offer the nationwide customer support Xerox provided.

Canon realized the only recourse was to create an advantage out of a disadvantage and develop a machine that didn't need such support. (If you can't fix it, feature it.) So, they invented the cartridge toner based copier, the innovation that eliminated routine service calls.

Canon's machines were smaller and less expensive but also slower than Xerox equipment. Innumerable customers proved that speed was not as important as the convenience of self-service. Xerox's prompt attention to their customers had been above reproach. Eliminating the need for service calls was better still.

Canon changed the market forever. All manufacturers now make machines that only need minimal routine care, but Canon retains its place as one of the industry's leaders.

Change

Remember, marketing is a commitment to serve the changing needs, wants, and buying habits of customers. You write the plan; your customers dictate what goes into it. Marketers who clearly hear spoken and unspoken needs, create the most successful plans. Needs change because the world changes. They also change because you and others offer products and services that permanently alter consumer expectations.

Cornerstones of a Plan

Your finished plan should be based firmly on these four questions. Experience has proven that most plans which fail do so because some element of this foundation was missing.

> 1) Does the plan define the company's goal, and estimate the time needed to reach it? As Yogi Berra likes to say, "If you don't know what you want, you might not get it." Without a goal, there's no way to tell if anything useful has been accomplished.

2) Does the plan spell out the help the company offers, and the strategy to provide it?
3) Does the plan identify the actions that'll make the strategy work?
4) Does the plan identify the person responsible for the creation and the follow-up of each element in it?

A Team Effort

Write your ideas down as you think of them. Notes on paper, unlike concepts drifting through your mind, allow you to review them, deliberately and systematically. Discuss the better ones with people in other departments. A successful marketing plan is rooted in two camps. It grows out of communication with customers and communication with the company's personnel.

A supervisor could say, "If you want my crew to do that, we'll need . . ." Manufacturing might tell you, "We can't do it that way. We'll have to . . ." Finance could reveal a fact that promptly relegates an idea to the wastebasket. Salespeople will ask questions you might have forgotten to ask for months. They can also refine your thoughts about when and where customers would buy the goods, and about preferred methods of payment.

Communicate the Plan

You've finished outlining the plan. You want to talk to people about it personally, instead of consigning it to paper and wondering who'll read it. Even if you could talk to each person individually, they'd lose track of the details. In written form, your plan enables your CEO to pinpoint responsibility, and evaluate performance and progress. It gives every department the same reference source, which promotes coordination. Anyone who reads it can link today's actions with tomorrow's occurrences. In essence, it enables everyone to look beyond procedures, toward results.

A restaurant could have forty employees, but many of them will only work part time. They could easily think the plan doesn't concern them. You want them to know that every employee plays an important part. Make it available and encourage them to read it. Each person need not have a copy, but even in large companies, most employees should have access to it.

By encouraging people to read the plan, you're doing more than helping them understand what the business is trying to do. You're proving that their understanding is important to you—and to the firm's success. It could encourage someone, who would otherwise drift on, to become a loyal and productive employee.

On occasion, there may be some details you don't want to make common knowledge. In reality, anyone who intends to pass information to a competitor can usually find a way to uncover crucial information. But few employees want to help the competition. They much prefer to help their employer grow, especially when they know they'll share in the proceeds.

With your well-laid plan in hand, your CEO can go forth, in search of the needed capital. With money in hand, you can together prepare to offer your company's brilliant idea—and advertise it.

Advertising, As Planned

20

Some years ago, bus lines in England wanted to attract more patrons. They embarked on an advertising campaign to familiarize non-riders with public transportation's excellent service. The buses ran frequently; they were clean; they went everywhere. Apparently, they were so punctual, a person could almost set her watch by them. The claims were credible, and the advertising extensive—but ridership did not increase. The bus company went looking for the reason. They discovered the people they'd hoped to persuade had no interest in any of the published facts. There was only one reason they didn't ride buses: they felt it would make them look "lower class." The whole program had been a waste of money.

Someone once summed up the frustrations of advertising, perfectly. The saying has been attributed to various persons, but no one can verify the author. Our anonymous sage said,

"Half the money I spend on advertising is wasted, and if I knew which half, I'd quit spending it."

Everything the bus company learned after the expensive ridership campaign, it could've learned ahead of time. Obviously, those responsible for the program were positive they knew what their prospective customers needed to hear. Consequently, they didn't even think to research it. It's an easily committed mistake: whenever we're certain we know something, it simply doesn't occur to us to verify it. Checking the validity of your message—no matter how obvious you think it is—can prove as profitable as checking dried beans, before cooking. In your whole lifetime, you may find only one pebble among the beans. Finding it could save you a large investment in dental work.

Lifeblood

Advertising is important to most businesses, and the lifeblood of some. Often, it's the only way a company can let enough people know their business or their goods exist. Yet it can be the most rapidly depleted portion of an annual budget. It is hard to tell what you get for every advertising dollar spent. Therefore, the money allocated usually represents an arbitrary figure. Management wants to advertise "as much as we can afford to," or "as often as possible." That type of loose definition allows the company to divert money from the advertising budget every time it faces unexpected expenses.

Customized Shopping

In the early 1980s, a unique retail grocery opened in West Los Angeles. It consisted of one huge warehouse and a loading dock. Their overhead was so low, compared to regular grocery stores, they could provide custom service at everyday prices. Patrons using a coded, well-indexed catalogue, placed their orders by telephone, and designated the time they'd arrive. At the pick-up dock, waiting attendants put the groceries in the car and accepted payment for the transaction. In a matter of minutes, the shoppers were on their way.

The service saved so much time and effort, at no extra cost, it quickly won loyal customers, yet the enterprise had only a brief existence. Their start-up costs had far exceeded their original estimate. Every extra dollar spent on construction and inventory came out of their advertising budget. When they opened, they couldn't afford to tell enough people what they were doing there. When they closed, few people knew they'd ever existed.

For advertising to be effective, you need more than the right message; you need to deliver it frequently. After you grow tired of running the same ads, the public just begins to notice them. My neighbor runs a newspaper ad for his business every Thursday. He opens the paper and looks for it before he reads the news. I only see it once in awhile.

To Whom Are You Advertising?

Advertising the right message, repeatedly, is only part of the job. You have to direct your ad to the person who decides which product to buy. Jim Palmer, the ex-baseball player, appeared in ads for men's Jockey shorts. I've yet to meet a man who says Palmer's recommendation prompted him to buy the brand. Still, the promotion was extremely successful — because women buy 70 percent of all men's underwear sold.

If you misdirect your message, it won't sail alone into thin air. Part of your precious advertising budget goes with it.

Before Nissan introduced the Infiniti, the vice-president in charge of the project conducted a public relations campaign. He described the aim of their advertisements by saying, ". . . we are going to hit right between the eyes the people we are trying to reach." That is exactly what you need to do. Know who decides to buy your goods, and direct your message at

them. Forget everybody else. The rule also applies to placement. Unless your target segment is very large and very
broad, forget about advertising in a magazine like *Business
Week* or *Time*. Their circulation includes too many people
who'll never be your customers. The cost of your ads, compared to the sales they may generate, could bankrupt you.

What Should Your Advertising Say?

It goes without saying that an ad should contain copy that
commands the attention of potential customers. But what
interests people? We all have one interest every advertiser can
take for granted: *ourselves.* This translates into a simple fact.
Customers don't want to hear about what you think of yourself, your company, or even your goods. They want to know
what the goods will do for them.

Glance through a legal or architectural firm's brochure.
Many of these professionals believe they should never convey
the impression of trying to "sell" anything. So, they don't talk
about what they do for clients; they talk about themselves,
instead. Every sentence refers to "I . . . , we . . . , our firm . . . ,
our staff. . . ." The closest they come, to mentioning the people they serve, is to call them "our clients"—as though they'd
branded them.

They expect us to make the leap from how wonderful they
say they are, to the help they can provide us. We could leap
the wrong way! We might see pictures of a law firm's posh
offices, note the company's civic involvements, and glance at
the list of impressive universities the lawyers attended. When
we're through, we could suspect it's a politically motivated,
pompous, and over-priced gang. We could look at pictures of
awesome buildings, and conclude that the architectural firm
only builds extremely expensive structures.

When reviewing a brochure, highlight all the "you" statements in pink, and the "we" phrases in yellow. If the copy
turns mostly yellow, it needs rewriting.

A gardening service ran an archetypal ad. It highlighted that catch-all phrase: "We tailor our work to meet client needs." One day, the owner of the gardening firm overheard a woman complaining about the gardeners employed by her condominium homeowners' association. She used an expression that made him realize he'd been thinking about what his company did, instead of what clients saw. His new ad opened with her words, "Does your gardener mow, blow, and go?" His phone started ringing off the hook.

How Should You Say It?

Every problem your advertisements depict needs an accompanying solution. Don't expect people to perceive the solution for themselves: spell it out. Listing features doesn't explain anything. Describe the value the features provide. Value could relate to saving money, time, or effort; the features of your service or product prove that value is provided.

If you read about a software program that "has multiple indexing capability" and "allows relational queries," would you know what the advertiser was talking about? Change the wording, and anyone can understand the message. "You can locate information easily because. . . ." "You can access related information quickly because. . . ." Such wording focuses on exactly what the user will do with the product, and the reason they can do it. A reader can believe this. Moreover, it employs familiar vocabulary, not an industry's esoteric jargon.

Recall Charles Schwab's advertisements. They aimed their message directly at the people who could be their customers. The ad said the company didn't maintain a research department. Hence, it operated on lower commission fees. Everyone could immediately see how and why someone would benefit. Furthermore, the copy clearly addressed only those persons who didn't want investment advice.

Elephants by Mail

Your ad, catalogue, or brochure needs to answer questions your customers would ask as well as those they could forget to ask. The answers should be whatever a salesperson would say. Explicit, written copy saves everyone's time, and prepares people to ask more specific questions.

A brochure or a catalogue requires a large investment of time and money. If it's a complete bust, the cost is significant, not just in production, but in future business. Well done, a brochure can help sell—and a catalogue can actually sell—almost any reputable goods. If you think that statement exaggerates the power of printed words and pictures, consider a story Roger Horchow tells, in his book, *Elephants In Your Mailbox*.

Horchow created the first upscale mail order catalogue not tied to a store. He gained his experience while running the catalogue department for Neiman-Marcus. In one of their editions, he happened to use a picture of an elephant. Soon, people were calling to ask if they could buy the elephant! That settled it. Horchow decided there was nothing a person couldn't sell through a mail order catalogue.

What's the Difference?

Most customers, most of the time, can't immediately see the difference between competing products or services, and won't bother to look for the difference. The more your advertising talks about the specific help your goods provide, the less your potential customers will remember other products.

Some years ago, General Motors ran an advertising campaign telling us, "It's not your father's Oldsmobile." I can't imagine the concept they thought their words would propagate, and it left me with no conception of their car. Nor did the ad pique my curiosity, if that was what they thought it might do. Why should it? The statement was a blanket fact that befits all new cars. If they were trying to tell the market that they had changed, the question is what had they changed to become? And why should someone be interested in finding out? It should be no surprise that in 1995, Oldsmobile was *still* trying to figure out what to become once they grew up. Their thinking was that they should become a step up from a Saturn upgrade, whatever that is.   Instead, in 2001, GM announced the closing of Oldsmobile.

Advertising That Works

Gary Stibel, of the New England Consulting Group, offers an easy way to know if you are buying "good advertising." He says, "Good advertising that doesn't sell is an oxymoron."

The job of advertising is to help sell your goods, by moving people through the buying cycle. The cycle begins with potential customers becoming aware of you and your offer. You know an ad is having an effect, when inquiries begin. Sales skills can sell anything once, but only the goods themselves can earn reorders and recommendations.

The Agency

Few businesses try to advertise without some professional help, even if it's only from their printer. If you employ an advertising agency, remember that it consists of two parts: account executives and a creative department. When an account executive hands you her card, draw a line through her title and write in, "Salesperson," and you will better understand her. Salespeople want to get and keep your account, and persuade you to buy more of whatever they sell. It is not the salesperson's persuasive ability you're buying, however. You'll be relying on the creative department to come up with that on your behalf.

If you meet members of that department, you may see some strange sights. Some of them might not dress or comb their hair as you and your associates do. Their refusal to behave like everybody else can reflect their innate individuality—a valuable quality in their profession. Or, it could bespeak an attitude completely unsuited to the world of commerce!

A banker was critiquing his new brochure for auto loans. At the time, four wheel drive vehicles were becoming popular. The brochure's cover pictured a truck precariously perched on a large rock. It was an eye-catcher, but someone could easily miss its implication.

The banker turned to the account executive and said, "I don't understand this. What's this truck doing on top of the rock?" The salesman replied, "It's a four wheel drive." The banker thought a moment, and offered a practical suggestion: "Maybe you should print 4×4 on the truck, in big lettering, so people will be sure to get the point." The salesman conveyed the idea to the creative department, and carried their one sentence answer back to the banker. "Conspicuous lettering on the truck would compromise the graphic integrity of the ad." They were serious!

On the other hand, some agencies will never disagree with you, even when they should. Consultants to all industries want their clients to like their work. There's certainly nothing wrong with that, unless they worry more about their client's feelings than their business needs. If they're primarily concerned with keeping you happy, they won't object to any change you make in their copy. Their silence can lead you to believe they agreed with you. More often, they let you do whatever you want, because they want you to like your ad. If this is the case, you have a graphics artist and a copy writer who are trying to keep your account—not advertise your goods, persuasively.

The message conveyed in your advertisements must be credible. If the agency returns copy that contains inaccuracies, tell them what's wrong. Have them rewrite it, because words are their specialty, not yours. If you don't like their style, change agencies. Don't move the graphics around. Don't replace one phrase with another because you prefer the sound. You created the concept you want conveyed; you pay them to communicate it effectively. They should know how to do it far better than you. Because we all succumb to advertising, we all think we're an expert. If you *really* think someone inside your company can create a better ad than any agency you can afford to hire, then go ahead and do it yourselves. Just be sure you're not fooling yourself.

Measuring Advertising Results

You ask an account executive, "How are we going to tell if our campaign is getting results?" She replies, "We measure readership." "We've won many awards." "We do surveys." You want to know how much the agency's work is helping your business. The agency is going to tell you a newspaper's circulation figures. From that, she expects you to extrapolate how many readers noticed your ad, and drew the right conclusion from it. Or you may learn that your ad won an award—for the agency that created it. Or you'll get to tell your employer that a survey proved people really enjoyed the ad!

Readership does not sell products. Memorable or enjoyable ads don't necessarily sell products. Nissan's "human race" series bored viewers. Isuzu's "Joe Isuzu" commercials amused viewers. Neither ad affected sales—for better or worse. Your advertising is only "good" when it accomplishes whatever you expected of it.

Your employer could ask you, "What's the purpose of this ad?" Your answer may be, "It'll improve our image," or "To sell product." Either answer is sufficient, for openers, so now the executive asks another reasonable question. "How are we going to tell if it's working?" The agency should have given you the answer.

Any agency may offer a caveat, at first. "There are many factors to consider. It's tough to measure the results." Tough it is; impossible it's not!

Some businesses need an immediate response to an ad, or they know it has failed. More often, it takes a while to see results. Virtually all advertisements, intended to increase sales, can and should include a call for action by the potential customer. Offer a free sample, or an audio or video tape, through an 800 number. Advise your commercial clients to ask for a brochure. Your ad won't have produced any sales, but it will be starting to reveal where and with whom the interest lies. Industrial sales, in particular, may require a multi-call process, but it always begins with an interested response. When people ask for more information, you gain a way to track the sales that eventually come from an ad.

The quality of the leads you get will vary according to the kind of ad you run. Bingo responses—the kind in which a reader circles a number to receive literature—produce a lower percentage of qualified leads than most. Many people circle numbers out of boredom, or by mistake. Often, by the time they get the information, they no longer need it.

If your sales force gets too many dead-end leads, they'll end up throwing away all the referrals from that source. They won't admit they're discarding them, because you might think they're wasting the company's money. Had someone tracked results, the ad's poor performance would've been obvious earlier. You can prevent the problem by qualifying the leads. Consider hiring college students, as qualifiers, who are specializing in subjects that fit your goods, like engineering. Or hire someone who is studying public relations or marketing.

You might hire an even younger person. One summer, my friend's teenage son couldn't get a job at a fast food outlet, because he was not sixteen. An insurance broker gave him some training in cold calling, and promised him a bonus for every card he filled out. He would also get a bigger bonus for every meeting he arranged. The youngster averaged three times the minimum wage for his summer's work. The broker said he was the best "cold call qualifier" he'd ever employed.

Where Are You Now?

Measuring the effect of an advertising campaign can be tedious, but it's the only way to know if you're getting your money's worth. The important point is that you advertise in ways that allow your sales department to track the response.

Difficult as it may be to measure a campaign's effect on sales, it's even harder to gauge an ad's effect on your company's image. Before you run "an image" or "an awareness" ad, you have to know your current position. You or the agency need to conduct some kind of survey, to determine how many people have even heard of your firm. After you advertise, the next survey should prove more people know about you, or about your goods—and that their impression is positive.

Whenever possible, do some of the work yourself. If you have direct access to customers, conduct your own survey over a series of weeks. For instance, in the restaurant or motel business, the job is particularly easy. Walk a few blocks away from your establishment, and ask anyone you pass to recommend a good place to eat or stay. If they don't mention your business, ask if they've heard of it, or where it is. In addition, instead of asking guests if they enjoyed themselves, ask what prompted them to come to your place. After an ad runs for awhile, ask the same questions. When you talk to people in "live settings," you can reach reasonable conclusions by questioning a comparatively small number.

On a cost per contact basis, advertising will never surpass public relations. Out of everything you can do, PR is usually the most cost effective way to generate leads. The problem is that publicity has to wait until the company has something newsworthy to report.

Some publications sell space for articles. A well conceived, series of articles can noticeably enhance awareness of your company, and sales, simultaneously. Poorly conceived, they become bad public relations and bad advertising, and can drive customers away. Remember well conceived means that you have thought through how these articles will create value for the proposed publications' readers while simultaneously presenting your message. This is a tricky balance that requires understanding the target publication's needs as well as your own. You're not buying advertising, but rather you are trying to influence your public.

Whenever possible, use public relations along with advertisements. The best agencies for mid-sized companies usually specialize in one or the other, however.

An agency that helps its clients establish an effective way to measure the results of their advertising, gains a strong competitive advantage. Granted, there's no perfect form of measurement, but less than perfect techniques don't equate with useless. When you buy other things, you know what you get for your money. You should have a realistic idea of what your advertising money buys for the company—but it requires continuous effort to get it.

Some agencies have begun to take a percentage of increased sales as their fee. The arrangement serves as a guarantee. Firms that won't offer such terms usually claim there are too many variables. After all, they can't control the way your salespeople behave. You pay the agency what you perceive as a small fortune. If your revenue doesn't increase, they tell you the fault probably rests with your sales force. While this may be true, it's possible that the agency may be telling you something else as well: they're in business to increase their revenue—not yours.

The most important lead to follow will always be an order. Yet most companies get a new order from a new customer, and leave it at that. Because someone buys something from your firm, it doesn't mean they know everything else you offer. Nor do you know what else they might want, unless you talk to them.

Research has revealed a strong correlation between persons who currently trade with a firm, and those who would, if the company caught their attention. Identify your customers' habits, and follow them to new customers. Auto repair shops, and car dealer service departments, learned to do it some time ago. They instruct their employees to write down the stations programmed on a car's radio before they start to repair it. That easy to perform, no-cost research tells them where to spend their advertising money.

Advertising Isn't Always Helpful

Of course, the help your advertising buys depends on what you expected. The word *help* is subject to interpretation.

Infiniti's sunlight, surf, and serenity series ranked third among the ten most remembered ads, in its opening season. A few months later, the unhappy dealers were screaming at Nissan. The memorable Infiniti ads were failing to motivate people to buy the car, while Toyota dealers were racking up Lexus sales. Nissan wanted advertisements that would create a long-term image; their dealers wanted to sell cars.

No matter what kind of help you seek, make sure to have a way to measure direct response, or don't advertise. You should never presume that any kind of advertising is better than none; sometimes an ad does harm.

A manufacturing firm wanted to determine the effectiveness of their promotions. They compiled sales statistics from all the stores carrying their goods, in Cleveland. Then they split the city in half, and ran two different advertisements. Each appeared in papers delivered to only one part of town. Sales went up in one half of the city—and dropped in the other. One of the ads was actually chasing customers away!

Experiment with your advertising. Vary the content, and medium, and watch the results. Try different devices to elicit inquiries.

Newspaper Advertising

Newspapers remain a leading advertising medium. They hold a 26 percent share of the national market. They make excellent conduits to mature consumers, but they don't effectively reach persons younger than thirty. A 1990 study, by the Times Mirror Center for the People & the Press, revealed an unequivocal fact. The younger generation "knows less, cares less, and reads newspapers less," than any group of consumers for decades past. You can reach young people through radio or cable TV, but not through the printed word. Many are functionally illiterate. People for whom reading is difficult don't even consult the Yellow Pages of telephone books.

When newspapers can do the job for you, the results can be dramatic. Two young men started The Wheel Works, alongside the Washington, D.C. Beltway. The company mounted and balanced tires. The men opened numerous branches, and built the business into a renowned success. After a while, they wanted to move "somewhere out west." By moving, they'd forfeit the profitable advantage of their well known and respected company name. The thought of losing their prominence made them realize they needed to invest in an all-out advertising campaign, in their new location. The decision prompted them to make the cost of advertising a primary factor in their choice of a location.

While researching different areas, they uncovered an unexpected fact. The circulation figures for San Francisco's leading newspaper and San Jose's were close to the same. Nevertheless, the cost of an ad, per capita, in the San Jose paper, was far less. They opened in San Jose, and reached the same number of readers for a much smaller investment. Several years later, they'd grown to more than twenty locations!

Conforming to the Company Image

Regardless of the medium used, keep in mind that management always has the last word on content. Everything said, implied, or pictured, must conform with company policy.

Years ago, one of my superiors hung a poster in his private bathroom. It was a copy of an ad that our company was planning to run in Germany. It featured a naked woman using one of our products while taking a shower. Fortunately, someone who saw it warned the people involved that the Chairman of the Board wouldn't tolerate such an ad, and it was stopped before it ran. Had the Chairman seen it, he would have fired everyone connected with it. There would've been no point in arguing that Europeans expect such pictures. In his opinion, anyone who approved of such advertising wasn't a person he wanted working for his company.

When the Going Gets Tough

There can be times when marketing should argue with management's decisions. Many employers are quick to say, "Business is rotten! Let's cut back on our advertising and save money." On the contrary, when business slows down, you may need to run even more of the advertisements you know worked before.

Employers will also use the same argument in reverse. "Business is great, so let's cut back on advertising." While people have money to spend and want what you offer, let everybody know you're there. Tell the world what you do well, tell them often and plainly, and promise to do it. However, if you simply advertise a "100% money back guarantee," you will be one of millions. Instead, talk about what you know your customers are *actually buying,* and guarantee to deliver it. Consider, for example, Enzymatic Therapy, a nutritional supplement company that offered its customers the following guarantee: "Feel healthy, feel great, or your money back."

The Truth

With or without a guarantee, plan to deliver everything you offer at least "99 and 44/100 percent" of the time. Procter and Gamble coined that still famous advertising slogan, over one hundred years ago.

William Procter and James Gamble became business partners in 1837. In that year, 600 banks closed and panic was spreading across the nation. The economic nightmare didn't prevent the two young partners from thinking about the future. Before they even got around to signing a formal partnership agreement, they signed personal notes for some land ". . . on which they hoped some day to build a factory."

Oscar Schisgall, a corporate historian, wrote a book tracing the history of P&G. He aptly entitled it, *Eyes on Tomorrow.* That is where every marketer must focus his vision. To help your firm be here *tomorrow,* your advertising needs to speak the truth at least "99 and 44/100 percent" of the time, *today.*

Harley Procter, the founder's son, was the father of that slogan, and the Ivory soap it described. The company had built their reputation on delivering "pure goods and full weight." When Ivory made its debut, the public considered castile soaps to be the most pure. In truth, no one had ever defined what a "pure soap" was.

Harley hired a chemical consultant to furnish a scientific definition of purity. The consultant analyzed the three leading brands of castile soap, and sent his report. A pure soap would contain ". . . nothing but fatty acids and alkali. Anything else that turned up . . . should be described as 'foreign and unnecessary substances.'" Harley then requested an analysis of Ivory, which proved that all but 0.56 percent of its contents were necessary. He simply turned the fraction into a positive statement: Ivory was 99 and 44/100 percent pure.

No one knows Harley's real motive for stressing purity and prominently advertising the mathematics revealed by the soap analysis. He may have acted out of an instinctive feel for advertising, or a strong desire for truth, or both.

Ivory soap also floats. That feature augmented the public's perception of its purity. In fact, it floats by accident. A workman went to lunch one day, and forgot to turn off the machine that stirred the mixture. After lunch, he discovered a frothy mess pouring out of the vat. His supervisor found the contents unaltered, so he allowed the over stirred batch to become bars of soap. Later, customers began to request more of "that soap that floats." Management didn't know what they were talking about, until the factory workers recalled the accident. Still, it was some time before Harley recognized the value of advertising the unique feature. He preferred to emphasize that Ivory was ". . . a soap so pure that it could safely be used to bathe babies . . ."

Much of our current advertising employs a different technique that was also popular during Ivory's early days. In those years, a druggist, offering a competing soap brand, advertised that it would, ". . . strengthen the muscles . . . thicken the hair and prevent baldness . . . cure the scurvy in the gums and prevent the teeth from rotting . . ." The manufacturer of that soap went out of business.

PART 5

A Glimpse of Significant Pieces

A Businessperson's Life

*Nothing doth more hurt in a state
than that cunning men pass for wise.*

Francis Bacon,
Of Cunning

Charles Kettering was an electrical engineer. Every time your car starts, automatically, Kettering deserves credit. His "Delco-Light" freed farmers from their dependence on kerosene lamps long before electricity lines reached farmlands. That lighting system also helped residents in the jungles of Yucatan. Kettering's numerous inventions still make life easier for everyone affected by them.

Thomas Boyd, in his biography, *Professional Amateur,* reveals many of the feelings and thoughts that motivated Kettering during his productive lifetime. The pioneer's thinking often addressed marketing's interests. Kettering also held strong opinions about workmanship, and customers and adjusting to changing conditions.

In the early part of the 20th century, Kettering said of market changes, "The trouble with many businessmen is that they are trying to find some way in which things will take care of themselves. . . . There are no places in an industrial situation where anyone can sit and rest. It is a question of change, change, change all the time."

These days, many businesspeople no longer wait for matters to take care of themselves. They demand government intervention when times are bad. The same source of help they solicit one day, they curse on another.

Government Impact

The undesirable changes, which government legislation impose on markets, don't always come in broad, easily identified strokes.

Most people dream of getting rich, but few like those who got there ahead of them. Consequently, when lawmakers need votes, they promise to increase taxes on the playthings the rich buy, like airplanes and yachts. If the additional tax makes the toy's price too high to be sensible, sales immediately drop. Wealthy people are like everybody else: they won't pay more than they think something is worth.

If the increased tax accompanies a recession—a common time for such maneuvers—many of the adult toy makers can't survive the double blow. They close their doors, and their personnel apply for unemployment benefits. The government spends money supporting the displaced workers from an industry they destroyed. Federal and state treasuries lose the revenue the industry produced, but the lawmakers get reelected. It takes very little research to realize that most voters simply don't understand the results of such legislation. The premise sounds sensible, so they presume it is. Besides that, they want "to punish the rich," and legislators know it.

Every time Federal or local officials help themselves to a perk, they consume tax dollars. They know that only a tiny drop of money from each taxpayer will replace the funds, and their presumption is correct. Individuals simply forego a few

movies, or eat a few less dinners in restaurants. Whole industries feel the cumulative effect, though they could never pinpoint the exact cause of their decreased revenue. Fact-based
television stories could dramatically portray these actual
events. Incredibly, businesses don't solicit such scripts. They
prefer to sponsor movies depicting innovative ways to commit murder.

Continental Motors and a Changing Market

During the 1970s, the market for single engine airplanes
expanded rapidly. Tax incentives had produced a torrential
demand. In the industry's peak year, manufacturers sold several thousand planes.

In the early 1980s, legislators perceived the thriving industry as a bountiful source for new revenue, so they changed
the tax laws. Without a tax break, few individuals could
afford to buy their own airplane. The price of planes, while
never low, had soared. Every airplane accident was followed
by a seven digit lawsuit. In turn, every business even
remotely associated with a plane's existence had to buy enormous amounts of expensive insurance, to protect its own corporate life. They passed a share of the increased insurance on
to their customers, which pushed their product's price higher.
When taxes changed, private airplane sales dropped to a few
hundred a year.

A shrinking market inevitably diminishes other markets,
and soon countless people were jobless. Only two engine
manufacturers remained in the nation by the 1970s. One was
Continental Motors, the firm that had made the engine for the
Spirit of St. Louis, Lindbergh's plane. That seasoned corporate
body sought the advice of outside consultants.

The consultants' reasoning followed the usual straight line.
Few persons could afford to buy a new plane. Therefore,
those who owned planes would be flying them longer.
Automobile owners can maintain their cars as they please,

but airplane maintenance must conform to FAA regulations. After every given number of flight hours, an engine must have specified service, and all flights are on public record. Continental only had to study the records to locate potential customers and remind them of their upcoming service needs.

Continental had found a way to respond to the drastic changes in the marketplace. Instead of closing, the firm has remained a major employer. In the late 1980s, they made the engines for the *Voyager,* the first plane to fly around the world non-stop, without refueling.

A Simple Lesson

In his youth, failing eyesight forced Charles Kettering to leave college for awhile. In the hope that outdoor, physical labor would improve his health, he took a job digging holes for the telephone company. He soon became the foreman of a line gang, installing telephone poles. One day, a hobo wandered on to the job site and asked for some food. Kettering took him into a restaurant and let him eat his fill. When he was through, the host asked his guest, "How would you like to have a good job so you could always have plenty to eat?"

The tramp didn't greet the offer enthusiastically, but he felt he should do something in return for the meal. He agreed to dig a hole. A while later, Kettering stopped by to see the man's progress, and found him laboring over a shallow, jagged cavity. He said to the inept digger, "Come with me and let me show you what a nice hole looks like." He showed him one, and then began to dig one himself. While he worked, he expressed his honest feelings to the hobo. "It's fun to dig a hole. And the rounder you dig it and the straighter you dig it, the more fun it is. It's fun to see how nearly perpendicular and smooth you can make the sides. . . ." He kept digging and talking, until the tramp asked to try his hand at it again.

The drifter decided to stay on with the line gang, and he eventually became the foreman. Years later, he spoke of that day, to Kettering. "You were the first person ever to tell me that work could be fun. If only years ago someone had taught me how much fun it is to work, when a fellow tries to do *good* work, I would never have become the bum I was."

"Good Work"

"Good work" can emerge from any reputable occupation, but a large bank account does not necessarily attest to it. Nor does it automatically accompany a college diploma. On that subject, Kettering also had something to say. "My definition of an educated man is the fellow who knows the right thing to do at the time it has to be done. . . . You can be sincere and still be stupid."

Lawyers, insurers, and doctors have each played their part in changing the nation's health care market. As costs have skyrocketed, each group has also proclaimed its own innocence and, by implication or direct statement, the guilt of all others.

Nevertheless, lawyers urged everybody into courtrooms to reach into "deep pockets." Insurers warned doctors to increase their malpractice insurance. Doctors denounced the nation's addiction to litigation, while they paid the ever-increasing insurance premiums. Their individual abuses of the system continued to breed counter abuses.

It took a long time, but finally the price of insurance began to hurt doctors' wallets badly. When the pain grew severe enough, a handful of doctors took the first step toward healing themselves, and helping the nation at the same time.

The American Society of Anesthesiologists did its own research into its members' practices. As a result, the society now demands that its members use monitoring devices, to reduce the chance of errors. Doctor-owned companies studied the causes of the most frequent lawsuits. They now insist their associates improve their skills in those areas. The day may even come when good work in the medical profession is once again more fashionable than driving a Mercedes.

The Double Profit

Charles Kettering's business philosophy grew out of his work as a research engineer, along with other pursuits. At one time, he considered it his obligation to a certain community to reorganize their failing bank. Since he knew nothing about banking, his lawyer warned him that he could easily lose his last dollar. If that happened, Kettering said, "I would do just what I did before when I didn't have any money. . . . I would create something people want . . . need, and would pay money for." He instructed his bank staff to treat every customer ". . . with unvarying courtesy, for the bank has nothing to build on except courtesy and service."

In later years, he coined a unique statement, expressing his view of all customers' rightful expectation. "I am for the double-profit system, a reasonable profit for the manufacturer and a much greater profit for the customer."

Focus on the Customer

Innumerable American businesses supply products or services that other companies use, in the production of their own goods or to maintain their business facilities. The suppliers think of the firms that buy their goods as "their customers." In turn, these firms think of themselves as the "well treated or mistreated customers" of certain suppliers.

Everybody knows customers are the source of profits. Everybody also knows it isn't a customer's obligation to worry whether their supplier makes a profit. Let those who can't compete effectively go out of business. There's always someone to take his place.

That sentiment is the essence of our national business weakness, and Japan's national business strength. The majority of Japanese businesspeople work together to supply the end-user of their goods: *their mutual customer.* In the United States our companies perceive each other with mutual caution as supplier and customer, and it's not always a friendly relationship.

Japanese industries use our weakness to their advantage. In essence, Japan has become a nation of united businesses. Together, they compete against our individual companies—and they do it very effectively.

We've never faced such competition. Through much of our nation's history, we've been the world's largest supplier of products and services. Our national philosophy proclaims that every person should be free to provide for himself, in whatever lawful manner he chooses. In practice, however, we've translated our philosophy into "every man for himself."

Dumping

Japan changed the rules of the marketplace. Our system, for all its productivity, is far from perfect. Japan's system is also far from perfect, but it does address a serious flaw in ours. Most of us do not stay in touch with our customers to any real extent.

There's nothing secretive and mysterious about Japan's way of invading and conquering one American market after another. For years, they've employed a monotonously repetitious procedure.

A Japanese business decides on the U.S. market they want to enter. They develop a product comparable to something already popular, and offer it at a ridiculously low price that gets everyone's attention. In essence, they're "making us an offer we can't refuse," at least to try.

Our industries react in one of two ways. Sometimes they accuse the Japanese of "dumping their goods," a euphemism for selling below production cost. Other times, they warn us we must "buy American," or face disaster. It makes no difference what our companies say. Time and again, the result is the same. Our firms get into financial trouble, and Japan's prosper.

For decades, this procedure has repeated itself, in our automobile, steel, and consumer electronic industries. Repeatedly, our businesspeople respond by concentrating on the price a Japanese company places on its goods. They fail to see that pricing is only a tool. The structure the tool helps to build is the subject of real importance. By going back a few years, we can watch how Japanese companies have used the tools and built the structures which threatened our semiconductor and computer industries. We can improve ourselves by meeting the challenge they pose.

Years ago, the American company Intel invented a memory chip that revolutionized computers. Intel's invention enabled the American semiconductor industry to become the leading world supplier of memory chips. These chips constitute 35 percent or more of the electrical components in a computer. A single computer uses hundreds of them. The number used the world over is beyond imagination.

When Japanese firms began to make the chips, theirs were similar to ours in quality and reliability. Recall that the semiconductor industry produces "me too" products, much of the time. Hewlett-Packard ran experiments for years before they found a measurable difference between Japanese chips and ours. (Although it was the Japanese product that finally became superior, it didn't happen quickly, nor did it last.)

Computer manufacturers are no different from other manufacturers. They won't suddenly start ordering all they need of a crucial part from one supplier. First, they have to see if the product suits their needs. They have to evaluate its quality. Moreover, they have to get to know the supplier, before they can trust its delivery. All this can take quite a while, but it follows a prescribed course that's easy to picture.

Gaining a New Customer

A Silicon Valley memory chip salesperson in the early 1980s goes to see her long-standing customer, a computer manufacturer in Massachusetts. She knows they're due to reorder, but this time the salesperson hears some startling news. She immediately calls her factory to report that a Japanese firm has offered chips at a 25 percent lower price. The factory's marketing department scoffs. They researched the price thoroughly before they set it. They know the alleged Japanese offer would be completely out of touch with the prevailing market price.

The marketers are right, but there's something of much greater importance they don't know. They don't know their customers. Like most other American marketers, they seldom bother to visit clients, in this nation or elsewhere. Consequently, they know little about their customers' problems and can't judge their veracity. Actually, they suspect somebody is playing fast and loose with the truth. Their salesperson could be after a price break, so she can write a big order. The factory firmly advises her to forget it. Nobody would make such an offer. "It's just some purchasing guy, fishing for a lower price from us."

Sure enough, the salesperson gets a reorder that convinces the marketers their suspicions were correct. Nobody bothers to verify the events. The fact is the Japanese company would never have received the whole order. They'd have to prove themselves and their product, first. The Japanese only got what they expected: a tiny, unnoticeable piece of the order, an evaluation quantity.

The time comes for the next order. Once again, the salesperson tells her factory that the Japanese were back with their low price. "They tried that last time, and it didn't work," her superior informs her. "Tell them we're not lowering our price. That's final." Once again, the salesperson gets an order. Though it's a little smaller than usual, the difference is not conspicuous—to the factory. Most of our high tech companies don't track their customers' purchases closely enough to realize their orders are gradually decreasing. Even if they do recognize it, many assume their customer's needs have diminished. When a firm also refuses to listen to their salesperson's opinion, they have no early warning system.

The computer chip orders grow steadily smaller, but the salesperson stops trying to convince her company that something is happening. Eventually, the customer decides they can trust the new supplier. They give them most of the next order, and that, finally, gets the American factory's attention. They investigate, and discover that a Japanese company has stolen *their* customer! The Americans are angry. How dare the computer company have the audacity to buy chips from the Japanese? Have they no loyalty to their old supplier? Have they no patriotism? The Americans are resentful and accusatory, while the Japanese firm is solicitously discussing their new customer's future needs.

Losing a Market

There came a point in the 1980s when most American computer manufacturers were buying most of their memory chips from Japanese companies. They based their decision on simple arithmetic. If they paid 25 percent more for chips than competitors were paying, they'd have to raise prices or take a smaller profit. Yet they couldn't raise the price of their "me too" computers in the intensely competitive marketplace. Nor did they want to take a smaller profit. So they joined the crowd, and bought the low-priced chips.

While all this was taking place, some American factories stopped producing memory chips, and concentrated on other products. Those that remained in the memory chip market began to fight back, by using the now familiar American technique of demanding legislation to protect their industry from "unfair Japanese practices." Eventually, our lawmakers succumbed to the pressure, and put a floor under the price of memory chips. The floor applied to all chips used in domestic production, whether bought here or purchased outside the country.

When Japanese factories could no longer underprice our manufacturers, they decreased the number of chips they offered us, by a small, but vital, percentage. You may think it strange that they refused to sell as many chips as they could, at the higher price. By restraining themselves, they gained an important advantage. In fact, they gained two advantages.

Our chip manufacturers hadn't dreamed the Japanese firms would cut back on their shipments. This unexpected response created a serious problem. Our companies couldn't always produce enough product to compensate for the decreased Japanese supply. This meant our computer manufacturers couldn't always meet their production schedules. Japanese computer companies immediately stepped in and provided the computers which our firms could not deliver. Consequently, by refusing to take full advantage of the high profit our laws offered them, the Japanese chip makers accomplished something else. They helped their nation's computer makers increase their own market share.

No one can prove the Japanese firms anticipated that result, but their expectations are of no importance. Their memory chip industry's self restraint obviously helped their computer industry.

The second advantage took a little longer to materialize. Our legally established price floor on chips was compelling our computer manufacturers to pay more than their competitors paid, in other nations. This forced them to accept the smaller profit they'd tried so desperately to avoid. American firms resent accepting a lower profit, and everybody, everywhere, knows it. (Japanese companies, of all kinds, quickly lower their prices to hold on to their market share, and then work to lower their costs.) Soon our computer industry was demanding that Congress rescind the law regulating the price of memory chips. Once again, although the Japanese firms have no reason to admit they anticipated it, their self restraint produced a result that benefited them. Our government abolished the price floor and negotiated a trade agreement.

Our computer makers regained access to chips at the lowest available price. However, our memory chip manufacturers were back where they started. One by one, they stepped out of the market, rather than compete against Japan's well established, low-priced goods. Today, we have only two U.S. based semiconductor companies producing DRAM chips.

The Japanese now hold a substantial portion of the memory chip market. As for new competitors, they offer little to worry about. It costs well over $500 million dollars to build a memory chip factory. Only countries such as Korea and Taiwan can afford it.

Thus, the majority of our computer manufacturers now depend on foreign suppliers for a "goes-into" they are obliged to buy. This in itself is not the problem. The trouble rests with the prevailing attitude of Japanese businesspeople: they love their country, and they want it to prosper. For their nation to flourish, their citizens need gainful employment. Therefore, the Japanese chip makers appear to favor their own nation's computer industry. Whenever demand for chips exceeds supply, Japan's computer factories get what they need first. Other nations get the leftovers. I can't imagine why anyone would expect them to do otherwise.

An Attitude

Shintaro Ishihara is Japan's foremost "America basher." In a recent book, he discussed Japan's role in the Persian Gulf War. He contends that the United States wouldn't have won the war if it weren't for Japanese technology. He points out that 92 of the 93 foreign-made semiconductors used in American weapons came from Japan. Their precision was all that enabled us to win. Ishihara misunderstands our

qualms—and underestimates our ability . . . as his countrymen did 50 years ago.

Some Japanese businessmen are uncomfortable with
Ishihara's views, especially in relation to one statement. He
advises his fellow citizens to ". . . just sit back and observe
how the United States and European countries get burned
. . ." In truth, there's nothing new about his attitude, and
that's exactly what makes some of his countrymen uncomfortable. They hear in his words a reflection of Japan's his-
torical isolationism. If nothing else, they fear the consumer
backlash it could unleash.

The Japanese have always sat back and observed the world
from within the confines of their own "closed club." We've
welcomed them into our business community, but they
haven't reciprocated. Our trade negotiators say it remains
extremely difficult for a westerner to become a member of
Japan's corporate groups. That nation simply doesn't have a
history of helping others. In fact, the last country they whole-
heartedly tried to help was Hitler's Germany.

Japanese firms were able to supply the superior semiconductors which helped our war effort, because Japanese citizens practice a superior allegiance to each other and their
nation. Their sense of unity has made them excel in marketing warfare. We need to learn how to work together, as they
do. (Let the Japanese look to whatever they think they need
to learn.)

Companies don't have "to dump their goods" in markets
where the margins have plenty of fat. In the memory chip
business, our factories always introduced each improved chip
at a high price. They wanted a higher profit for putting more
memory in less space. Thus, Japanese firms could cut the
price of their chips by 15 percent, and simply remove some
of the fat. Another 10 percent drop produced a 25 percent
lower price than ours. That percentage proves too tempting
for most people to ignore, in any marketplace. For the company offering the lower price, the lost profit becomes the cost

of marketing their wares. It's not a costly tactic, considering the rewards.

To be sure, some foreign businesses occasionally dump their goods, but not as promiscuously as our businesspeople claim. Moreover, even when dumping occurs, the firm making the charge rarely gains anything. It can take years to settle the lawsuit. Hence, every time someone makes the accusation, it signals the beginning of a lengthy process. In the meantime, the low-priced goods remain in the marketplace, driving others out. If a guilty verdict finally withstands the procession of appeals, the penalties are sometimes high enough to reimburse the accuser. Even so, the company may not have survived the wait. Nor does a guilty verdict mean that all foreign firms are always dumping. More often, they're simply benefiting from our insatiable national appetite for immediate and high profits . . . and *our willingness to let our fellow businessperson go under.*

A Response

The time to act is when a Japanese company makes its first move in your marketplace. Don't immediately presume that your salespeople—or your customers—are lying, and never assume the Japanese won't maintain their low price. They don't care about today's profits; their eyes are on the market share and profit they'll have tomorrow . . . and the next day.

Look at their product or service as your customers see it. Why would people want it, aside from the price? What do your customers value? If you realize the low-priced goods are equal or superior to yours, expect your customers to do more than just try the offer. They'll probably like it—more than yours.

Improve your goods as soon as you can. In the meantime, explore the idea of dropping your price to within 10 percent of the Japanese offer. Customers, en masse, do not chase a 10 percent discount. Of course, this presumes you have a profit margin that allows the drop. If you don't, then your operation may be inefficient. Or their costs may be lower than yours because of their research methods.

Their factories take apart and study their competitors' goods. They learn which products are superior to theirs, and then find a way to improve their own, while making it cheaper. Their strategy is to capture a market, and then make a profit. Americans try to make a profit from day one.

If you can find nothing significantly wrong with your operation, the Japanese firm could be dumping. Report your suspicions to your Congressman, and prepare for a long ordeal.

If you can lower your price, however, you could create a far different end to the story—provided you and the companies you supply perceive each other *as partners*. This means they'll want to help you stay in business. It also means you will understand their need to buy material at competitive prices. When you lower your price to them, they can lower their price, and hang on to *your mutual customers*.

Remember, you may call another business your customer, but they exist for the same reason you do. They're only a link in a chain. Your *real customers* are the persons the Japanese companies have joined each other to serve. They're the people Charles Kettering said should enjoy "a much greater profit" than everyone else.

A Brighter Future?

One company that appears to be finally relearning what American businesspeople knew a hundred years ago is General Motors. Before accountants and lawyers began to run our major industries, the entrepreneurs who started the companies understood what a business had to do. They must try to please their customers, and they won't adequately please them with anything less than "good work."

General Motors worked hard to produce the Saturn, the first new line they've introduced in decades. Shortly afterwards, customers began to report leaky radiators. Texaco had supplied the radiator coolant. Texaco discovered they'd shipped a bad batch, which the Saturn factory had used in some vehicles. Texaco publicly acknowledged their responsibility, and assured consumers they'd taken steps to prevent a recurrence. In turn, Saturn didn't simply recall the faulty cars for repair—they replaced them with new ones.

At first, the publicity had looked ominous for GM. They'd counted heavily on the Saturn to begin restoring their credibility. The incident actually helped them. The public discovered the company was standing behind its product in an unprecedented way, and sales increased.

Something else came out of the experience: evidence of a new kind of relationship. The Saturn factory didn't simply buy material from different suppliers. They gained working partners. Together, all are striving to build a better car, at a lower price. In addition, each is taking responsibility for its own contribution to the product.

Alfred Sloan, Jr., as the President of General Motors beginning in the 1920s, led the company to prosperity. He created the concept of different GM models, to serve everybody. No matter how much or how little money a customer had, he could find a GM car to fit his needs. The firm owes much of its astounding success to that marketing concept. (After Sloan retired, management increasingly blurred the differences between models.)

Sloan was a close friend of Charles Kettering. Today, we find their names permanently linked, as the Sloan-Kettering Institute for Cancer Research, in New York.

Twenty-five years after Kettering graduated from Ohio State University, he returned to give a commencement address. He closed his speech with words which reflected his own life.

"There are . . . three things, which if you get your point of view right, you will have no trouble with. The first is that you are going to be a servant to somebody or something. . . . The next is that to be a good servant implies two things, willingness to work and willingness to learn, because no one of us knows very much. . . . And if, when you pack your bag for this eventful journey . . . you pack egotism and selfishness and all that sort of thing down in the bottom of the bag, and if you lay your servant's uniform on top, the passports will not have to be opened, and they will pass you through the line."

A Marketer's Life

Nothing great was ever achieved without enthusiasm.

Ralph Waldo Emerson,
Essays, Circles

You have an idea you know will work. The plan is sitting waiting for approval. Every day you mention something more about it. Your mate, coworkers, and friends have begun to sound like a chorus. "Come on," they plead, "let's talk about something else for a change."

You're a "true believer" in whatever it is you conceived. That makes you exactly what a business needs to make a plan a success. Government regulations won't discourage you. A lack of cooperation won't deter you. Changes in the marketplace will only slow you down—until you find a satisfactory response.

When a marketer behaves like a true believer, put other matters aside and evaluate the plan. Ask questions and listen carefully to the answers. Are the milestones and jump off points defined? Is everything thought through, to your satisfaction? If so, and if you can afford the venture, run with it.

Or you may wish you had such an enthusiastic marketer. In that case, it's time to hire one. At the same time, you'd prefer to have no marketing program than to spend your time and money traveling in the wrong direction. How can you identify a person who has a better than even chance to make you a winner?

What to Look for in a Marketer

One school of thought says you should hire a marketer from inside your own industry. You'll immediately gain the advantage of not having to wait while he or she learns about your business. To find this person, aside from regular recruiting methods, try luring a competitor's employee. Look for someone you suspect could be unhappy with their company's policies. On the other hand, their previous experience can be a disadvantage. They may have developed strong biases about which tactics will and won't work. Familiarity with any subject inevitably increases the possibility of "pig/sow" thinking.

Another school of thought indicates that marketing is a mind-set, unrelated to a particular industry. Marketers ask the right questions, and continue to ask them until discovering what needs to be known. They can become any company's theoretical customer, in thoughts and feelings. They're intuitive and creative, but practical enough to understand the importance of careful research. Given those traits, they can soon become familiar with any kind of business that doesn't require highly specialized knowledge.

I lean toward the latter theory. John Sculley went from the soft drink business to the computer business. The only attribute those two industries have in common is that they both sell their products to people.

On balance, it may not matter whether a marketer has experience in your industry or not. Look for someone who expresses real interest in your kind of goods, but not because of the profit potential. Their thoughts need to center on why people use your product or service. Watch how the conversation progresses during an interview. Both of you should be talking about the people who use your goods, more than about the goods themselves.

Someone who has enjoyed a successful career in advertising usually can't double as a skillful marketer. Advertising communicates information. Marketing relies on intercommunication, to identify problems and solve them. Though a marketer seldom creates the solution, she can articulate her ideas to those who can produce the actual answer.

Advertisements tell customers that an answer exists, and a company should advertise with planned regularity. Salespeople persuade consumers to buy their company's solution instead of the competition's. Selling must be a deliberate, organized effort, or the company will go broke. On the other hand, small companies often do marketing on an informal, "think of something and try it" basis.

If you can't afford a full time marketer, your most cost effective alternative may be to hire a marketing consultant. You only have to employ one to answer specific questions. A consultant can learn why customers prefer your competitors' goods, or discover the reason some of them never tried yours. You may want them to evaluate your advertising, or the promotional material your sales force uses. The consultant can help you locate a new distribution outlet, or a geographical area where you have a real opportunity to become a leader.

Marketing consultants are expensive. Still, by hiring a consultant on a project by project basis, it could cost less than a full-time employee. Realize that you'll probably have to teach them about your business, and pay them while they learn. It's going to cost you a few thousand dollars before they actually go to work for you. It could annoy you to pay someone to learn your business when they're not becoming a part of your staff. Keep in mind that you're buying their expertise. They can't employ it, until they become thoroughly acquainted with your current business.

You can also hire a public relations firm and use them to help fine tune your marketing concepts. Their job is to influence public opinion. To do so, they'll need to ask you numerous questions. While answering them, you'll have to express succinctly the value your goods provide, and discuss many other marketing subjects. Some advertising agencies provide similar help. Bear in mind that PR and ad agencies make their money by conducting public relations, or by creating and placing advertisements. Expect them to offer marketing advice that focuses on their line of work.

What to Expect From a Marketer

A marketer must respect and adhere to the president's view of the company's future. This means he has to understand the kind of business the president wants to be in—and the kind that she'd never want to own. If the marketer thinks the president has adopted the wrong limitations, he may pursue ideas the company could never entertain. He might show how the company's retirement community would unquestionably profit by adding nursing home facilities. The unauthorized plan could lead the president to ask, "What are you going to tell me next? I should get into the funeral home business!"

Nonetheless, a conscientious marketer will not hesitate to argue with management about specific tactics. It's common for a CEO and a marketer to butt heads occasionally. You're both trying to guide the business, but marketing must defer to the president's decisions. If he has ideas he really believes in, and the president consistently discards them, he'll find his job too frustrating. It isn't necessary to agree with the marketing manager before letting him implement a tactic. The president should only reject marketing's suggestions when she's certain they'll send the company in the wrong direction. Any time the president can't make up her mind, defer to marketing's judgment. A standoff goes to marketing, because marketing is his job. If the president continually overrules marketing, then the president will be doing her own marketing, and he'll become a "yes man." A talented person won't remain in that position for long.

To gauge the value of a marketing tactic, most industries can use an accepted rule of thumb. You should begin to see results in approximately two times the buying cycle of your wares. A buying cycle varies according to the goods involved.

A product or service that people use and replace frequently has a short buying cycle. The manufacturer of a goes-into could have a long wait. The product that uses the goes-into may require its own development period and introduction in its marketplace. It can take two years to determine if a new high tech widget is a bust or a bonanza. An innovation on a diaper service can prove itself much faster.

What Does the Marketer Do First?

After hiring a marketer, what is she going to do, starting from her first day on the job? The company may have an idea for expansion that she needs to explore. Or, there could be nothing more to tell her than the bare facts. "We need better marketing. We've done some, but it wasn't all it should've been. We call on customers regularly but, the truth is, we're always hoping to leave with an order. We have a fine sales force. Most of our clients have been with us for years, but we need to broaden our focus. Put a plan together, and let's get this business growing."

How should a marketer receiving such instructions proceed? Early on, she'll probably have to determine which of the four directions for growth the firm should follow. The company may need to concentrate on improving its goods, or finding something new to offer. It could be ready to invest in pursuing new customers. Or she might have to show her employer why the expansion idea is a separate business, in need of its own name and capital. It can take three months, or longer, to reach a decision. The time will vary, depending on how much she has to learn about the business, and the complexity of its problems. She needs to identify the company's current market position, examine competitors' strategy and tactics, and pick customers' brains.

As she gets to know customers, she may detect an underlying note of resentment. Without saying it, customers could be telling her, "Sure, we've given your company plenty of business, but so what! If we ask for anything out of the ordinary, you always act like you're doing us a *big* favor."

The company doesn't have the relationship with its clientele that it thinks it has. Although they've traded with each other for years, they haven't created a working partnership, or friendly vendor/customer relations. She needs to learn the reason the disgruntled customers have continued doing business with this firm, for so long.

Sometimes a company can hold on to many dissatisfied clients for obvious reasons. The supplier offers the best solution in the whole world—or the only one that's readily available. Whatever the reason, she may see that a capable competitor could've lured a large portion of the company's customer base. If this is the case, eliminate the cause of customer resentment and win their loyalty, before someone else does. The fact that no one has done so doesn't mean no one can—or will. Recall that Searle did not bother to develop friendly relations with the food companies using their popular sweetener, until they finally recognized what could happen.

The company's management could express its own brand of resentment. "Customers never talk about what we've done for them in the past. It's always, 'What're you going to do for me tomorrow?'"

A business that delivers on its promises yesterday and today earns credibility. Nevertheless, a customer isn't buying what the company did for her yesterday. She already paid for that satisfaction. A business wants new money for whatever it does tomorrow; customers want new satisfaction.

Businesses fail because they don't profitably satisfy *enough* customers. There's no other reason. They could be trying to deliver something not enough people want. Or they're offering it in an unsatisfactory way, compared to how someone else offers it. Many executives believe they take a personal hand in satisfying their clientele. They cite how they're readily accessible to anyone with a problem. In reality, the only customers they talk to are the ones who are angry! When a company officer speaks solely to people who are complaining, or asking for favors, she can easily begin to resent her own customers. Remember, satisfied clients can tell you what your firm does well. Then, you can deliberately plan to do more of it.

As the marketer gets to know the firm's personnel, he may discern another source of ill will. Past management errors could have left pockets of simmering resentment.

Some employees become genuinely upset when their employer perceives them as the cause of mistakes, especially when they believe themselves innocent. Obviously, they're concentrating on management's fluctuating, and sometimes faulty, perception of them. The leaders of a firm need to focus the staff's thinking on the customers being served, instead of on management.

A publisher of a new magazine encountered an attitude among his production staff that caused him recurring aggravation. In some issues, an ad appeared in the wrong place. The client would promptly announce, "I'm not paying you." The mistake usually occurred because of a clerical or production blunder. Occasionally, it was hard to know why it had happened.

If the publisher couldn't place the blame, he became angry with everybody, but most of all with the production department. Since it was an infrequent problem, he finally learned to ignore it. He reran the ad, at no cost to the client, and stopped guessing who was at fault. His original outbursts had rankled the production crew, however. They wouldn't forget anyone's error. At every opportunity, they were back, pressing the argument of their past and present innocence. The more they talked about it, the more they aggravated their employer. He began thinking about whom he should fire, instead of looking for the simple solution.

The production department needed to think about the mistake from the customer's point of view. The only reason a company buys advertising space is to increase sales. There are very few errors in placement that will make an ad completely worthless. It may become less persuasive, but most of the time, it will be better than no ad at all. Mistakes are inevitable, so a company needs to learn how to use them constructively, while it works to eliminate them. Any error that involves a customer should become an opportunity to turn a dissatisfied client into a loyal one.

The publisher could have erased the after-effect of his anger by expressing his new attitude, plainly. "I've come to realize that occasional mistakes can help us. Any time we have to run an ad again, our client gets two ads for the price of one. He finds out he can depend on us to do the job he hired us to do. In the meantime, we have another opportunity to get people interested in his goods, and show him our magazine is just what he needs."

Before employees can believe that customer satisfaction is the only important subject, management must prove it. Only then will a staff stop concentrating on pleasing "the boss," and start working to please customers, so everyone can win.

By going on calls with salespeople, a marketer or president not only meets customers, but also gets to know the sales staff. A firsthand acquaintance helps them understand salespeople as individuals. Then, if Tom says his customer is "really upset," they'll know what he means. He could be saying someone is angry because an order is late. He could also be saying the person is getting ready to trade with a competitor. A marketer's touch might calm the waters.

Remember, the marketing and sales departments work hand in hand, with neither subordinate to the other. A sales rep in Phoenix might call and say, "I can't sell this new stuff." Her problem doesn't appear to make sense. Paul is selling it in Dallas; Marge is doing great in Seattle; Pete has no problems in Indianapolis. Even if the sales manager insists it's the salesperson's fault, marketing's personal acquaintance with her could leave them wondering.

A marketer could call her and say, "Why don't I come down there and make some joint calls with you? Let's see if we can figure out what's unique about Phoenix." Previous experience with her would let her know marketing's coming there to help. You're also applying the adage, "Don't fix the blame, fix the problem." What works in six places may not work in the seventh. In certain locations, just modifying an offer makes the difference; in other areas, nothing helps.

Why Do They Buy?

The fun aspect in marketing is working with an endlessly long test tube. There's no absolute answer to why consumers buy goods. Giant corporations have been studying buyer habits for decades, and they've never found an All-Encompassing Truth.

As customers, we don't always know exactly why we choose certain goods instead of others. Nor do we know whether the first advertisement we saw, or the tenth, finally impressed us. Each time we buy something, we're drawing on an accumulation of experiences. After a while, we can say exactly what we like or dislike about a company, but we rarely remember what originally caused us to trade with them. Sometimes, it was simply their name.

Ordinarily, as soon as we believe a firm will provide what we want, we stop looking elsewhere. Therefore, when a company's name plainly reveals the help they offer, they can win the first chance to capture us.

Years ago, it was commonplace for people to name their business after themselves. In today's world of instant communication and rapid travel, a name can journey far and quickly. Linking a firm to a person's name could slow down or limit growth.

Owners, especially of service companies, frequently believe they should build their business on their own reputation. Later, clients realize the key person only hustles new clients, and then no one sees her again. They begin to suspect they're paying extra for something they're not getting.

Huckster & Company doesn't make much sense. Who cares about Huckster? It can take a lifetime to make his name famous. If he succeeds, his son may profit from it. On the other hand, a name that speaks of what people are actually buying can command attention in any locale.

A woman became a manufacturer's representative for ventilated shelving, used in custom closets. She opened her business in a town with a population of around 7,000 people. In a small town, she knew that most of the homeowners would become aware of her company. She would also get to know many of them personally. This gave her a perfect reason to put her name on her front door, but she hesitated.

There was ample room for development for miles around. Between new houses and remodeling jobs, there would've been enough clients to support a very small business. She realized that was not all she wanted. She had her eye on working with builders and remodelers in more diverse areas, like San Jose, San Francisco, and Sacramento.

She looked up "Closets" in the Yellow Pages of various telephone books. There were listings for "Mr. Wonderful's Closets," and "Closets Designed by Marvelous Me." Firms that refrained from using a personal name were "Closet This" or "Closet That." She was beginning to wonder if it was possible to differentiate her business name, when she finally recognized the concept she needed. What, after all, did her product do for someone? It gave a home "Added Dimensions."

When you start a new business, take a look at the six word definition of the help your firm provides. Try reducing it even further. If you can say it in two or three words, you could have your company's name.

Common Sense

Making sense in the marketplace, as you now know, relates to a myriad of subjects that affect us all, since we're all consumers. A business name that describes what we're actually buying makes sense to us. Advertisements that make sense hold our attention. We're all willing to listen to sensible salespeople, and we want to shop in a sensible atmosphere. We don't expect to walk on thick carpeting in a Kmart store, or see paint peeling off the walls at any Neiman-Marcus location. Neither would make sense. Nothing, however, is more important to us than finding goods that make sense.

Ann Landers, in her famous advice column, printed a letter from a man who had a problem. He had a 39 inch waist, the wrong size for every brand of boxer shorts. If he bought a 36-38, they were unbearably tight. If he bought a 40-42, washing them weakened the elastic waistband, and left him with drooping underwear. He closed his letter with words that apply to all businesses, no matter their wares. "Retailers are complaining that business is slow. One way to generate sales is to manufacture merchandise that fits the needs of the consumer. It's as simple as that."

Miss Landers' reply was equally simple. She advised manufacturers and retailers to ". . . listen to what this man is saying. He makes sense."

Listen to your customers, so you can provide something they need and want: your goods will make sense to them. Listen carefully to your company's personnel, so you can help them speak sensibly when they talk about the business that supports them. Listen to and watch your competitors, to discover when their words and actions don't match, so that you can take advantage of their lapses. And, while you're watching and listening to everybody else . . . never forget to listen to yourself. It's not rocket science!

About the Author

A recognized expert in marketing, planning, strategic positioning, and customer relationships, Mitch Goozé has addressed groups throughout North America, winning high ratings for his energetic presentation style and results-oriented approach to marketing.

His ideas have helped senior executives from more than 4,000 companies define their market niches, develop and implement practical, workable marketing plans, and realign their marketing efforts to focus more closely on the customer.

Mitch Goozé is an experienced general manager with operating experience in the high technology and consumer products industries. He has experience running divisions of large companies, as well as being CEO of mid-sized companies. Mr. Goozé was president of Teledyne Components, a division of Teledyne, Inc. from 1985 through 1990.

Mr. Goozé is a graduate of the University of California, Los Angeles. He did graduate work in electrical engineering at the California State University, Long Beach and graduate business studies at Santa Clara University and holds a MBA from Heriot Watt University, Edinburgh, Scotland.

Mr. Goozé is a member of the Board of Directors of Intisys, and Telesensory Systems. He's a past member of the Board of Directors of The American Electronics Association and ASU-CLA, and the Board of Advisors of the Leavey School of Business at Santa Clara University. He is also a Founder of the International Center for Professional Speaking in Phoenix, Arizona.

He has been President of Customer Manufacturing Group since 1991. Customer Manufacturing Group helps increase marketing/sales performance through process improvement management. He can be reached at 800-947-0140 or mgooze@customermfg.com.

About The Institute for Marketing & Innovation

The Institute for Marketing & Innovation is a research and publishing company specializing in forward thinking information to improve your bottom line. The Institute conducts primary marketing research and publishes management tools (books, research reports, and audio and video tape products) to help increase your effectiveness.

If you would like to hear, see, or read more of what Mitchell Goozé or our other experts have to say, or if you'd like a free copy of our management tools catalog, please contact us by mail, telephone, or fax.

The Institute for Marketing & Innovation, Inc.
3350 Scott Boulevard, Building 30
Santa Clara, CA 95054-3104 USA
Telephone: 800-944-9491
Fax: 408-727-3949

Also From The Institute for Marketing & Innovation

The Secret To Selling More
It's Not Where You've Been Looking
If It Were, You'd Have Found It Already
by Mitch Goozé

Index

Western Union company, 165
Wheel Works, The, 270
Windermere Associates, 194–195
Wine cooler industry, 110–112
Wisk laundry detergent, 168
Worlds of Wonder Company,
   160–161
Wristwatch retailing
   digital watch and
     semiconductor industry,
     151–154
   Timex, failure to adapt,
     154–155
   two views, 57–58

Xerox Corporation, xerography,
   165, 253–254

Yellow Pages advertising, 134–135

Zitter, Mark, 223